# Judicial Review of Administrative Discretion in the Administrative State

Jurgen de Poorter · Ernst Hirsch Ballin ·
Saskia Lavrijssen
Editors

# Judicial Review of Administrative Discretion in the Administrative State

ASSER PRESS

Springer

*Editors*
Jurgen de Poorter
Department of Public Law and Governance
Tilburg Law School
Tilburg, The Netherlands

Ernst Hirsch Ballin
Department of Public Law and Governance
Tilburg Law School
Tilburg, The Netherlands

Saskia Lavrijssen
Law Technology Society and Markets/LAW
Tilburg Law School
Tilburg, The Netherlands

ISBN 978-94-6265-306-1 ISBN 978-94-6265-307-8 (eBook)
https://doi.org/10.1007/978-94-6265-307-8

Published by T.M.C. ASSER PRESS, The Hague, The Netherlands www.asserpress.nl
Produced and distributed for T.M.C. ASSER PRESS by Springer-Verlag Berlin Heidelberg



This T.M.C. ASSER PRESS imprint is published by the registered company Springer-Verlag GmbH, DE part of Springer Nature
The registered company address is: Heidelberger Platz 3, 14197 Berlin, Germany

# Preface

## Rethinking the Constitutional Design of Administrative Law: Judicial Review in the Administrative State

### Constitutional Design of Administrative Law and the Rise of the Administrative State

In the traditional constitutional framework, administration is strongly identified with the executive branch. In other words, the constitutional design of administrative law must be understood in light of the concept of the *trias politica*, in which the executive power is seen as implementing what has been decided by the legislator, subject to that latter's permanent political control and democratic political accountability. It is in the initial legislative policy choice, subject to this subsequent political control and accountability, that the executive branch finds its legitimacy. This constitutional design also affects how we customarily perceive the interrelationship between the executive branch and the judiciary. The role of legal oversight, whether by judicial or administrative courts, must also be understood from the perspective of separation of powers. The courts are supposed to review administrative action in a restrained way, for example, by applying the standard of unreasonableness or manifest error. The rational underpinning of this restrained form of judicial review is found in the presumed democratic legitimacy that administrative decision-making derives ultimately from the initial legislative policy choice and subsequent political control and accountability of the executive.

The question arises, however, as to the extent this traditional constitutional framework corresponds to the actual relationship between the different actors in what is called "the administrative state". If we look to the field of comparative constitutional law, we see special emphasis placed on the independent role of agencies as a fourth branch within the overall scheme of government.[1] We can also

[1] McLean J and Tushnet M (2015) Administrative bureaucracy. In: Tushnet M, Fleiner T, Saunders C (eds) Routledge Handbook of Constitutional Law. Routledge, London/New York, pp. 121–130.

see this development in the Netherlands as well, with the proliferation of "authorities", i.e., agencies that are expected to be to some extent independent from politics.[2] Take, for example, the Consumer and Markets Authority, which has, since its inception, developed both stronger political independence in combination with broader discretionary powers. But even as to bureaucracies with less formal independence, i.e., working under full political accountability, similar observations could be made. Consider, for example, the so-called IND (Immigration and Naturalisation Service). Outside the field of asylum law, where either the Minister of Justice or his Secretary of State take the key decisions, the large majority of the administrative action escapes direct political control. This means that those who are politically responsible may only set the broader policy goals but administrative actors otherwise operate free from direct instructions. In this sense, in the modern administrative, including the many independent agencies, administrative actors necessarily play an ordering and correcting role. This role cannot be solely understood as the application of rules that have been developed by the legislator or even those at the political summit of the executive branch. Rather, often the operative rules are by the administration itself—the regulating agencies—or they operate pursuant to rules that give the administration substantial discretion.

The reality of administrative autonomy and discretion makes an approach to administrative law grounded in the classic *trias politica*, in which democratic legitimacy is derived ultimately from the legislature, problematic in a certain way. From this perspective, it is inapt to qualify "bureaucrats" as the executors of the political will, or as "alter egos of the political actors." Whether by law or simply, in fact, administrative actors operate with some degree of independence from political control.[3] Therefore, over time, this fourth branch has been subjected to special forms of accountability, not solely based on (often limited) political oversight—legislative and executive—but also on an indirect democratic legitimacy by means of external transparency, which serves as an essential support to judicial review. As Lindseth has argued: "this sort of mediated legitimacy provided for a workable reconciliation of historical notions of representative government (which continued to regard the elected legislature as the cornerstone of self-rule) with the executive-technocratic reality of the administrative state after 1945."[4]

## The Constitutional Role of the Courts: Rethinking the Tripartite Approach to the Separation of Institutional Power

The traditional concern of judicial review is democratic accountability. It is reflected in the vestigial attachment to the old *transmission belt theory*, in which the role of the administration is understood to consist of faithfully applying the instructions set by the legislature. This attachment is further reflected in the

[2] It should be noted that in this context the term independency is used in a sense that must not be confused with the term independency usually used in relation to the judiciary.

[3] McLean and Tushnet (2015, p. 122).

[4] Lindseth P (2010) Power and Legitimacy: Reconciling Europe and the Nation-State. Oxford University Press, Oxford, p. 90.

insistence of judges, in reviewing administrative action, that there be an identifiable statutory basis for any claimed delegated administrative power. This legal basis provides an essential link between the administrative action and the consent-based legitimacy of the elected organ, while also ensuring that the powers ultimately exercised operate within the scope of clear statutory instructions or policy choices.

It is often difficult, however, to locate such instructions and choices in many pieces of legislation, particularly those which merely provide a framework (*lois-cadres*) but otherwise delegate or even subdelegate significant normative power. It seems remarkable that, in Dutch administrative law, the judiciary has responded to these legislative developments not with greater scrutiny but with increasing judicial restraint. The rationale seems to be that, to the extent the legislator does not set instructions, it implicitly intends the administrative sphere to enjoy greater discretion, thus justifying a diminished judicial role. But is this what is really to be expected of the judiciary in the modern administrative state? Can we build a theory of judicial review on this model of democratic accountability or should the model of judicial review evolve, seeking to do justice in the face of new forms of administration and governance at the national, European, and international levels?

A different approach seems possible if we understand the aim of judicial review from a different constitutional point of view. The core function of judicial review should be, from this perspective, to ensure the nonarbitrary character of all exercises of administrative power, rather than simply ensuring the democratic accountability of the administrative decision-making process. The potential of a doctrine focused on preventing nonarbitrary exercises of administrative power, however, is hampered by a deeply fundamental and conceptually flawed reliance on separation of power anachronisms.[5] The separation of powers, with its *a priori* insistence on legislative primacy (and, indeed, exclusivity) in particular affairs, thus can represent a debilitating force in the prevailing institutional structure if it leads to excessive judicial restraint. The tripartite theory reinforces the judicial reluctance to scrutinize the exercise of administrative discretion in a way that is normatively unjustifiable. "Administrative law doctrine … goes astray when it assumes (or pretends) that judicial deference is equivalent to political neutrality… Broad deference to the agency amounts to an alliance by the judiciary with the executive, which disservices the system of checks and balances; it abdicates any direct judicial responsibility for the quality of governmental actions."[6] Carolan has argued in this respect that the traditional tripartite approach to the separation of institutional power is both descriptively and normatively inadequate, and that the question arises as to whether it ought to be replaced by a new separation of powers system that shows due regard for both the realities of contemporary governance and the normative notions of nonarbitrariness.[7] Instead of focusing on a strict separation of powers, the

[5] Edley Jr J (1991) The Governance Crisis, Legal Theory and Political Ideology, Duke Law Journal 41:561–606, p. 562.

[6] Ibid.

[7] Carolan E (2009) The New Separation of Powers: A Theory for the Modern State. Oxford University Press, Oxford, p. 106.

alternative should be to seek sufficient checks and balances to hold accountable an administrative power that is coming to enjoy ever greater discretionary powers and autonomy in its decision-making processes.

### The Interrelationship Between Courts and Administration: Modalities of Judicial Review of Administrative Power

In our ongoing research project of which this book is a part, we seek to understand developments in Dutch administrative law against a broader comparative, European, and transnational backdrop. The focus is on how courts review administrative decisions in various regulatory domains, such as competition law, energy law, environmental law, and asylum law, comparing the emerging modalities of judicial review as well as the changes that have been visible in the case-law of supreme administrative courts. From a normative point of view, we ask whether these modalities meet the needs of a changing system of administrative governance noted in Section 0.2 above. To this end, we include comparative analysis with German, UK, and US administrative law as well as with the modalities of judicial review applied by the European Court of Justice.

One of the rationales behind administrative discretion is what we would call "discretion as policy". This form of administrative discretion arises precisely because the legislature, in adopting the statute, cannot foresee the characteristics of every single case. Therefore, it leaves leeway to the administration to balance interests and take a decision that suits best the particular situation. Here, judicial review is traditionally hampered by the dichotomy that exists between law and policy. Traditionally, courts were supposed to limit their review to matters regarded as judicial (or, subsequently, quasi-judicial) in nature. This meant that the review of arbitrary action in areas formally defined as nonjudicial was understood to be beyond the presumed parameters of legitimate judicial action. This lack of judicial oversight meant that the administrative bodies came to enjoy, in some corners of their work, an effectively rule-free environment. From our perspective, normatively, this raises the question whether the traditional distinction between law and policy is still adequate in the context of the administrative state. Courts cannot take responsibility for the policy choices made by the administration, but they can assess whether the decision-making process used by the administration has been reasonable in the light of the principles of subsidiarity, proportionality, transparency, and precaution, along with human rights.

An interesting question in this respect is what factors should determine the modality of judicial review, including the actual existence of political control, as well as its nature and extent. Another factor would be the court's relative institutional capacity, notably its lack of expertise as compared to the administration. This could give rise to another basis to justify judicial deference to administrative discretion, i.e., "discretion as expertise", grounded in the professional expertise of administrative bodies. Deference here would accept the place of administrative discretion within the state's governing structures, but that deference cannot be so absolute as to ignore the possibility of (normatively objectionable) arbitrary outcomes. Claims of expertise sometimes posit the idea that there exists an objectively correct conclusion, to which the specialist administrator will reflexively come without having to balance conflicting interests. Courts should be on guard against claims of expertise that are in fact a guise for political trade-offs, thus undertaking a sufficiently searching review of delegated powers to ensure that they are "be exercised in the coldest neutrality."

The question arises, however, whether the judicial concern to prevent arbitrary exercises of administrative power may lead courts to do more and enter directly into this domain of purported expertise. One response could be that judicial deference in relation to "substantive outcomes" will be counterbalanced by a strict process review. Courts could do this by assessing more intensively the way the administration has established the facts and distributed the burden of proof. On the other hand, we could also in principle question whether it is an oversimplification to assume administrative bodies are always better equipped to consider broad questions of (scientific) expertise. Courts must indeed be conscious of their constitutional role but this does not alter the fact that they could develop standards regarding, say, who should be regarded as an "expert" or what guiding principles might be adopted to improve the quality of the expertise-base of the administrative decision-making process. In this respect, it seems to be interesting to question what could be learned from the evidentiary standard announced in *Daubert v. Merrell Dow Pharmaceuticals*, which governs the admissibility of expert testimony in federal courts and many state courts in the U.S.[8] In its *Daubert* judgment, the U.S. Supreme Court made clear that courts are to ensure that expert testimony is both relevant and reliable, with the reliability inquiry focusing on: a. testability or falsifiability; b. peer review and publication; c. the known or potential rate of error; and d. the degree of acceptance in the field's community. At its core, *Daubert* is aimed at ensuring that scientific evidence meets the same standards of reliability that the relevant scientific field itself would require.

Another interesting question to be addressed in this project is to what extent it is still justifiable that, in principle, Dutch administrative courts are not allowed to review generally binding regulations.[9] Article 8:3 of the Dutch General Administrative Law Act (GALA) says that no appeal lies against a decision laying down a generally binding regulation or policy rule.[10] Some specific acts, like the Electricity Act and the Gas Act, provide exceptions to this general rule, making direct appeal against generally binding regulations possible. The dichotomy between law and policy underlies the prohibition of Article 8:3 GALA for the courts. However, we must admit that there is also an exception to this in case

[8] 509 U.S. 579 (1993).

[9] Article 8:2 of the General Administrative Law Act.

[10] Initially, this prohibition ought to be temporary. Later, it was turned into a permanent exemption of administrative appeal.

litigants question the legality of an administrative order on the basis of the unlawfulness of the underlying statutory provision on which the order is based.[11] Besides this, so-called "residual legal protection" is provided by the civil courts.[12] But for this type of review, the Dutch Supreme Court set a standard in its landmark *Landbouwvliegers* case in 1986,[13] that there is no rule prohibiting secondary legislation to be declared void because of an arbitrary use of regulatory powers. Nevertheless, the court also ruled that the nature of the legislative power as well as the constitutional position of the judiciary calls for judicial restraint when it comes to regulatory decisions that imply policy choices.

Among legal scholars there seem to be some debate about whether the prohibition laid down in Article 8:3 still suits the realities of contemporary government. Legal scholars have added, as well, that if we consider lifting this prohibition, the judicial review of these generally binding regulations should have more substance than this *Landbouwvliegers* standard. But what does that mean? Here, we could possibly learn from the way US courts assess the legitimacy of regulations set by regulatory agencies. Regulation still seems to be a blind spot in Dutch administrative law. So, the question arises if and to what extent the administrative courts can play a role in the development of principles of administrative regulation.

## Conference on Judicial Review in the Administrative State at Tilburg Law School

With these considerations in mind, Tilburg Law School hosted a conference on judicial review of administrative decision-making on January 18–19, 2018. We would very much like to express our gratitude to the Royal Dutch Academy of Sciences (KNAW) as well as to the board of Tilburg Law School for making this conference possible. This conference sought to raise questions about the traditional assumptions regarding judicial review of administrative discretion in light of changes in the constitutional framework. Particular focus was given to whether other models of review are more appropriate considering the changing political and legal landscape in which administrative authorities and courts operate. Different perspectives were brought to bear on the role of the courts and the developments in different EU Member States, the EU, and the US across different social sectors and legal domains. The aim of the conference was to build a bridge between academic research and the realities of administrative law and judicial review of administrative decision-making on a daily basis.

---

[11] Bok A (1991) Rechterlijke toetsing van regelgeving (Dissertatie Groningen University). Kluwer, Deventer, pp. 4–5.

[12] See recently HR 22 May 2015, ECLI:NL:HR:2015:1296, JB 2015/125 (Privacy First). This residual protection is only possible in case of a lack of sufficient legal protection in the proceedings before the administrative courts. In practice, this means that as long as there is a possibility to lodge an appeal against an administrative decision before an administrative court requesting a test on the legality of the underlying regulation, the civil court will declare a complaint on the lawfulness of this regulation inadmissible because of the existence of sufficient legal protection before the administrative court.

[13] HR 16 May 1986, Landbouwvliegers arrest.

The conference consisted of four different parts. The first part addressed the changes in the constitutional framework and dealt with the changing role of the judge in the evolving administrative state, going beyond the traditional borders of the *trias politica*. The keynote speech was delivered by John Bell (Cambridge University) and dealt with the topic of judicial review in the administrative state. Joanna Mendes (University of Luxembourg) gave a critical account of the judicial paradigm of administrative discretion and Peter Lindseth (UConn School of Law) talked about the development of the modern administrative state. In the second part, we approached the topic from a comparative perspective, comparing different models of judicial review across different jurisdictions. Ittai Bar Siman Tov (Bar-Ilan University) talked about models of judicial review from a constitutional point of view, Anna Gerbrandy (Utrecht University) elaborated on challenges for judicial review in the supervision of markets and Deni Mantzari (University of Reading) spoke about the institutional dimension of judicial review of administrative decisions in the UK regulatory state.

In the third part, starting on the second day of the conference, the results of the first conference day were related to Dutch constitutional and administrative law. Ernst Hirsch Ballin (Tilburg University) reflected on the Genealogy of constitutional law: judicial review in the administrative state. Rob Widdershoven (Utrecht University) discussed the evolution of the standard of review applied by the European Court of Justice and judicial review in the administrative state 2.0. Jurgen de Poorter (Tilburg University) reflected on developments in the standard of review of generally binding regulations applied by the Administrative Jurisdiction Division of the Council of State. The final part of the conference tried to bridge the gap between academic discourse and the practice of the Supreme Administrative Courts in the Netherlands with contributions of Saskia Lavrijssen (Tilburg University) on energy regulation reviewed by the Trade and Industry Appeals Tribunal, Heiko Kerkmeester (Trade and Industry Appeals Tribunal) on Dutch competition law seen from a judge's perspective, Tom Barkhuysen and Michiel Van Emmerik (Leiden University) on judicial review in Dutch environmental law and Bart Jan van Ettekoven (President of the Administrative Jurisdiction Division of the Council of State) on judicial review in Dutch environmental law seen from a judge's perspective.

We are happy to present this book with the edited versions of the papers presented during the exciting and successful conference. It is a unique collection that links state-of-the-art academic research on the role of the courts in the administrative state with the daily practice of the higher and lower administrative courts struggling with their role in the evolving administrative state. We have noticed that with the changing role and forms of the administrative state, courts across the world and across sectors are in the process of reconsidering their roles and the appropriate models of judicial review. Learning from the experiences in different sectors and jurisdictions, the conference and the book provide theoretical and empirical foundations for reflecting on the advantages and disadvantages of different models of review, the constitutional consequences, and the main questions that deserve further research and debate.

We are grateful to our student assistants Camille Colard and Ron de Martines and to our secretary Yvonne Sminia for their help in bringing this book to its present form.

Tilburg, The Netherlands

Jurgen de Poorter
Ernst Hirsch Ballin
Saskia Lavrijssen

# Contents

# Editors and Contributors

## About the Editors

**Jurgen de Poorter** is Professor of Administrative Law at Tilburg University and Deputy Judge in the District Court of The Hague.

**Ernst Hirsch Ballin** is Distinguished University Professor (Tilburg University), Professor in Human Rights Law (University of Amsterdam), and President of the T.M.C. Asser Institute for International and European Law. He is also a member of the Scientific Council for Government Policy (WRR).

**Saskia Lavrijssen** is Professor of Economic Regulation and Market Governance of Network Industries at Tilburg University.

## Contributors

**Tom Barkhuysen** is Professor of Constitutional and Administrative Law at Leiden University, the Netherlands and partner at Stibbe Amsterdam.

**John Bell** is Professor of Law at University of Cambridge.

**Fatma Çapkurt** is a Researcher at the Department of Constitutional and Administrative Law at Leiden University.

**Peter Lindseth** is Olimpiad S. Ioffe Professor of International and Comparative Law and Director of International Programs at the University of Connecticut School of Law (USA).

**Despoina Mantzari** is a Lecturer in Competition Law and Policy at University College London, Faculty of Laws.

**Michiel van Emmerik** is Associate Professor of Constitutional and Administrative Law at Leiden University and Deputy Judge at the District Court Midden-Nederland.

**Bart Jan van Ettekoven** is Chair of the Administrative Jurisdiction Division of the Council of State in the Netherlands and Professor of Administrative Law at the University of Amsterdam.

**Rob Widdershoven** is Professor of European Administrative Law at Utrecht University, the Netherlands, a Researcher at the Montaigne Centre for Rule of Law and Administration of Justice, and Advocate General in Administrative Law of the Netherlands.

# Part I
# Judicial Review from a Constitutional and Comparative Perspective

# Chapter 1
# Judicial Review in the Administrative State

**John Bell**

## Contents



**Abstract** Judicial review is not the only form of accountability for the administration. Successful accountability requires a "braiding" of different mechanisms, a careful combination that ensures that they work together. Administration involves different activities, e.g. policy-making, running services or purchasing them from the private sector, regulating the private sector, and arranging for participation in decision-making. Each requires different forms of accountability. For the public sector, the most important model is not the principal-agent model, but the trust model: the official is granted power to work for the benefit of a third party beneficiary. The official must therefore be accountable not only to the person conferring the power, but also to the beneficiary. Judicial review's distinctive contribution is to focus on legality and respect for process, as well as transparency in justification. The paper illustrates the process of braiding by two examples. The first examines the way standards of good administration developed by the ombudsman and judicial review can be mutually influential and can help to work together to improve administrative practice. The second looks at how standards of public sector ethics and policies of avoiding corruption can be brought together from both judicial

Professor of Law (1973), University of Cambridge; e-mail: jsb48@cam.ac.uk.

J. Bell (✉)
University of Cambridge, Cambridge, UK
e-mail: jsb48@cam.ac.uk



J. de Poorter et al. (eds.), *Judicial Review of Administrative Discretion in the Administrative State*, https://doi.org/10.1007/978-94-6265-307-8_1

review and other monitoring bodies. The paper suggests braiding works where the different standard monitoring bodies are institutionally close, where there are possibilities for informal interaction and where the values put forward by the different institutions fit the culture of the institutions subjected to them.

**Keywords** Judicial review · accountability · braiding · public services · ombudsman · England · the Netherlands

Judicial review is one of a number of mechanisms of accountability of the administration. We need to recognise its special, but limited place in achieving accountability. Its place is primarily in ensuring processes of decision-making are respected and, at the margins, defending certain fundamental values against encroachment. It needs to operate consciously in conjunction with informal and non-legal standards and mechanisms of accountability if it is to contribute effectively to an overall scheme of accountability.

This argument is presented in a number of stages. The first section argues that the "administrative state" performs a number of functions that require different forms of accountability and to which judicial review makes varied contributions (Sect. 1.1). The concept of accountability if then explored (Sect. 1.2). It is suggested that judicial review has a limited contribution to play in relation to the accountability of public authorities. That leads to the question of what is special about the contribution of judicial review (Sect. 1.3). Given that judicial review is only one mechanism among many for securing accountability, then it becomes important to understand the way in which it works in a coherent fashion with other mechanisms. I suggest that the concept of "braiding" (Sect. 1.4), borrowed from studies in contract law, offers a regulatory ideal for the way in which judicial review should work with other forms of accountability.

## 1.1 The Role of the "Administrative State"

Is it right to characterise contemporary public administration as the "administrative state"? I have my doubts. "Administration" conveys the sense of taking care of a machinery that has been programmed to deliver specified outcomes.

It is as if the politicians have decided a policy, such as the level of rents in public housing, and then the administrators simply have to implement it by sending out the bills and collecting the rent. In the past, it required a bureaucracy to delivery such outcomes, but many of them can now be delivered by machines. Indeed "e-government" is all the rage. But that picture of "administration" is certainly not adequate. Contemporary public administration does a number of different things.

First, the classical task is to implement decided policy, often to complex facts (which is why a machine cannot do it). The administrator, at the very least, has to interpret the rules and characterise the facts. That involves judgment (or what might be called "weak discretion"). Even the Immigration Rules, which contain a lot of very specific details, still require human judgment mainly because it is simply not possible to design a programme that will fit the complexity of human lives. In recent months in the UK, there has been a lot of discussion of the way in which such judgment has been exercised in the so-called "Windrush" cases, where migrants who came to the UK in the 1950s and 1960s without formal documents (because they were not necessary then) were finding that they were being told by officials that they were unable to prove that they were lawfully in the UK.[1] Officials chose to adopt a narrow approach to the issue of what constituted sufficient proof of entitlement to residence, insisting on very specific documents that are readily available today, but were not necessarily available (or kept) in the past. That scandal showed that we need human decision-makers to over-ride, and to build a body of administrative case law to articulate the meaning of the rules.

But the example of immigration also shows that administrators often have to develop policies in order to deliver very broad policy goals, such as the "hostile environment for illegal migrants". There are choices to be made—how easy is it for people to offer alternative types of information to that which the administrators say they want? How far will the immigration authorities make use of data held, for example, by the Department of Work and Pensions or the Inland Revenue about whether people have been employed in the UK over the past few years and where they lived? Or does the applicant have to demonstrate these facts from their own personal records? How strong does the evidence have to be? These are procedural points about the implementation of a policy. But there will also be matters of interpretation. Where there have been short time gaps between ending one job and beginning another, does this prevent the applicant having the status of a person who has been "continually employed" during the previous five years?

Once we look at other areas of policy, the range of potential choices by the administration is greater. The Bank of England has to use the various economic tools at its disposal to keep down inflation. But it has a variety of options.[2] A planning authority has considerable scope to develop a planning policy for an area and then apply it to the various applications which are made to it. In reality, administration involves varying degrees of discretion that is authorised.

If a body is asked to exercise significant discretion in designing policies to implement a broad policy objective, it is not enough for the administrator to say "I was only doing what I was instructed to do". The existence of significant discretion requires that the policy choices be explained and justified. This cannot be undertaken simply by citing the authorising statute. It is necessary to explain both the interpretation of that power and the reasons why this was the best choice available to carry out the policy. That is a task of accountability which is similar to the

[1] Khomami N and Naujokaityte G (2018) How the Windrush Scandal led to fall of Amber Rudd – Timeline. https://www.theguardian.com/uk-news/2018/apr/30/how-windrush-scandal-fall-amber-rudd-timeline. Accessed 31 May 2018.

[2] Bank of England (2018) Monetary Policy. https://www.bankofengland.co.uk/monetary-policy. Accessed 31 May 2018.

accountability of a politician, because both are in effect policy-makers. Judicial review is good at requiring certain formalities in justification, but it is not very good at engaging with the substance of the reasons given for the decision.

Judicial review may intervene where the decision is outrageously disproportionate, but there is a line between reviewing very bad decisions and challenging bad decisions or ones that the administration could have decided differently.

Secondly, for many years, public administration has exercised discretion in order to achieve goals of public health and welfare by providing services. The provision of public infrastructure and public services became classic in the 19th and 20th centuries. The control of these activities is exercised by the way people were chosen to be on the boards which designed and ran the service or by reporting to a central or local politician. That is not done by rules, but by empowering employees of a public body to use their judgement to provide appropriate outcomes to individuals or groups. There were significant debates about the extent to which those running public services were indeed accountable. Many are run as public corporations and so treated rather like private corporations in terms of their freedom to run their business. The role of any oversight body is just to ensure either a minimum level of welfare or to delivery agreed levels of public service. Questions may be asked by the oversight body about value for any public money put in, but rarely about the local operational decisions. Instead, there are complaints mechanisms, either within the hospital or public service or through an ombudsman.

In the last 30 years, there has been a shift from direct delivery of services to more of a purchaser-provider relationship. The public body defines the service and engages the private contractor to run it, typically requiring the private sector to provide investment and return a profit to the public. So, the cleaning service or the catering service or the transport service in a public hospital may be put out to public tender and awarded to a private contractor.[3] Public accountability relates to the design of the service which is tendered, the tendering process, and the monitoring of performance. But such control is often considered inadequate, especially when there is a significant failure in performance. Unless accountability and powers of intervention have been built into the design of the tendering process, then the powers of intervention will be limited.

All the same, the public administration also has to shoulder a level of risk which exceeds that of the private sector, even if the service is contracted out. It is no use a public hospital turning away people injured in a coach crash on the motorway on the ground that it has not employed enough staff to cope with this sort of emergency. The public sector has to fund the redundancy of the public service, in the sense that there is a level of over-provision that covers a level of emergency. This is

[3]E.g. the running of English hospital transport by a subsidiary of Deutsche Bahn: https://www.arrivatransportsolutions.co.uk/. Accessed 31 May 2018.

not what the private sector would do. So there are different principles of operation and different expectations for which a public service needs to be answerable.

Thirdly, public bodies have been regulating the private sector since Roman times (e.g. in markets). Nowadays, we have bodies set up by government to perform such tasks over a wide range of activities, e.g. insurance, financial services, pensions, and so on. These are designed to provide sufficient skilled supervision to enable the consumer to invest with confidence and to structure the market where bargaining is not realistically possible. The accountability of the public regulator is not the same as that of the body which is regulated. If a pension fund goes bankrupt, then its managers are the primary people responsible. The regulator will be answerable only to the extent that it failed to identify the warning signs of an impending collapse. The regulator and others may also attempt to salvage the pension fund.[4] The accountability here is secondary, not primary. The regulator has a duty to supervise and to act, rather than to manage the fund or to bail it out when it has inadequate funds. Because much of the activity involved is of positive action, then there is often little room for judicial review which is involved in quashing decisions.

Unless the regulator oversteps its wide powers of supervision, there is little room for the courts in judicial review. More often the claim in the courts will be for compensation resulting from a failure to act in a timely fashion.[5]

Fourthly, the public administration is responsible for arranging processes of policy formulation. Many policies are decided by politicians who are elected or rejected from time to time. New Public Management involves a much more timely consultation on policies and a feedback on performance. Those who benefit from policies are expected to contribute to their formulation and to respond with complimentary or critical comments on how the performance is conducted. This expects citizens and experts to bring their knowledge and insights on very significant issues. It involves a commitment of time well beyond four or five-yearly voting. While citizens may still be trying to scramble for time across part-time jobs, commuting and other pressing issues of their own, they have to find time to be constructive citizens. "Active" citizens in a real position to be involved in the decision-making are becoming the new administrative "elite", the few privileged who have the mental and social resources to inquire about technical topics and to develop arguments in a way of which the administration will be able to make use. The public administration provides the information needed.

There is not one single role which the public administration performs. So there is no single role which judicial review can be expected to perform.

[4] See on the collapse of British Home Stores: G. Ruddick, S. Butler and N. Fletcher, The Guardian 25 April 2016: https://www.theguardian.com/business/2016/apr/25/bhs-heading-for-administration-as-rescue-deal-fails. Accessed 3 October 2018.

[5] See the Barlow-Clowes scandal: Gregory and Drewry 1991.

## 1.2 The Role of Judicial Review as a Mechanism of Accountability

The different tasks of government call for different forms of accountability including different roles for judicial review. If a body is asked to exercise significant discretion in designing policies to implement a broad policy objective, it is not enough for the administrator to say "I was only doing what I was instructed to do". The existence of significant discretion requires that the policy choices be explained and justified. This cannot be undertaken simply by citing the authorising statute. It is necessary to explain both the interpretation of that power and the reasons why this was the best choice available to carry out the policy. That is a task of accountability which is similar to the accountability of a politician, because both are in effect policy-makers. Judicial review is good at requiring certain formalities in justification, but it is not very good at engaging with the substance of the reasons given for the decision.

The term "accountability" has a particular resonance in English. Whilst "acceptability" relates to the rightness of either the outcomes or the reasons of decisions reached by officials, "accountability" involves justifying what you have done, not necessarily in an individual case, but certainly in a pattern of decisions. It is "a legal, political, social or moral duty on the part of the accountor to explain and justify his or her action or inaction to particular bodies demanding explanations".[6] This goes beyond behaving in a professional (bureaucratic) manner. You are expected to be responsive to those on whose behalf one is supposed to act.

In his work, Cane has identified six categories of accountability mechanisms in relation to the resolution of complaints.[7] Starting with the original decision-maker, he identifies also internal review by the bureaucratic reviewer and then by the bureaucratic complaints handler. Each of these people internal to the bureaucratic administration has their own focus of attention.

Each looks at legality and merits, but in different ways and with different degrees of accessibility by the complainant. He also identifies three external bodies that deal with complaints.

They are the ombudsman, the tribunals, and the courts. The first two look both at legality and merits, whereas the courts only look at legality. Furthermore, the bureaucratic complaints handler and the Ombudsman (as the external complaints handler) are permitted to look not only at compliance with specific rules, but more generally at consistency with administrative practice and standards of fairness. In his account, Cane is suggesting that accountability can be organised in different ways depending on what we want the complaint-handler to examine, and the speed and formality with which this is to happen, and how easy it is for the complainant to access this form of accountability.

---

[6] Oliver 1991. More generally, Harlow 2002, Chapter 1.

[7] Cane 2009, pp. 256–259.

How far is judicial review an exercise in accountability in Cane's sense? His focus is on the redress of grievances by citizens. Rightly, he points to the way, other mechanisms established by law provide better forms of redress. There are two foci of attention in dealing with grievances. On the one hand there is the feature of compensation. On the other hand, there is the prevention of future or past excesses of power. Judicial review is not primarily a mechanism for providing compensation. In many legal systems, including English law, the provision of compensation is governed by the ordinary rules of law, not by rules which are distinctive for the public administration. So the procedures of administrative law have no special place and, accordingly, the complainant will rarely rely on judicial review. When it comes to judicial review, then its focus is on the legality of administrative decisions. The administrator is asked to demonstrate the legal basis for decisions. Often this will be satisfied by showing that the decision-maker had competence to make the decision, without having to show that she exercised any available discretion correctly. But, the complainant is not typically concerned with the niceties of whether another decision-maker was invested with better authority to make the decision. The question of legality is also quite narrow from the complainant's perspective. It asks whether the interpretation of the law (and possibly the characterisation of facts) conform to the proper interpretation of the law. Those sorts of question are of less interest to individual complainants than they are to administrative superiors. Keeping lower administrators acting within the purposes set by the law ensures that they continue to do their job. It is a valuable process, even if there is no complainant. But again, judicial review is usually not the best procedure to achieve that result. If the lower administrator is within the organisation, then hierarchical communications (or even discipline) will suffice. Judicial review has its place where the administrative authorities are not integrated and where one body does not possess supervisory powers in relation to the other. The function here is essentially prospective—to ensure that the lines of authority are set out for the future (and sometimes for the past). Put in this way, judicial review is only marginally a process of complaint resolution.

To add to this complexity about the place of judicial review, we should note that, in our society, we work with at least three paradigms of accountability. The first, and most very ancient, is the *principal-agent model*, which corresponds most to Mulgan's "authority" model.[8] One person, the principal, commits a task to another and then expects that other, the agent, to answer for how he has performed that task. As the word "account" implies, this is often about money. So a landlord employs an agent to collect rents from tenants, and then requires the agent to provide an account showing the monies he has received. The agent is acting on behalf of the principal and must demonstrate that he had discharged that responsibility. The relationship is essentially hierarchical. The agent has to show she did as she was told. In our own society, a second model has become important, the *representative-elector model.*[9]

[8] Mulgan 2000, p. 555.

[9] Dowdle 2006, pp. 4–6.

Here the electors vote into office a representative. The representative may have a specific mandate, but will often have wider authority to act in the best interests of society (not necessarily just the best interests of the electors).

Through periodic elections, the representative has to show the electors she acted responsibly in the exercise of her mandate to account by the electors and can be replaced. Essentially the people governed have the right to answers from those who govern them. This model is prevalent not just in politics, but also in spheres such as commercial companies where the directors are elected by the shareholders. It is also a model used in relation to trades unions or school governors. Being accountable here does not mean that the representative has to show that he or she did what the electors instructed. Rather it is a matter of showing that the representative has behaved responsibly in the decisions he or she made in the interests of the community, company, union or school in relation to which authority was exercised authority. (Sometimes political discourse confuses this with the principal-agent model. The representative may be seen as simply the agent of those who voted her into power, e.g. the parent governor of a school. But it is more normal to expect independent judgment to be exercised.) Hence this is distinct from the principal-agent model.

Importantly, the model of accountability in relation to the exercise of discretion is different. The third model is the trust model. The distinctive feature of the *trust model* is that it imposes accountability in two directions. The trustee or fiduciary is accountable on the one hand to the person who gave her the task (the legislature). That is like the representative-elector model. But she is also accountable to the beneficiary, the person for whom the task has been entrusted. The narrative of public service is a narrative of a common project in which those with expertise and power exercise them for the good of others, not in a unilateral, paternalistic manner, but in response to and quite often in dialogue with those who benefit from that service. This trust model is captured in the idea of the Citizens' Charter. Over 16 years after it began in 1992, a British Parliamentary committee wrote:

> The initiative's underlying principles retain their validity nearly two decades on – not least the importance of putting the interests of public service users at the heart of public service provision. We believe this cardinal principle should continue to influence public service reform, and encourage the Government to maintain the aims of the Citizens' Charter programme given their continued relevance to public service delivery today.[10]

The beneficiary is not a superior, but has an independent claim to call the trustee to account because he is the person for whom the trust exists. The combination of the need for active citizenship in New Public Management and a trust model of accountability creates the need for active engagement both by citizens and by officials.

Yseult Marique has studied this phenomenon in relation to Public-Private Partnerships. School buildings are now financed by being built and run by a

[10] Public Administration Select Committee, *From Citizens' Charter to Public Service Guarantees: Entitlements to Public Services* (2007-8, HC 411), Recommendation 1 and [17].

construction firm at an annual rent paid by the local education authority or by an academy school for the benefit of pupils, staff and parents for periods often of 25 years. It would be too complex to draw up a list of performance promises for such a long period. Instead there needs to be trust generated between the parties that the school will be run in a way which enables the basic purpose of promoting pupils' education to happen.[11] There needs to be an ethos of a common project in which each party will perform its role. As she puts it, such trust is driven ultimately by an element of altruism, not a self-interest which will take advantage of every loophole to avoid doing something or charging more. It requires a "self-distancing" which redirects attention to the common project. It needs an ethic of care, rather than one of self-interest.[12] In trust law, we talk of a "fiduciary duty", a duty to promote the interests of the beneficiary.[13]

But I think I prefer Marique's notion of an "ethic of care" on the part of the person trusted towards the third party as the salient characteristic of the trust model.

The distinctive feature is the duty of altruism that arises from the nature of the project in which all parties are engaged. The "ethic of care" requires not simply that the servant anticipates the needs of the person served and responds proactively. It involves a respect for the dignity of the person served and allowing him or her a voice in the way in which they are served.

The trust model is not simply a model for complaints. It is a model which fits into an ongoing relationship between the parties. If the intervention of the beneficiary occurs, it is to ensure that her interests are respected not only in relation to specific transactions in the past, but also in relation to the future of the ongoing relationship.[14] Now the ongoing relationship requires the interests of the beneficiary are properly acknowledged and taken into account. This requires both a focus on the beneficiary's interests as relevant considerations that are taken into account when making a decision (and these are checked) and that this is reflected in the reasons that are given for a decision. On the whole, judicial review can check that these processes have been followed, but cannot engage with the content. That is the long recognised distinction between the review of legality and that of merits. Judicial review ensures that the framework of the relationships established by law are respected, but then lets the parties get on with the framework of that relationship.

Judicial Review operates as one mechanism, among many, by which officials are asked to explain their decisions. It is not a good forum for dealing with helping either active citizenship or the trust model of accountability. It is much better at supervising the principal-agent model. It can really only deal with two process

[11] Marique 2014, pp. 218–219.

[12] Ibid., pp. 259–271.

[13] *Roberts v Hopwood* [1925] A.C. 578. In this case, a local authority was held to have failed in its duty to its local taxpayers in paying excessive wages to its workers.

[14] See *Al Nehayan v Kent* [2018] EWHC 333 (Comm) at [167]–[176].

features of accountability. But all the same, judicial review comes to be called upon to perform these wider tasks of accountability.

Where does this impinge on administrative law as applied by the courts?

## 1.3 The Special Tasks of Judicial Review

Cane's analysis demonstrates that judicial review is predominantly focused on legality. Now, as has been said, legality involves both a question of whether the decision-maker has the power to decide as he did and a question about the process by which this was achieved. The special features of judicial review, alongside other accountability mechanisms, is its distinctive attention to these questions.

The first of these features is to ensure participation before decisions are taken. The right to have a say in decisions which affect you becomes essential to the modern form of administrative action. Judicial review can ensure that processes are respected. The *Miller* decision in the UK on triggering Article 50 TEU is a good example. The debate in court was about who was to make the decision, the Executive or Parliament, not what was the right decision.[15] It is the process and its design which secures involvement and accountability. If you have your ability to make an argument in a planning application process or a planning inquiry reviewing that decision, then you have been involved and the justifications offered for the planning decision are a form of accountability which legitimates the decision (even if it made against you).

The second feature is transparency of justification. The justification must engage with the arguments and interests of those affected by a decision. It is not a form of paternalist government, but requires the official to explain themselves to those about whose future they have decided. That implies a duty to provide adequate reasons after decisions are taken.

The difficulty for the court is how far it should go in assessing the adequacy of those reasons. The concept of transparency suggests that the reasons given for decisions should be genuine, explicit and comprehensible to the people to whom they are addressed.

The concept of active citizenship will encourage the losers to seek to use the judicial process where the individual or group has lost the political or administrative process. So, the court has to decide how far it will respond by interfering with the content of the decision. One way forward is the concept of deference, which is encapsulated in the normal concept of "margin of appreciation" used in moderating standard of judicial control. Will the court only intervene where there has been a serious failure to justify a decision by reference to the prescribed standards? This is the normal sense of proportionality. This fits the representative-elector model. The

[15] *R (on the application of Miller and another) v Secretary of State for Exiting the European Union* [2017] UKSC 5.

representative is given authority by the elector to decide and must be allowed to exercise judgment about what is best, even if the elector does not agree with the specific decisions. Therefore, it would be inappropriate for a reviewer to be more stringent in what is required. Adequacy of reasons primarily serves the purpose of explaining the decision to the person in respect of whom the decision was made. But it also serves to secure the accountability process by which the decision is justified to those who conferred the mandate in the first place. If the reasons are sufficient to enable both those processes to take place, then the reasons are adequate. It is not for the reviewer to add further requirements. The job of the reviewer in judicial review to ensure the integrity of the process of decision-making.

But the trust model of ensuring accountability to the recipient of services creates potential problems here. The recipient of services is concerned not so much with authority to decide as with the rightness of the decision. Two features of this are a precautionary approach and an interest approach. The first, more interventionist stance might best be described as the "expectations approach" or legal certainty approach. Under this, established positions are not to be changed without very good reasons. This goes beyond the classic idea that the rights of an individual must be respected. In relation to public services, this approach suggests that expectations of service should be respected. An example is where a local authority provides a care home for an elderly person. The person gives up their own home in return for a promise of lifetime care. Changes in the budget of the local authority lead it to wish to move the elderly person. To what extent is the local authority entitled to rely on the changed situation?[16] Is the legitimate expectation of the old person the basis for preventing the administration changing the way her care is given? The interests of the beneficiary focus less on the quality of the reasons offered by the administration, but more on the result which the beneficiary was expecting. If we focus principally on the discretionary power of the administration and only interfere where the reasons do not enable the person conferring the power or the person receiving the service to engage in political or administrative review of the decision, then we have a very limited form of judicial review.[17] If we go down the route of enforcing the expectations about the outcome which a potential beneficiary has been led to have by the administration, then we move away from tight conceptions of legality and more into the realms of "administrative fairness", which did not have a place in Cane's analysis of judicial review. The trust relationship depends on a sense of fairness and encourages a broader scope for judicial review here.

The other type of claim is *R v Cambridge HA, ex p B*.[18] Here the parents of a sick child sought to challenge the decision of a health authority not to give their child an experimental treatment. The judge refused to order the treatment. Whereas the decision of a medical body used to be treated with deference, nowadays Wang

[16] *R v North and East Devon HA, ex p. Coughlan* [2001] QB 213; Hughes 2017, p. 181.

[17] Compare the Australian decision of *Re Minister for Immigration and Multicultural Affairs, ex parte Lam* (2003) 214 CLR 1. See Elliott 2016, Chapter 10.

[18] [1995] 1 WLR 898. See, generally, Wang 2017.

argues that the courts are exercising stricter scrutiny over the evidence for any rationing decisions in the public health service. Thus a blanket decision that a drug would not be used has had to be replaced by a more careful scrutiny by the doctors of the benefits in the individual case.[19] The focus is on giving reasons, but they must be rational reasons that justify the high level of scrutiny required, especially in their focus on the needs of an individual patient.

There is an underlying idea of the level of care which an individual is entitled to and from which the Health Authority cannot depart without good reason. There is obviously a "margin of appreciation", but the scope of judicial review is broadened, particularly where decisions are being taken by quangos, rather than by elected bodies. Again, this is much closer to a conception of fairness and of attention to the individual than would be required by a more classical analysis of judicial review.

The trust model also creates a particular concern about the rules of standing in applications for judicial review. Whereas, under the principal-agent model, the question of competence might be confined to specific office holders (those who represent the people by whom power is given), the trust model requires accountability to the beneficiaries of a service or an exercise of power. That requires that standing be extended. The UK courts have moved away from a rights-based model of standing for judicial review to a public interest model. As long as a person has a legitimate interest in the matter at issue, it is not necessary that his or her right is affected. The case in the Supreme Court concerned the Scottish Parliament and its legislation to give a right of action to the victims of asbestos.[20] This matches the concern about enforcing legitimate expectations. Judicial review becomes one of the mechanisms of ensuring that the concerns of beneficiaries are taken into account and that there is a process of accountability towards them.

What I have argued is that the trust model of accountability lets in the beneficiary of services both to have standing and to complain about the levels of service, even where she does not have a right to a level of service, but merely an expectation. Much of the accountability is satisfied by reasons, but they have to be transparent and objectively justified reasons that are applied consistently.

The trust model is not simply a model for complaints. It is a model which fits into an ongoing relationship between the parties. If the intervention of the beneficiary occurs, it is to ensure that its interests are respected not only in relation to specific transactions in the past, but also in relation to the future of the ongoing relationship. Now the ongoing relationship requires the interests of the beneficiary are properly acknowledged and taken into account. This requires both a focus on the beneficiary's interests as relevant considerations that are taken into account (and are checked) and are reflected in the reasons that are given for a decision. On the whole, judicial review can check that these processes have been followed, but cannot engage much with the content. That is the long recognised distinction between the review of legality and that of merits. The trust model and its concern to

[19] See Wang 2017, p. 650, citing *Salford Primary Care Trust, ex p. Murphy* [2008] EWHC 1908.
[20] *AXA General Insurance Ltd. v Lord Advocate* [2011] UKSC 46, [2012] 1 AC 868.

protect expectations tends to blur the line somewhat. Judicial review ensures mainly that the framework of the relationships established by law are respected, but then lets the parties get on with the framework of that relationship.

## 1.4 Influences on Judicial Review: Braiding

Maurice Sunkin has argued that we need to have a focus on the perspective of the administrator if we are to understand the impact that judicial review has on decision-makers.[21] In particular, legal scholars need to appreciate the way judicial review decisions are received and interpreted into the ongoing flow of administrative decisions. For example, there may be regular discussions between the representatives of local and central government about the formulae to be used for providing state funding to local government. In the course of those conversations, ministers may make decisions which are then challenged by way of judicial review.[22]

But the judicial review process is not the end of the matter, and the real point of the litigation is to ensure that there are changes in administrative practice by the minister in relation to future discussions and negotiations.

In many countries, judicial review actions are brought either directly by non-governmental organisations (NGOs) or are funded by them.[23] Their social function is to support groups of citizens and to lobby the government on their behalf. They are frequently treated as privileged interlocutors within the processes of formulating and implementing policies.[24] They bring judicial review actions typically as part of their campaigning to put pressure on government.[25] It therefore makes sense to assess judicial review in its administrative context, a context in which legal and non-legal considerations are closely connected.

Public officials are subjected to an inter-connecting mix of legal and non-legal standards. These are "braided" together like the locks of hair to form a strong constraint. "Braiding" is a term I borrow from the literature on the enforcement of contracts. Gilson and colleagues use "braiding" to signify the combination of formal and informal methods of enforcement which are integrated in such a way as to build trust between the parties.[26] What applies in the consensual contract field, also

[21] Sunkin 2004, p. 69.

[22] For example, *R v Secretary of State for the Environment, ex p. Association of Metropolitan Authorities* [1981] 1 WLR 1; *R v Secretary of State for the environment, ex p. Hackney LBC* [1984] 1 WLR 592.

[23] See Baldwin and McCrudden 1987.

[24] See Hilton et al. 2013.

[25] See, e.g., Jans and Marseille 2010.

[26] Gilson et al. 2010, p. 1383. The article develops the idea of combining formal and informal methods of enforcement. In my use, I go much further and look at standards. In presenting this, I am very grateful to Pablo Baquero whose thesis develops the concept of braiding much more fully:

applies in the non-consensual world of administration. There is a longstanding body of literature in the UK on the place of informal mechanisms in the control of the administration. It is for the courts, amongst others, to ensure that their standards braid, rather than fray.

*Illustration of "Braiding" 1: The Ombudsman*

The UK does not have a concept of "the administration" (*l'administration*) in the French sense of an organically collected body of those who carry out the will of the legislature. There are a vast number (which no one can count) of bodies which could be treated as "administrations". Each has its own legislation creating it and setting standards for its performance. The traditional way of handling complaints was to set up bespoke mechanisms, often a tribunal or conciliation body. So the natural question has always been, "how is this administrative body expected to work?" and complaints resolution mechanisms use the answer as a benchmark.[27] As Harlow and Rawlings explain, despite the initial intentions of those establishing tribunals, they have been seen by lawyers as "court-substitute" bodies and have gradually been moved in the years 1957 (Franks) to 2007 (Tribunals, Courts, and Enforcement Act 2007) into becoming an integral part of the judicial system, specialist in dealing with complaints against the administration.[28] The emphasis here is on conformity to rules of substance and procedure. Alongside the tribunals, there also grew up ombudsmen first in the public sector (from 1967) and then in the private sector. These have been important in establishing standards for the way the administration behaves. The standards are those connected with ideas of "good administration".

The fragmented character of the UK administration has meant that we have failed to establish formally or informally any general statement of standards with which the administration should comply. Instead, there have been the occasional public inquiry or committee. The Franks Committee of 1957 and the Nolan Committee on Standards in Public Life are the two most famous.[29]

But there is no equivalent to the Dutch GALA (*Algemene wet bestuursrecht 1994*) in terms of legislation or the *Guidelines of Proper Administration* adopted by the NO. As a result, the courts and the ombudsmen have effectively constructed their standards on a case-by-case basis through their grievance settling processes,

"Networks of Collaborative Contracts for Innovation" (Cambridge 2018), especially Chapter 2 in which he focuses on institutional arrangements as well as standards which ensure the coordinated interplay of formal and informal elements.

[27] See Stebbings 2006; Rawlings 1987.

[28] See Harlow and Rawlings 2009, pp. 437–444.

[29] The Committee on Tribunals and Inquiries (Cmnd. 218, 1957); *Standards in Public Life* (Cm 2850-I, 1995). The Franks Committee was set up to look at tribunals and inquiries, but its principles of openness, fairness and impartiality were the touchstone of broader reforms of the culture of public administration. The Nolan Committee looked in particular at the ethics of political life, but this also went further into all areas of public life: see below text in footnote 49.

with little systematic overview. The relationship between legal and non-legal standards can be seen through two illustrations.

As Cane makes clear, the courts and the Ombudsman are alternative forms of remedying complaints made by citizens. Each has procedural and substantive advantages. But, from the point of view of both the administrator and the citizen, they are able to make criticisms of how an administrative decision has been made in the past and how decisions should be made in the future. So there is an obvious concern that the interventions of each body should be laying down broadly similar requirements and standards.

A Dutch doctorate writer, Milan Remáč, has written there is no formal mechanism of coordination between the British courts and the British ombudsmen.[30] At best one can expect that there will be some synergy between what they produce. Although Remáč does not articulate this very fully, his underlying idea is that there should be coherence in the standards to which the administration is held accountable.

Remáč presents the idea of "normative coordination"—that the standards applied by courts and ombudsmen should set broadly similar standards. In relation to both England and the Netherlands, he sets out in some detail how there are normative similarities in what the courts do in the name of controlling the legality of the administration, and what the ombudsmen do in sanctioning maladministration. Of course, there are differences. The judge is concerned to ensure that formal requirements in terms of competence and procedure are complied with. The ombudsman is concerned to ensure that standards of good administration are upheld. These are naturally higher standards, and he points out that values such as *courtesy and civility* in dealing with citizens and *seeking continuous* improvement are values which go beyond the requirements of legality.[31] He makes similar points in relation to the Dutch legal system. He notes that from the Guidelines of Proper Administration drawn up by the Dutch National Ombudsman principles 7 (courtesy), 13 (leniency) and 15 (de-escalation) go beyond what would be expected of judges. Whereas the court applies proportionality allowing a margin of appreciation to the administration and only intervenes where there is manifest disproportionate conduct. The ombudsman, by contrast, requires that the action of the administration must be moderate and be the least burdensome for the citizen.[32] The result is that he concludes that, even in areas of substantive overlap, normative standards of the ombudsman can have a different application form those of the courts.[33] There is not an integrated set of standards.

The worry articulated in Remáč's research is the rather casual lack of knowledge on the part of judges about what the ombudsman would do. In his report on the Netherlands, he states that "the NO [Nationale Ombudsman] and the courts

[30]Remáč 2014, Part II, Chapter 3.

[31]Ibid., p. 216.

[32]Ibid., p. 116.

[33]Ibid., p. 351.

mutually acknowledge the existence of their findings."[34] He illustrates this from a number of cases where the findings of the NO are acknowledged in the judgment of a court.

They may not be binding, but they provide a guide to whether something has gone wrong in an administrative decision or not.

By contrast, there is more limited awareness in England. There is some reference, but it is ad hoc.[35] Overall, the Ombudsmen look at the judges more than the judges look to the Ombudsmen. The JUSTICE-All Souls Review of 1988 suggested that there should be an "Administrative Review Commission" which should "keep under constant review all the procedures and institutions whereby the individual may challenge administrative action".[36] But nothing came of it, although the Commonwealth Ombudsman in Australia does perform this role.[37] Such a function is a more general, audit role, rather than the resolution of complaints.

Yet it is clear that the work of lawyers within non-legal bodies, such as the Council on Tribunals (which functioned from 1958 to 2007) and the Administrative Justice and Tribunals Council (which replaced it until 2013), helped to identify where the law needed to be reformed in relation to judicial review in England. So there is a major point in ensuring the perception of the administration gained in the ombudsman's complaints process is shared with those involved in judicial review.

The development of English administrative law shows the standards of good administration are developed extra-legally and these influence the way judicial review imposes duties such as to give a hearing or to give reasons or not to give the appearance of bias. Judges sometimes offer a valuable corrective to such public standards, but they are not the primary standard-setters. In the UK, standards may well be set by the administration itself. A good illustration is the *Citizens' Charter* of 1992 under which "information and openness", "courtesy and helpfulness", "choice and consultation","putting things right" were among the six principles of public service. These standards were referred to by the Ombudsman, but were not seen as exhaustive.[38] The key to this reform was to have a Unit within Government which followed up implementation. A reliance on complaints to trigger action will inevitably produce a patchy result.

But there are areas, such as human rights, where the judges have to intervene to protect vulnerable groups from abuse by the majority. Major areas are the administration of prisons and immigration, where people are not able to defend themselves and political imperatives disregard the interests of those who are the subjects of administration. Of course, there are administrative standards enforced by

---

[34] Ibid., p. 90 and more generally, Part II, Chapter 4.

[35] Ibid., Part II, Chapter 4 and p. 201.

[36] JUSTICE-All Souls Review of Administrative Law in the United Kingdom, *Administrative Justice. Some Necessary Reforms* (Clarendon Press 1988, Oxford), p. 74.

[37] See Cane, above note 7, pp. 261–263.

[38] Select Committee on the Parliamentary Commissioner, *Implications of the Citizens' Charter for the Work of the Parliamentary Commissioner for Administration* (HC 1991-2, 158), para 3. More generally, see p. 1999, Chapter 5.

inspectors, but these often need reinforcing by the courts, particularly as they involve international standards.

The idea of braiding picks up Remác's approach which suggests that there needs to be some effort at connection between the formal (legal) and the more informal (administrative or other non-legal) standards of good administrative conduct. Remác's attention focuses mainly on the use of normative standard setting. But there is a need for some institutional structure to support it. In addition, there is a proper place for the formal. As Michael Harris pointed out, there is evidence that the effect of relying on informal systems may not be to the benefit of citizens.[39] It is therefore important to know the effects of each process.

Institutions vary between countries. To a great extent, the French model of *l'administration* is hierarchical. The Paris government exercises control through prefects and the ministry of finance over regional administrations and various other ministries have oversight powers or, in the case of public education, have very strong powers of direction. As a result, informal standards can be set by circular from the Prime Minister or some other minister.

The French situation provides examples of how the interaction of the legal and the non-legal can be supported by a formal legal framework establishing relationships between the courts and the Ombudsman.[40] The French Ombudsman was created as the *Médiateur* by legislation in 1973 and became constitutionally enshrined as the *Défenseur des droits* in 2008. Implementing that constitutional amendment, legislation of 2011 sets out a number of ways in which interaction between the courts and the Ombudsman are institutionalised. In a first way, judges from the administrative courts are appointed to various bodies which advise the *Défenseur*, especially those dealing with the ethics of security and combatting discrimination. The *Défenseur* is also able to obtain an advisory opinion from the Conseil d'État on the interpretation of legislation. The function of this process is to enable the *Défenseur* to reduce the amount of litigation which may arise. For example, following the decision of the Cour de cassation in the *Baby Loup* case,[41] the question arose about whether people who helped with the public service, such as teaching assistants in schools, had to follow the prescriptions of religious neutrality required by the constitutional principle of secularism (*laïcité*) that applied to the public service as a whole. Because the private sector and private individuals are involved in various ways with the delivery of public services, this ruling was able to anticipate many potential disputes.[42] The *Défenseur* is also authorised to intervene in litigation as a kind of amicus curiae in order to secure a similarity of approach between the courts and the Ombudsman. For example, this did occur in relation to the prevention of discrimination in relation to handicapped people.[43] These various

[39] Harris and Partington 1999, Chapter 2.

[40] See De Saint-Sernin 2018. On the Médiateur see Brown and Bell 1998, pp. 32–34.

[41] Cass. Ass. Plén, 25 June 2014, JCP 2014 J 903. See Hunter-Hénin 2015; Bell 2017, p. 240.

[42] See avis, 19 December 2013, JCP adm 2014, 2005.

[43] See CE 20 November 2013, case no. 362879.

institutional procedures do not change the function of the French Ombudsman. He is still only allowed to recommend, not to impose solutions on the administration. But the functions of the courts and of the Ombudsman are to be coordinated. Originally, this was achieved only by informal processes.[44] Now the more formal procedures have both institutionalised the exchanges between the two institutions and have enhanced them. The Ombudsman has a place in the court room, and the administrative judge has a place in the formal advisory mechanisms of the Ombudsman. In this way, it is easier to ensure that both institutions are coordinated in their advice or requirements to administrators and in their dealings with the public, especially in the resolution of complaints.

*Illustration of "Braiding" 2: Bias and Corruption*

The issue of corruption and bias demonstrates a significant interplay between judicial review and more informal standards. The "rule against bias"[45] established in judicial review started with the idea that a judge or administrator could not have a pecuniary interest in the matter which he was deciding. In the light of developing national standards and also of Article 6(1) the European Convention on Human Rights, the test has been expanded to prohibit situations in which the "fair-minded and well-informed observer" would consider that there was a real possibility that the decision-maker would be biased.[46] The result of this expansion is that courts and administrators must be careful to remove potential appearances of bias.

As the public service has grown and diversified, the informal mechanisms of ensuring common ethical standards have no longer sufficed. When the functions of the state were limited to maintaining order and minimal public services, and these were often provided by local authorities, then it was possible to ensure a relative similarity in the understanding of standards. But the demands for state intervention have grown and there are large public services on a national level.

For example, France has almost 5.5 million civil servants in 1700 *corps*.[47] In the UK, as in many other countries, there has been an effort in recent years to involve the expertise of the private sector far more in the provision of public services. Whatever values are shared among those who work directly as part of the public sector, these are not necessarily shared by those engaged by the private sector. There needs to be training and monitoring to ensure that these are adopted. Among those elected to public office, most will come from a variety of public and private sector backgrounds that are different one from another. They too will not necessarily come to their roles with a deep understanding of public sector values in areas such as the appearance of bias. The result is a growing heterogeneity among those

[44] See Braibant 1977, p. 287

[45] See Wade and Forsyth 2014, Chapter 13.

[46] *Lawal v Northern Spirit Ltd.* [2003] UKHL 35; *Porter v Magill* [2001] UKHL 67.

[47] See (2017) La fonction publique d'État – Le portail de la Fonction publique [The Public Service of the State—The Public Service Portal]. https://www.fonction-publique.gouv.fr/la-fonction-publique-detat. Accessed 11 June 2018.

involved in the delivery and management of public services. One cannot make assumptions in societies with a plurality of ethical beliefs about common standards. It has therefore become a significant issue in most western countries to reinforce existing ethical standards. In 1998, the OECD produced its "Principles for Managing Ethics in the Public Service" [C(98)70/FINAL], and these are now incorporated in the Recommendation of the Council on "Guidelines for Managing Conflict of Interest in the Public Service" of 2003.[48]

National concern with these issues has not been simply following international trends. The UK Report notes that the Nolan Commission reported already in 1995 with a very substantial statement of "Standards in Public Life" that has been expanded into a wide range of areas.[49] In particular, Principle 2 (Integrity) provides:

> Holders of public office must avoid placing themselves under any obligation to people or organisations that might try inappropriately to influence them in their work. They should not act or take decisions in order to gain financial or other material benefits for themselves, their family, or their friends. They must declare and resolve any interests and relationships.

In addition, Principle 4 on accountability requires that officials hold themselves accountable for their decisions and Principle 5 requires openness in decisions. This goes beyond requiring that public officials give reasons for decisions, it also requires that the key documents involved in the decision are open to inspection.

These principles sit alongside criminal law sanctions against specific forms of corruption and also the potential for judicial review to be taken against a public body decision.[50] The Committee on Standards in Public Life provides independent guidance to public bodies based on investigations which it has conducted. Such reports can identify particular areas of public life where there is concern and can make recommendations. For example, in May 2018, this body provided advice on ethical concerns in relation to the use of private, voluntary and charitable sector bodies in the delivery of public services.[51] The need arose from the increased use of outsourcing by government departments to deliver public services and concerns about the growing size of certain firms who were capable of delivering such services and the ethical standards they adopted, e.g. in relation to their employees and their pensions.

These concerns go beyond corruption in the narrow sense of public officials putting money into their private pockets, but they do relate to the broader concern about the values that are exhibited in the public sector, particularly Nolan Principle

[48] See Managing Conflict of Interest of the Public Service—OECD. http://www.oecd.org/gov/ethics/managingconflictofinterestinthepublicservice.htm. Accessed 8 June 2018.

[49] *Standards in Public Life* (Cm 2850-I, 1995): see generally Jowell and Oliver 2007, Chapter 17, and the Committee on Standards in Public Life (2018). http://www.public-standards.gov.uk. Accessed 8 June 2018.

[50] See the facts of *Jones v Swansea City Council* [1990] 1 WLR 54 and 1453: premises leased by a council to a woman whose husband was a member of that council.

[51] Committee on Standards in Public Life (2018) The Continuing Importance of Ethical Standards for Public service Providers. https://assets.publishing.service.gov.uk/government/uploads/system/uploads/attachment_data/file/705884/20180510_PSP2_Final_PDF.pdf. Accessed 8 June 2018.

1 (selflessness): "Holders of public office should act solely in terms of the public interest."

The Dutch experience is similar. In a Report to the World Congress of Comparative Law in 2006, the Dutch approach was explained as going beyond legal rules:

> The Dutch authorities adopt policies based on the consideration that established rules alone are not enough to promote integrity among administrative bodies. They rely on civil servants' conscience with regard to integrity problems. The main focus of the current Dutch policy on integrity is that administrative bodies: are aware of the importance of integrity; promote awareness; identify vulnerable spots in their organisations; take measures to reduce risks; have the capacity and the will to cope with violations of the integrity principle; and keep integrity at the top of the agenda.[52]

In that analysis, there was a combination of both legal rules (such as in administrative law and criminal law) and "soft law" instruments, such as codes of conduct, which together helped to create an environment in which the avoidance of corruption is encouraged and biased conduct seen as inappropriate. At the same time, there are institutional mechanisms which help to support the implementation of these values. For example, The Dutch authors described the way that a central office within the Ministry of Justice supports authorised local authorities in enforcing the law on corruption in the public sector. When such a public body applies, this Office investigates the integrity of applicants for licences and subsidies. To perform this task, the Office has numerous sources of judicial, financial and police information. As a result of its investigations, the Office assesses the risks and likelihood that applicants will abuse the required facility. These findings will be formulated in a written advice for the local authority, articulating the level of potential concern of corruption.

The EU Anti-Corruption Report of 2014[53] wrote positively about the work of this Office for the Promotion of Public Sector Integrity (BIOS, *Bureau Integriteitsbevordering Openbare Sector*). The institutional mechanism of supporting prior identification of problems avoids the need to undertake judicial review of decisions for bias or the criminal prosecution of those who took the decision for corrupt motives. That Report also notes that the rules applicable to prevent conflict of interests of civil servants are in detail described and explained in the Conflict of Interests Manual. In addition, those rules are supported by a self-assessment tool known as "SAINT" (Self-Assessment INTegriteit) which was developed to assess risks and to self-assess the impact of the integrity policy of public bodies.[54] Some local authorities go further and produce their own toolbox to aid decision-making. It is the braiding of legal rules, non-legal standards, and institutional procedures and mechanisms that produces the robust solution. Now, the Report also makes clear

---

[52] Addink and ten Berge 2007, p. 14.

[53] COM (2014) 38 final, Annex 19 Netherlands, pp. 5–7.

[54] Ibid., p. 5.

that these different kinds of rule build on longstanding traditions and values within the Dutch public sector and community, but they do manage to take them further.

One of the ways of gaining trust in public decision-making is to develop codes of practice which are enforced. In France, these have recently been reformed by the creation of the commission de déontologie de la fonction publique.

Created originally in 1993, its function was completely overhauled in 2016. Its function is to examine issues connected with corruption and transparency in public life and public procurement.[55]

The area of corruption is a good illustration of "braiding" at work. If we take an overview of national systems, then we can see that many of the issues in the area of corruption translate not simply into concerns about bias in decision-making, but form part of larger concerns about good government.[56] Sanctioning the decision that has been taken in a biased or corrupt fashion is only one tool in a large toolbox that is concerned with ensuring that the right decisions are taken in the first place. The mechanisms used in specific countries reflect national traditions, but they are often taken in the light of international pressures from bodies such as the EU, the Council of Europe, the OECD and so on. Most of these exercise "soft law" influence. Even at national level, the legal rules on how decisions are made and what is impermissible fit together with procedures and standards of a soft law kind about how decisions should be made. The judgement on the rightness of decisions is not limited what is legally allowed, but fits the broader set of ethical values.[57]

## 1.5 What Are the Conditions for "Braiding" to Work?

Braiding is about the integration and coherence of judicial and other forms of accountability. Ideally, the standards set by the judiciary ought to fit coherently with those of the other bodies. But how does that work? If we go back to the studies of the Ombudsman, then some pointers emerge. One issue is the distance between the institutions. The British Ombudsman was created as an adjunct to Parliament. Indeed, members of the public could originally only gain access to the Parliamentary Commissioner for Administration (as he was originally called) through a member of Parliament. The Commissioner then reported to Parliament for action to be taken. He has since gained independence of action and direct powers of recommending remedies. But this institutional position inevitably set him apart from the more independent courts. It is only when the Ombudsman became more independent that the courts would have seen a degree of similarity. Furthermore, the legislation creating the Ombudsman specifically excluded the jurisdiction of the

[55] La commission de déontologie – Le portail de la Fonction publique [The Commission of Ethics —The Public Service Portal.

[56] See Bell 2007, p. 796.

[57] Ibid., pp. 80–807. See also Bell 2006, pp. 1273–1274.

Ombudsman where a redress was possible before the courts. Of course, this was less critical in the early days, because judicial review had barely developed as a form of redress for the citizen. It is much more a concern today, when judicial review is more active. There is a contrast here with the French position which started with a similar restriction of access only through members of Parliament. But the competition between institutions was less of a problem. The workload of the administrative courts was increasing at the time at which the Ombudsman was being created and especially again at the time when the office was being revised by the creation of the *Défenseur des droits* in the period 2007–2011. The administrative courts perceived the need to reduce the flow of litigation, and they saw the Ombudsman as a potential mechanism of resolving cases in a non-binding way. The Balladur report of 2007[58] sought to provide redress in relation to the good functioning of the public administration, rather than just interference with rights. This complementarity of mission was reassured, as has already been said, by institutional mechanisms. When it comes to corruption and public sector ethics, the British experience was easier because the chair of the committee established to look into the question was a senior judge.

The second dynamic needed to secure braiding is informal interaction. This is most obvious within the contractual setting which was the original source of the concept. Within a contractual setting, interaction between parties and the formalisation of understandings go hand-in-hand.

The field of innovation contracts starts with the informal arrangements between the parties and then leads them to put some down in more formal documents. There is not the same collaborative enterprise between the different groups who seek to regulate the public administration. Informal interactions between them depend on a much looser sense of common enterprise. It is clear that the French and the Dutch have managed this much more than the British. British courts remain within a professional legal world and do not see the same kind of shared function being performed by others, such as Ombudsmen.

The area of corruption suggests that a third dynamic is the fit with the existing political and administrative culture. The reports on the Netherlands argue that there is an underlying culture which is supportive of the ideals of integrity which the informal codes of practice and procedures within the administration are trying to secure. The Committee on Standards in Public Life has as similar grounding within the culture of the public service on which to work. It is that which brings the examples here back to the original idea of "braiding" as it appeared in the contract law literature. There common projects provide the bedrock on which the common standards are developed.

[58] Comité de réflexion et de proposition sur la modernisation et le rééquilibrage des institutions de la Ve République, *Une Ve République plus démocratique* (Paris 2007), pp. 91–92.

## 1.6 Conclusion

Judicial review has an important, but limited place within the array of mechanisms available to ensure the accountability of public bodies. There are matters on which it excels—notably the control of the competence of a decision-maker and an instance on following procedure in making a decision. At the other extreme of providing a remedy for complaints or compensation, it is less well placed. It is often cumbersome and expensive. In terms of setting standards, judicial review is necessarily hit and miss. Some issues will come to the courts and some issues will not, depending on the vicissitudes of litigation. Even when they come to court, not all aspects of a topic will be covered. By contrast, a systematic code of practice can be produced by regulatory bodies or others. So the standards set by judicial review are likely to be fragmentary and episodic. A court may have the opportunity to lay down important points, but it has to recognise that the bulk of the standard-setting will be undertaken by others. That necessarily leads to the need for coherence in what is required of the administration. A French model of hierarchical superiors and central supervisors (préfets, recteurs de l'académie) enables centralised guidance to communicate standards produced by different bodies (including the courts). The more recent French model of cross-membership in advisory committees to the *Défenseur des droits* and standing for that person to plead before the courts institutionalises communication between the different bodies dealing with complaints and setting standards. But both features of the French system are illustrations of the specific ways that braiding can be made to work. It does not result simply from the enactment of standards (even coherent standards) by different authorities. Those only produce the different strands of hair. The braiding is a more deliberate process and cannot be left to the poor administrator to sort out for herself. Of course, we will not get perfect coherence. Anyone who has tried to undertake the braiding of hair will know that it requires more time than the client usually has. But it is worth doing, because it produces a better product. In relation to administrative law, it produces better instructions to officials and better protection for the citizen.

## References

Addink GH, ten Berge JBJM (2007) Study on Innovation of Legal Means for Eliminating Corruption in the Public Service. 11 (1) Electronic Journal of Comparative Law

Baldwin R, McCrudden C (1987) Regulation and Public Law. Weidenfeld and Nicolson, London

Bell J (2006) Comparative Administrative Law. In: Reimann M, Zimmerman R (eds) The Oxford Handbook of Comparative Law. Oxford University Press, Oxford, pp 1259–1286

Bell J (2007) Legal Means for Eliminating Corruption in the Public Service. In: Boele Woelki K, van Erp S (eds) General Reports of the XVIIth Congress of the International Academy of Comparative Law. Bruylant, Brussels, pp 785–807

Bell J (2017) Secularism French Style. European Public Law 23:237–244

Braibant G (1977) Les rapports du Médiateur et du juge administratif [The Ombudsman's rapport and administrative judge]. AJDA 1977:283–288

Brown N, Bell J (1998) French Administrative Law. Oxford University Press, Oxford
Cane P (2009) Administrative Tribunals and Adjudication. Hart Publishing, Oxford
De Saint-Sernin J (2018) Le Défenseur des droits et le juge administratif [The Defender of Rights and the Administrative Judge]. RFDA 34(2):332–342
Dowdle M (2006) Public Accountability: Designs, Dilemmas and Experiences. Cambridge University Press, Cambridge
Elliott M (2016) From Heresy to Orthodoxy: Substantive Legitimate Expectations in English Public Law. In: Groves M, Weeks G (eds) Legitimate Expectations in the Common Law World. Hart Publishing, Oxford, pp 217–44
Gilson R R, Sabel C F, Scott R E (2010) Braiding: The Interaction of Formal and Informal Contracting in Theory, Practice and Doctrine. Columbia Law Review 110:1377–1448
Gregory R, Drewry G (1991) Barlow Clowes and the Ombudsman. Public Law: Summer 2:192–214
Harris M, Partington M (eds) (1999) Administrative Justice in the 21st Century. Hart Publishing, Oxford
Harlow C (2002) Accountability in the European Union. Oxford University Press, Oxford
Harlow C, Rawlings R (2009) Law and Administration. Cambridge University Press, Cambridge
Hilton M, McKay J, Crowson N, Mouhot J F (2013) The Politics of Expertise: How NGOs Shaped Modern Britain. Oxford University Press, Oxford
Hughes K (2017) R v North and East Devon Health Authority [2001]: Coughlan and the Development of Public Law. In: Juss S, Sunkin M (eds) Landmark Cases in Public Law. Hart Publishing, Oxford, Chapter 9
Hunter-Hénin M (2015) Religion, Children and Employment: The Baby Loup Case. International Comparative Law Quarterly 64(3):717–731
Jans J H, Marseille A T (2010) The Role of NGOs in Environmental Litigation against Public Authorities: Some Observations on Judicial Review and Access to Court in the Netherlands. Journal of Environmental Law 22(3):373–390
Jowell J, Oliver D (2007) The Changing Constitution. Oxford University Press, Oxford
Marique Y (2014) Public-Private Partnerships and the Law. Edward Elgar Publishing, Cheltenham
Mulgan R (2000) Accountability: An Ever Expanding Concept? Public Administration 78(3):555–573
Oliver D (1991) Government in the United Kingdom: The Search for Accountability, Effectiveness and Citizenship. Open University Press, Milton Keynes
Rawlings R (1987) In the Jungle. Modern Law Review 50:110–117
Remáč M (2014) Coordinating Ombudsmen and the Judiciary. Intersentia, Cambridge
Stebbings C (2006) Legal Foundations of Tribunals in Nineteenth-Century England. Cambridge University Press, Cambridge
Sunkin M (2004) Conceptual Issues in Researching the Impact of Judicial Research on Government Bureaucracies. In: Hertogh M, Halliday S (eds) Judicial Review and Bureaucratic Impact: International and Interdisciplinary Perspectives. Cambridge University Press, Cambridge, pp 43–75
Wade H, Forsyth C (2014) Administrative Law. Oxford University Press, Oxford
Wang D (2017) From Wednesbury Unreasonableness to Accountability for Reasonableness. Cambridge Law Journal 76(3):642–670

# Chapter 2
# Constitutional Genealogy of Judicial Review in the Administrative State

**Ernst Hirsch Ballin**

## Contents



**Abstract** Administrative procedural law has long been based on the idea that the administration enjoys freedom in the execution of laws that are established through democratic procedures, and that the administration is therefore primarily subject to political, not judicial, oversight. Public administration has however become increasingly complex, and rule-making occurs more and more by specialized administrative agencies. This high degree of professionalism makes it difficult for democratic bodies to properly check the administration. Therefore, administrative

---

Ernst Hirsch Ballin is distinguished university professor (Tilburg University), professor in human rights law (University of Amsterdam), and president of the T.M.C. Asser Institute for International and European Law. He is also a member of the Scientific Council for Government policy (WRR). Ernst Hirsch Ballin was from 2000 a member and from 2003 the president of the Administrative Jurisdiction Division of the Council of State, until he was reappointed as the Minister of Justice of the Netherlands (2006–2010). He recently published on the future of the European Union, citizens' rights and fundamental rights protection, and trust in the rule of law.

---

E. Hirsch Ballin (✉)
Tilburg University, Tilburg, The Netherlands

University of Amsterdam, Amsterdam, The Netherlands

T.M.C. Asser Institute, The Hague, The Netherlands



J. de Poorter et al. (eds.), *Judicial Review of Administrative Discretion in the Administrative State*, https://doi.org/10.1007/978-94-6265-307-8_2

procedural law has to enable administrative courts to move beyond the 'margin control' on the exercise of discretionary powers by the administration and facilitate an effective legal protection against the administration.

**Keywords** Administrative procedural law · judicial restraint · the administrative state · judicial review · proportionality principle

The ways in which administrative acts are reviewed by the judiciary arise from constitutional changes in the 19th century and afterwards. The recognition that no power in the state can be absolute, and that a *Rechtsstaat* (or state governed by the rule of law) demands that all powers be based on and restricted by democratically legitimate law, required the gradual replacement of internal review (i.e. administrative appeals to higher levels in the state structure) by independent judicial review. In the course of this evolution, the different legal traditions of the *Rechtsstaat* and *État de Droit* in continental Europe, and that of the Rule of Law in Anglo-American contexts, finally arrived at 'a kind of convergence'.[1] However, this certainly did not mean an end to the dynamics in the constitutional and socio-economic context of administrative law. Indeed, the effects of some of the changes that started in the 20th century have still not yet been seen in full. This chapter starts with some observations concerning the nature of judicial review, against the background of the current debate on the relationship between judicial review and administrative authority, and then situates this in the evolving functioning of public administration. From there, a constitutional genealogy of the judicial function in administrative law can be delineated.

## 2.1 The Significance of the Law of Procedure

The law of procedure ('procedural law') is often viewed as an arid, but indispensable branch of law. As well as judicial procedures, procedural law includes the decision-making process preceding any legal disputes, both in administrative and other branches of law. Procedural law obviously has to function efficiently if we wish to do justice to conflicting interests. At the same time, and especially with regard to appeals against administrative decisions, concerns have been mounting about certain abuses of procedural law that serve to delay political and administrative decision-making. From both perspectives, however, procedural law is obviously intimately connected with the very purposes of substantive law and its development. Jannes Eggens, one of the sharpest minds in Dutch civil law of the 20th century, emphasized the dynamic character of legal relations and how they

[1] Lindseth and Rose-Ackerman 2010, Chapter 1 (introduction).

'proceed' in legal procedures.[2] The classical Roman maxim of *da mihi factum, dabo tibi ius* correctly summarizes that the legal process transforms evidence and arguments into the determination and legal validation of formerly contested legal relationships.

The specific features of a legal relationship used to be reflected in the applicable procedural law. During the course of the 20th century private law changed as much as administrative law. At present, private law protects vulnerable interests through mandatory rules and has considerably reduced the scope for individual autonomy, while values underlying fundamental rights are impacting more and more on rights and obligations.[3] The way in which private law is applied is embedded in public law structures, such as the administration of real estate and patents, and the redistribution of benefits under copyright law and 'neighbouring rights'. At the same time, the traditional demarcation between administrative law and criminal law has become porous. Law enforcement with respect to essential general interests—like the integrity of the financial system, the reliability of the distribution of information, and public security and counterterrorism—nowadays requires coordinated efforts under various legal regimes.[4] While it may still be correct—not only in common law—to view private law as the skeleton of a legal system, much of the musculature that steers the skeleton's movements now comprises administrative procedures that are applied primarily by public bodies and ultimately, in the case of disputes, by the courts.

By definition, all these functions of administrative law are related to acts of public bodies. However, administrative law does not cover the functioning of the state in every respect as its procedures do not generally apply to acts of the institutions associated with the deploying of sovereign powers and governing. The government (the head of state, or the government and its ministers) decides on the direction of politics. In the Netherlands, this task is attributed to the Council of Ministers (under Article 45 of the *Grondwet*, i.e. the Constitution), while at a European Union level a similar role is fulfilled by the European Council. As Article 15 of the Lisbon Treaty states, 'The European Council shall provide the Union with the necessary impetus for its development and shall define the general political directions and priorities thereof. It shall not exercise legislative functions.' These sovereignty-bearing institutions (*soevereiniteit-dragende instellingen*)[5] take their decisions under specific rules, which we may refer to as constitutional procedural law. This is a subject fundamentally different from that of administrative law: its purpose is the expression of political will, in the past often as absolute rulers, but currently in accordance with the principles of the *Rechtsstaat* and every individual's fundamental rights. While any review by a constitutional court has to examine questions of a possibly deeply political nature, it must resist the temptation to seek

[2] Schoordijk and Smits 1998, p. 505.

[3] Meder 2011, p. 459.

[4] Hirsch Ballin 2018.

[5] Van der Hoeven 1958.

to take control of politics:[6] it should express neither more nor less than arguably constitutional viewpoints. The Netherlands makes no provision for constitutional review of legislation by a court. Indeed, under Article 120 of the Constitution, courts are forbidden from meddling in the constitutionality of parliamentary legislation and treaties.

Maybe because its government ministers are ideally and typically decision-makers in matters of administrative law, the traditional Dutch aversion against judicial meddling in state affairs has spilled over into the view that judicial restraint is required precisely *because of the political legitimation* of administrative decision-making. In this theory, executive power is supposed to entail not only the execution of laws, but also, in the event of discretionary powers, the execution of policy decisions taken by ministers and other authorities who are politically accountable to parliament or local representative bodies. Here, discretionary powers are framed as a domain of administrative ‘freedom’, upon which judges should not encroach and which should be exclusively subject to hierarchical and, ultimately, political control.[7]

Administrative law has traditionally been viewed as law resulting from the statutory *empowerment* of administrative bodies—which is constitutionally correct—and therefore as nothing other than the *execution* of laws by bodies (jointly referred to as ‘the executive’) subject to political oversight, and accountable in a democratic context to representative bodies such as parliament and municipal councils. This, however, is a distortion of the political and administrative realities. This identification of empowerment (attribution of powers) with the execution of laws has produced two dogmatic assumptions in traditional administrative law theory: on the one hand, the assumption that the administration is legally ‘free’ to deploy its discretionary powers within the limits of its empowerment (hence the judicial review yardsticks of *ultra vires* and *abus de pouvoir*) and, on the other hand, that the way in which administrative bodies deploy their discretionary powers should usually be subject only to democratic political control, with the heads of these bodies accountable to representative bodies.

These two basic and related assumptions—discretionary powers constitute executive *freedom*, while executive freedom is subject to *political oversight*—emerged in the late 19th and early 20th centuries.[8] Until recently, these assumptions were dominant and indeed are still influential, especially among lawyers who focus on administrative law for attributing competences and among politicians trapped in the notion of politics as empowerment. However, these assumptions no longer hold true in view of the transformations of administrative law that have been seen in the recent past, especially since the final quarter of the 20th century. Any reassessment of administrative procedural law therefore has to include the administrative decision-making process itself.

[6] Maus 2018.
[7] Möllers 2016, p. 111.
[8] Donner 1987, p. 49.

## 2.2 Changes in the Constitutional Context

While the constitutional structure of three neatly distinguishable 'powers', including the executive power subordinated to politically accountable ministers, still serves didactical purposes, the workings of administrative law demonstrate a large degree of administrative self-sufficiency, and not only in 'new' domains. Although decisions on whether, for example, to admit non-citizens to the Netherlands are taken in the name of the Minister (or Deputy Minister) of Justice, only exceptional situations have to be submitted for consideration at a political level. Professional expertise within the framework of guidelines, including those in the *Vreemdelingencirculaire* [Aliens Act Implementation Guidelines], must be leading in the assessment of the facts and in the way the minister's discretionary powers are applied, and new guidelines will emerge if situations arise that are not sufficiently covered by existing standards.

This is just one example of a fundamental transformation in the modern state as a whole. Public bodies' intense involvement in economic and social life necessitates a profoundly different relationship between the state and other actors, which Peter Lindseth and others have referred to as the administrative state.[9] The development of the administrative state undermines the notion of an executive power merely following the generalized instructions of the laws that have to be 'applied'. These days, public administration comprises an extremely complex system of laws, legal decisions and physical interventions (the constructing of roads and railways, for example) aimed at stabilizing and facilitating activities of private, semi-public and public agents, and at protecting interests that are insufficiently strong in themselves.

The underlying constitutional principle in Western democracies has long since been that the freedom of action of the individual and the individual's organization is the appropriate default position. Interventions on behalf of the state require legal justification, in accordance with the legality principle enshrined in modern democratic constitutions. Depending on the evolving assessments of the needs and risks in a free society,[10] as well as technological developments, the priorities and intensity of administrative actions give shape to the economic order associated with the political system. In Western Europe, especially in the Member States of the European Communities founded in the 1950s, the organized market economy associated with the idea of *Ordoliberalismus* has profoundly influenced the development of administrative law and indeed has characterized the *Wirtschaftsverfassung*, or economic constitution, of these states and the EU.

Gradually the national political and economic order has transformed into a pluralism transcending national borders and including transnational 'regimes' and networks. The constitutional developments in the final decades of' the 20th century brought about considerable changes in the economic constitution, specifically its fundamental overhaul by the arrival of neoliberalism, with its aversion to political

[9] Lindseth 2010, p. 90.
[10] Vermeule 2014.

influence and its blind trust in the 'invisible hand' of the market. The ensuing privatization of state enterprises and state subsidies, which have since started increasing again, amounted to a redefinition of the economic constitution. These days, information processes, alongside economics, now define the constitutional set-up. Similar to the economic constitution, the constitutional arrangements for giving and receiving information could very well, therefore, be referred to as the 'information constitution', evoking a whole new array of administrative interventions. The availability and processing of information are such important resources of power that they require oversight, based on the ideas of transparency and countervailing powers.

Such new areas of public policy—market functioning, information, fraud, terrorism and other fields of international crime—are usually the domain of independent agencies. Administrative law now thus surpasses the traditional contours of the 'executive' in several ways. Its rules demand a swift and professional application that exceeds the reach of parliamentary legislation. The functioning of the bodies to which regulation is entrusted requires such a degree of professionalism that the hierarchical structure of a ministry, subject to political direction, is no longer suitable for this purpose. Although judicial oversight is essential in the absence of a clear set of legal norms, it will fail to achieve its intended purpose if it is constrained by antiquated notions of executive freedom and political oversight.

## 2.3 The Emancipation of Administrative Law from Being the Law of the Executive Function

What has not changed is the fact that all administrative bodies are bound by legislation, and that such legislation is in turn bound by the Constitution, EU law and international law. The legality principle requires a legal pedigree for all decisions and measures with an impact on the rights and freedoms of individuals, whose fundamental rights have to be respected and fulfilled. In traditional theories of administrative law, the constitutional requirement for a legal pedigree reflected the view that administrative law entailed merely the execution of laws and nothing else. But the—still not unusual—qualification of the administration as 'the executive power' fails to recognize that administrative bodies wield discretion to an extent that cannot be reduced to implicit or explicit instructions given by politically accountable authorities.

Nevertheless, this institutional imaginary has long served—and in some people's eyes still serves—as the justification and even as a compelling reason for judicial deference towards the administration. This view usually emphasizes the 'separation of powers' and relies on spatial metaphors to describe the nature of this separation.[11] In this view, all three branches of the *trias politica* (i.e. the legislature, the

[11] Hirsch Ballin 2015, pp. 7–58.

executive and the judiciary) have their own 'domain' upon which the other powers should not encroach. Courts, therefore, should limit themselves to checking that the law has not been violated, that the margins of the discretionary power have not been violated ('marginal control'), and that formal principles, such as the requirement to give reasons for decisions, have been observed. In the same language of spatial metaphors, a court failing to observe this restraint will be reproached for 'sitting on the administration's stool'. This view has profoundly influenced the nature of judicial review that has prevailed in the case law of the Administrative Jurisdiction Division (AJD) of the Council of State (the highest court for general administrative law in the Netherlands) since the final decade of the 20th century, with the result that the 'administration' enjoys the permanent benefit of the doubt. Until recently, for example, a typical reason for the AJD to reject claims of negligence in cases involving possible conflicts of interests would be that the court 'cannot conclude that the weighing of interests cannot be said to be sufficiently motivated'.

The judicial practice based on this theory of spatial separation of the powers has tended to follow a more or less fixed pattern of reasoning, starting with questions about the legal pedigree and followed by questions about administrative guidelines (in the form, for example, of instructions, plans and policy rules). If the administrative body has observed the law and the guidelines, the decision will be upheld by the court, unless a general rule of good administration (such as the need to give reasons) has been violated. In 1994, the proportionality principle—at that time already well known in German, French and European administrative law—was introduced into Dutch law through an amendment of the General Administrative Law Act [*Algemene wet bestuursrecht*]. The AJD, which at that time strictly adhered to the theory of judicial restraint, quickly responded through case law in which application of the proportionality principle was limited to situations involving misappreciation of a grave and manifest nature (*willekeur*).[12]

In 1968 H. D. van Wijk published a theory on law-making in administrative law, which he referred to as a 'stepping-back by the legislator'. In this theory, the legislator made room for the administration by substituting precise legal norms for discretionary powers softly regulated by guidelines, policies and plans. Remarkably, the traditional practice of judicial restraint supplements this stepping-back by the legislator with a simultaneous stepping-back by the court. This is now the weak spot in the practice of judicial restraint as it is exactly where the democratically legitimate legislator steps back that the court fails to step in, thus creating a gap in oversight.

The negative consequences of this stepping-back are aggravated by the extending of judicial restraint to the administration's assessment of the *facts*. Administrative procedural law does not contain many rules on evidence. In the doctrine applied by the AJD, however, at least until recently, the process of establishing the facts was viewed as the administration's own responsibility and to

[12] ABRS (*Afdeling bestuursrechtspraak van de Raad van State*) 9 May 1996, ECLI:NL:RVS:1996:ZF2153.

be assessed ahead of the decision-making (*ex tunc*), which could only be marginally checked by the court. This doctrine is unsatisfactory, firstly because factual assessments are typically something for which courts are competent (if necessary, assisted by independent experts), like in other branches of law, and secondly because this doctrine is seriously detrimental to the effectiveness of judicial protection regarding status decisions and other continuing legal relations. For this reason, Article 83 of the Immigration Act was amended in 2010 and now requires a factual assessment to include developments *after* the initial decision. This change is now being applied, albeit with some delay, in the Division's case law.

Once again it was a change in immigration law that paved the way for a reassessment of the restraint doctrine. Decisions on refugee protection belong to a legal domain that is highly value-laden and embedded in human rights. The persistence of this vacuum in domestic legal protection amounts to an invitation to the European Court of Human Rights to step in, even though serving as an ultimate court of appeal is not one of the latter's core tasks. Since 2015, Article 46 of EU Directive 2013/32/EU has required 'a full and ex nunc examination of both facts and points of law' of negative decisions. Cautious attempts in legislation to elicit a more far-reaching judicial review, including the introduction of the proportionality principle in Article 3:4, second paragraph, of the General Administrative Law Act, and the requirement for a full judicial review of asylum decisions, were ultimately accepted.[13]

Since the turn of the century, obligations under international and EU law had also been pushing the AJD in its case law to accept its role as a court with full jurisdiction, albeit still with some reservations. In recent years, therefore, the AJD has moved away from the restraint doctrine and endorsed a new approach, in which judicial reviews have assumed the characteristics of judicial assessments in general, similar to their role in civil and criminal jurisdiction. Along with their full jurisdiction on facts and the interpretation of the law, administrative courts are gradually proceeding in the direction of an effective *judicial* review of the use or failure to use discretion. Obviously, their yardsticks must be of a legal nature, including general principles of administrative law.

In its 2017 Annual Report, the AJD abandoned the terminology that was previously used in this respect, as if the administration enjoys 'freedom' of policy or assessment (*beleidsvrijheid* or *beoordelingsvrijheid*) in deploying its discretion.[14] Indeed, back in 1974, Jo van der Hoeven noted that public authorities never enjoy freedom in the way we do or may do.[15] What is meant by the term 'freedom' is, instead, the obligation to assess the kind of decision that is most suitable in the light of the underlying policy principles. The new preference for terminology referring to

[13] Including ABRS, 11 June 2014, ECLI:NL:RVS:2014:2052 (alcohol lock) and ABRS 13 April 2016, ECLI:NL:RVS:2016:890, ECLI:NL:RVS:2016:891.

[14] 2017 Annual Report of the Council of State: http://jaarverslag.raadvanstate.nl/2017/visueel/uploads/2018/03/Webversie-jaarverslag-2017-Raad-van-State.pdf, p. 61.

[15] Van der Hoeven 1974 RM Themis.

a margin of appreciation ('policy space' and 'assessment space') is definitely more appropriate and paves the way for a diligent proportionality review, as applied in many other jurisdictions: 'The principle of proportionality takes all benign purposes as given and evaluates the means by which they are pursued and their effects and the relationships between all three. It is a universal ideal in large part because it is so solicitous of local rule.'[16]

## 2.4 Conclusion

Daniel Halberstam offers a constitutional theory that is suitable for the present conditions and that distinguishes between three foundational constitutional values: voice, rights and expertise.[17] Public administration in the administrative state is a function that operates on its own professional account—the '*expertise*'—but requires legitimizing legislation, which is the expression of the *voice* of the citizens, and the confrontation with their *rights*. The first of these two aspects, the voice, relates to democratic constitutionality, and the latter, the rights, to the functioning of an administrative jurisdiction. The genealogical approach in this chapter, based on research published in Dutch, has shown us that the traditional notions of executive freedom and political oversight have become obsolete under the constitutional conditions of the administrative state. A rapprochement between administrative procedural law and other branches of procedural law with respect to the nature of the judicial function is, therefore, both inevitable and desirable. Three further steps would appear to be required in administrative procedural law:

- A different approach to evidence. The complex constellation's usual reliance on the facts as established by the administrative body should be replaced by an equitable burden of proof. This should comprise assessment of the reliability of the establishment of facts, using methods of certified expertise.
- Better use, following international examples, of proportionality assessment methods with respect to discretionary powers, especially the three-step method.[18]
- Recourse to fundamental rights and principles, like those of the EU Charter of Fundamental Rights, where, in the absence of normative parliamentary legislation, the interests of persons and organizations have to go beyond the results of administrative law-making.

The attitude of administrative courts (i.e. how they proceed in administrative legal procedures) is conditioned not only by views on their constitutional positioning, but also by these procedures being embedded in the wider ambit of the administration

[16] Beatty 2004.

[17] Halberstam 2010, p. 193.

[18] Barak 2012.

of justice, including the proximity to and distance from advisory tasks, the caseload and the ability to concentrate on questions of law. The need to apply a rather mechanistic and reductionist approach to the judicial function has been conditioned, at least partly, by the AJD's huge caseload of cases of a mostly routine nature. That is very different from the way in which cassation case law has been established. While the Grand Chamber of the highest courts of administrative law and the introduction of 'conclusions' certainly represented a step forward, further steps are still needed. I suggest creating a 'general' chamber within the AJD, to which cases can be referred by the other chambers, in order to establish a truly leading layer in AJD case law. Other cases meanwhile should be the work of specialized chambers or a chamber for residual cases.

Administrative procedural law has to be assessed not only in terms of the speed of delivery of a 'final' judgment, but also by the extent to which it serves as a beacon of trust amidst the hypercomplex conditions of public administration in the 21st century.

## References


Barak A (2012) Proportionality: Constitutional rights and their limitations (Cambridge Studies in Constitutional Law). Cambridge University Press, Cambridge

Beatty D M (2004) The ultimate rule of law. Oxford University Press, Oxford

Donner A M (1987) Nederlands bestuursrecht: Algemeen deel [Dutch administrative law: General part]. Samson H.D. Tjeenk Willink, Alphen aan den Rijn

Halberstam D (2010) The promise of comparative administrative law: a constitutional perspective on independent agency. In: Lindseth P L, Rose-Ackerman S (eds) Comparative administrative law (Research Handbooks in Comparative Law). Edward Elgar Publishing, Cheltenham, pp 185–204

Hirsch Ballin M F H (2018) Over grenzen bij bewijsvergaring - Grondslagen voor geïntegreerde normering van strafrechtelijke bewijsvergaring (oratie V.U. Amsterdam). Boom Juridische Uitgevers, The Hague

Hirsch Ballin E M H, Ortlep R, Tollenaar A (2015) Rechtsontwikkeling door de bestuursrechter [Legal development by the administrative judge] (VAR-reeks 158). Boom Juridische Uitgevers, The Hague

Lindseth P L (2010) Power and legitimacy: Reconciling Europe and the nation-state. Oxford University Press, Oxford

Lindseth P L, Rose-Ackerman S (2010) Comparative administrative law (Research Handbooks in Comparative Law). Edward Elgar Publishing, Cheltenham

Maus I (2018) Justiz als gesellschaftliches Über-Ich: Zur Position der Rechtsprechung in der Demokratie [Justice as societal superge: On the position of jurisprudence in democracy]. Suhrkamp, Berlin

Meder S (2011) Rechtsgeschichte - Eine Einführung [Legal history: An introduction]. Böhlau Verlag [Böhlau Publishing], Cologne

Möllers C (2016) Constitutional foundations of global administration. In: Cassese S (ed) Research handbook on global administrative law. Edward Elgar Publishing, Cheltenham, pp 107–128

Schoordijk H C F, Smits J M (1998) Eggensbundel: Een selectie uit het werk van Jannes Eggens [Eggens Collection: A selection from the work of Jannes Eggens]. Belvédère, Overveen

Van der Hoeven J (1958) De plaats van de grondwet in het constitutionele recht; Enkele opmerkingen over betekenis en functie van de grondwet in het geheel der constitutionele verhoudingen [The place of the constitution in constitutional law: Some remarks about the definition and function of the constitution in all constitutional relations]. W.E.J. Tjeenk Willink, Zwolle

Van der Hoeven J (1974) De grenzen van de rechterlijke functie in de administratieve rechtspraak [The borders of the judicial function in administrative case-law]. RM Themis 1974, afl. 5–6, p. 658–678.

Vermeule A (2014) The constitution of risk. Cambridge University Press, Cambridge

# Chapter 3
# The European Court of Justice and the Standard of Judicial Review

**Rob Widdershoven**

## Contents



**Abstract** In this chapter the standards of judicial review applied by the ECJ when assessing Union acts and decisions and those that are imposed by the ECJ on the

---

Rob Joseph Guillaume Marie Widdershoven is professor of European Administrative Law at Utrecht University, the Netherlands, and researcher in the Montaigne Centre for Rule of Law and Administration of Justice. Moreover, he is Advocate General in Administrative Law of the Netherlands.

---

R. Widdershoven (✉)
Utrecht University, Utrecht, The Netherlands
e-mail: r.widdershoven@uu.nl

 
J. de Poorter et al. (eds.), *Judicial Review of Administrative Discretion in the Administrative State*, https://doi.org/10.1007/978-94-6265-307-8_3

national courts when reviewing decisions within the scope of Union law, are examined in comprehensive way. It is proposed that the ECJ is strengthening its grip on the level of national judicial review of those decisions and that the formerly applied national autonomy approach is gradually but surely vanishing. Instead the ECJ increasingly transports its standards of review of EU acts to the review to be conducted by the national courts of similar acts and decisions. These standards include a process-oriented review of discretion and margins of appreciation. This process review combines a strict review of the authorities' establishment of the facts with a test of the statement of reasons. Therefore, it could better be qualified as semi-procedural. This test provides for the necessary compensation for judicial deference in relation to the substance of the decisions concerned.

**Keywords** Judicial review · process review · substantive review · national procedural autonomy · effective judicial protection · fundamental rights · discretion · margins of appreciation · establishment of the facts · appraisal of the facts · duty to examine · rights of defence · statement of reasons

## 3.1 Introduction

This contribution explores the standard of judicial review in administrative law cases from a European Union law perspective. The EU legal order may be characterized as a shared or composite legal order, within which Union and national legal order cooperate together to implement Union law.[1] In the shared legal order, Union law is sometimes directly applied towards individuals by a Union institution or agency.[2] This, for instance, is the case in European competition law, wherein the Commission is empowered to impose fines and penalty payments on companies who have violated the EU competition rules. These decisions may be contested by the companies involved before the Union courts, in first instance the General Court and in appeal the European Court of Justice (hereafter: ECJ or Court) on the ground of Article 263, fourth paragraph, TFEU. Obviously, questions of judicial review's intensity may be at stake in these judicial procedures. Usually, however, the application of Union law *vis-à-vis* individuals takes place at the national level by national authorities. In that case, these national acts within the scope of Union law may be contested by an individual before the national (administrative) courts,[3] who have the opportunity or obligation to refer preliminary questions concerning the

[1] Prechal et al. 2015, pp. 7–9; Besselink 2007.

[2] Cf. in respect of decision-making powers of agencies, the contributions in Scholten and Luchtman 2017.

[3] The term national acts 'within the scope of Union law' is synonymous—and used interchangeably—with the term national acts 'implementing Union law'. Both terms refer to the scope of Article 50(1) CFR, as interpreted in Case C-617/10 Akerberg Fransson, ECLI:EU:C:2013:105. They include (a) national decisions implementing specific EU obligations prescribed by secondary

validity or interpretation of Union law to the ECJ (Article 267 TFEU).[4] The issue of judicial scrutiny may play a role in these national judicial procedures as well and might be the subject of a preliminary reference.

From the foregoing it is clear that in the context of Union law questions of the intensity of judicial review may rise at two levels, the Union level and the national level, and that at both levels the ECJ is or may be involved. In this chapter it is proposed that the ECJ is strengthening its grip on the level of judicial review of national decisions within the scope of Union law, *inter alia* by transporting its review approach in cases concerning EU acts and decisions to the judicial review of national decisions within the scope of Union law by the national courts. As a result, regarding the intensity of review national procedural autonomy is gradually but surely vanishing. Moreover, certain tendencies regarding the ECJ's judicial scrutiny of EU acts are becoming relevant for judicial review of national decisions by the national courts as well. They include the tendency to apply in relation to decisions which leave the authorities a margin of discretion a process-oriented review to compensate for judicial deference as regards the substance of those decisions.[5]

To substantiate these claims, I will—after an introduction of the autonomy approach which was the dominant ECJ approach until fairly recently (Sect. 3.2)—examine the different standards of judicial review the ECJ prescribes to the national courts and connect them, as far as possible, to the standards of judicial review the ECJ applies when assessing EU acts. These different standards are: unlimited jurisdiction (Sect. 3.3), strict legality review (Sect. 3.4), differentiated review standards on the basis of Article 47 of the Charter of Fundamental Rights of the EU (hereafter: Charter or CFR, Sect. 3.5) and the process oriented review of margins of discretion or appreciation (Sect. 3.6). Section 3.7 contains some reflections on the outcomes of the analyses in Sects. 3.2–3.6, more in particular on the two developments which have already been indicated above: the decreasing autonomy of the Member States as regards the intensity of judicial review, and the tendency in the case law of the ECJ to apply and prescribe a more process-oriented review. The most important findings are summarized in Sect. 3.8.

## 3.2 Procedural Autonomy and Beyond?

Up until quite recently the ECJ approached—and sometimes still approaches—the issue of judicial scrutiny by national courts of acts, implementing Union law, in the framework of the principle of national procedural autonomy.[6] Therefore, as long as

or primary Union law, (b) national acts derogating from the fundamental free movement rights and (c) the enforcement of category (a) and (b). Cf. Van den Brink et al. 2015, pp. 150–155.

[4] See for this possibility or obligation in more detail, Broberg and Fenger 2014; Lenaerts et al. 2014, Chapters 3 and 6; Ortlep and Widdershoven 2015, pp. 350–360.

[5] Lenaerts 2012; Bar-Siman-Tov 2012.

[6] Prechal 2015, pp. 43–58; Ortlep and Widdershoven 2015, pp. 399–403.

Union law had not laid down binding rules as regards the issue in sectoral EU legislation, the MS were allowed to apply their national standards of judicial review, provided that the minimum *Rewe* principles of equivalence and effectiveness were met. According to the first principle the rules governing a dispute with a Union dimension may not be less favourable than those governing similar domestic actions. On the ground of the principle of effectiveness national procedural rules must not render virtually impossible or excessively difficult the exercise of the rights conferred on an individual by Union law. The test on in particular the effectiveness principle by the ECJ was quite deferential and allowed the Member States' courts much leeway to apply their own, sometimes very different standards of review.

Within the boundaries of the principle the marginal test on *Wednesbury* unreasonableness applied by the UK courts,[7] and the more strict legality control of margins of interpretation exercised by the German courts were both allowed.[8] This appeared from the cases of *Upjohn* and *Arcor*.[9]

*Upjohn* was concerned with the preliminary question of the English Court of Appeal whether it should be empowered to substitute its appraisal of the facts for that of the Licensing Authority on Medicines when revoking the market authorisations of several medicinal products of Upjohn. The ECJ observed that the applicable directive did not contain any rules for the exercise of the right of review and that therefore the national court could apply its national review standards, subject to the principles of equivalence and effectiveness. On the ground of the latter principle it was not necessary that the national court should have the power concerned. In this regard the ECJ also referred—by analogy—to its own review of decisions of Union institutions in areas where they enjoyed a wide measure of discretion by reason of complex economic assessments, which is limited to the verification of whether the measure was not vitiated by a manifest error or misuse of power, or that the institution had clearly exceeded the bounds of its discretion.[10] Therefore it could not require the English court to conduct a more strict review.

[7] The UK standard of Wednesbury unreasonableness was set in Court of Appeal 7 November 1947, *Associated Provincial Picture Houses v. Wednesbury Cooperation* [1948] 1 KB 223. According to it a court only intervenes if the administrative decision constitutes a misuse of power or is 'irrational', meaning that it is 'so outrageous in its defiance of logic or of accepted moral standards that no sensible person who had applied his mind to the question to be decided could have arrived at it (cf. Lord Diplock in *Council of Civil Service Unions and Others v. Minister for the Civil Service* [1985], 1 AC 374 (410)). So, it refers to blatant or manifest errors. See for more details, Thompson 2018, pp. 246–253.

[8] See Pünder and Klafki 2018, pp. 88–90. According to German law indefinite legal terms such as 'public interest' of 'public safety' are fully reviewed by the courts. Moreover, only in exceptional cases the courts recognize a 'margin of interpretation' (*Beurteilungsraum*), which is controlled with limited scrutiny.

[9] Case C-120/97 *Upjohn*, ECLI:EU:C:1999:14, Case C-55/06 *Arcor*, ECLI:EU:C:2008:244, respectively.

[10] *Upjohn*, point 34. See for this substantive ECJ standard, Section 6, hereafter. From that section it appears that nowadays this judicial deference in relation to the substance of the act is counterbalanced by a strict process review.

The issue of scope of judicial review was again put on the agenda of the ECJ in the *Arcor* case, which concerned a preliminary question of a German court about the intensity of judicial review of a decision in the field of telecommunication. In the case the German government and a third party had argued, relying on *Upjohn*, that the decision constituted a complex economic assessment and that therefore judicial review of it had to be limited. The ECJ again approached the question in the framework of procedural autonomy, subject to the principles of equivalence and effectiveness, and declared that Union law does not lay down any rules requiring the national court to apply a specific means of review of the decision in question.[11] Thus, the German court, are allowed—and, arguably, on the ground of the principle of equivalence even required—to exercise their usual more strict judicial scrutiny of administrative decisions.

In more recent case law of the ECJ this autonomy approach is not applied very often anymore, although it has not disappeared completely. More in particular the ECJ applied it in the 2015 case of *East Sussex County Council.*[12] In it an English court had raised the preliminary question whether it would be inconsistent with Article 6 of Directive 2003/4, which prescribed the right of access to the national courts in cases concerning access to environmental information, if the reasonableness of a charge for supplying environmental information is subjected only to a limited judicial review as provided for in English law, namely on *Wednesbury* unreasonableness. In its judgment the ECJ observes that Article 6 does not determine the extent of judicial review required by the directive and that it is, thus, for national law to determine that extent, subject to the observance of the principles of equivalence and effectiveness.

Therefore—and in line with *Upjohn*—the English test on *Wednesbury* unreasonableness is as a matter of principle not contrary to Union law.[13] What is new in the judgment is that the Court continues by stating that national courts are obliged to test whether the charge in question is in line with the conditions of Article 5(2) of Directive 2003/4, more in particular with the condition that the charge should be 'reasonable'.[14] In the literature it has been argued that the latter test is stricter than the *Wednesbury* test on manifest errors or misuse of power,[15] and this observation seems to be correct. After all, a test on 'reasonableness' is more strict than a test on manifest unreasonableness. Therefore, the case perhaps indicates a new approach of the ECJ according to which the national courts are, as a matter of principle, allowed to apply their national standards of judicial review as long as it results in a judicial assessment of whether the conditions set by Union law are fulfilled.

---

[11] *Arcor*, point 169.

[12] Case C-71/14 *East Sussex County Council,* ECLI:EU:C:2015:656.

[13] *East Sussex County Council*, point 58.

[14] *East Sussex County Council*, points 58 and 59.

[15] Eliantonio and Grashof 2016

In this possible new autonomy approach the Court stays away from the fundamental discussion on the intensity of judicial review by the national court, thus avoiding possible tensions or even collisions with the national courts, while at the same prescribing the result of judicial review in the concrete case, namely to test whether the charges concerned are reasonable. Future case law may clarify whether this 'result-driven' approach is really intended by the ECJ.

To conclude, although *East Sussex County Council* might indicate a partly new line, under the autonomy approach the ECJ is as a matter principle deferential as regards the standard of judicial review of national courts when assessing acts within the scope of Union law. In addition, from the *Upjohn* case it appears that the ECJ will not require from the national courts a level of judicial scrutiny which is stricter than the intensity of judicial review applied by the Court itself. This does, as shown in *Arcor*, however not preclude a more intense scrutiny by national courts on the basis of national law.

## 3.3 Unlimited Jurisdiction

As stated in Sect. 3.1, in the following sections I will in a comparative way examine the different standards the ECJ applies when reviewing EU acts and/or prescribes to the national courts in case they are reviewing national decisions in the scope of Union law.

### *3.3.1 Unlimited Jurisdiction Before the Union Courts*

The most intensive ECJ review standard is the standard of unlimited jurisdiction. This standard is applied when it assesses whether a competition law sanction (fine or penalty payment), imposed by the Commission, is proportionate to the seriousness of the violation of the competition rules. As has been clarified in the case of *KME*,[16] this test implies that the EU Courts are empowered and obliged to:

> substitute their own appraisal for the Commission's and, consequently, to cancel, reduce or increase the fine or penalty payment imposed.[17]

As regards the assessment of the amount of a fine or penalty payment the ECJ does not exercise any judicial deference. The EU Courts should substitute their own

[16] Case C-389/10P *KME*, ECLI:EU:C:2011:816, point 130.

[17] *KME*, point 130.

assessment for that of the Commission's and—if necessary—cancel, reduce or increase the sanction imposed.[18]

This unlimited review, however, is not concerned with the question whether a company has indeed violated the competition rules of Article 101 and 102 TFEU. The assessment of this question is subjected to a review on legality on the basis of Article 263 TFEU,[19] and is discussed below, in Sect. 3.6.

Furthermore it is important to note that in *KME* the Court connects the requirement of unlimited jurisdiction to the right to an effective remedy of Article 47 CFR. More in particular it states that:

> the review of legality provided for under Article 263 TFEU, supplemented with the unlimited jurisdiction in respect of the amount of the fine, [...], is not therefore contrary to the requirements of the principle of effective judicial protection in Article 47 of the Charter.[20]

From this consideration it may be derived that unlimited jurisdiction in respect of the amount of the fine is required in order to guarantee an Article 47 CFR consistent legal protection in competition sanctioning cases.

## 3.3.2 *Unlimited Jurisdiction Before the National Courts?*

The next question is whether the *KME* standard of unlimited jurisdiction applies to the imposition of national sanctions for breaches of the European competition rules as well. As yet this question has not been referred to—and, consequently, not been answered by—the ECJ. To my opinion there are two reasons for expecting that the question, if referred, will be answered in the affirmative.[21] First and foremost, because the ECJ connects the standard of unlimited jurisdiction to Article 47 CFR, a fundamental right which applies to national sanctioning of the European competition rules as well.[22] Secondly, because this seems the logical consequence of the enforcement system of competition law, provided for in Regulation 1/2003.[23] Under this system, similar violations of the EU competition rules might be sanctioned by either the Commission or by a national competition authority. Given this freedom of choice, it seems to me imperative that the intensity of judicial review of the national sanctioning of violations of EU competition law should be at least very

[18] The exercise of unlimited jurisdiction does, however, not amount to a review of the Court's own motion (*KME*, point 131). So, it is for the applicant to raise pleas in law against the decision and to adduce evidence.

[19] *KME*, point 121.

[20] *KME*, point 133.

[21] Ortlep and Widdershoven 2015, pp. 402–403

[22] When sanctioning EU competition law violations the Member States are undoubtedly implementing (or acting within the scope of) Union law. See for both terms note 4, above. Therefore, Article 47 applies to these national sanctions as well.

[23] Official Journal L 001, 04/01/2003.

similar (and preferably the same) as the intensity of the ECJ's review. Otherwise the system would facilitate forum shopping to the jurisdiction with the lowest level of scrutiny. That seems unacceptable.[24]

In addition, as the standard of unlimited jurisdiction is based on Article 47 CFR, I expect the ECJ to impose this standard also to the national review of administrative sanctions of a criminal nature within the scope of Union law in other areas than competition law. An additional reason for this expectation is that, in the case of *Menarini*,[25] the European Court of Human Rights (hereafter: ECtHR) prescribes the national courts a similar intensive scrutiny of administrative sanctions qualifying as a criminal charge on the basis of Article 6 ECHR.[26] In the wordings of the ECtHR the national courts should exercise 'full jurisdiction' when assessing such sanctions. According to Article 52, third paragraph, CFR, this ECtHR interpretation of Article 6 ECHR, is, as a minimum requirement, binding for the ECJ when interpreting and applying the corresponding Charter right of Article 47 CFR.

## 3.4 Strict Substantive Legality Review of Interferences with Fundamental Rights

Outside the area of competition law sanctions and possibly other administrative sanctions of a criminal nature (criminal charge) within the scope of Union law, the ECJ conducts a legality review only. Typical for such a review is that the Court is in principle not allowed to substitute its own appraisal of the facts for that of the Commission. Nevertheless this review may be strict indeed.

### *3.4.1 Strict Substantive Review in Fundamental Rights Cases*

A substantive strict review may apply in particular to assessment of acts seriously interfering with a fundamental right. In this respect the landmark case of *Digital Rights Ireland* is very relevant.[27] The case concerned the validity of the Retention

---

[24] Widdershoven and Craig 2017, pp. 335–336.

[25] ECtHR 27 September, *Menarini*, App. No. 43509/08.

[26] The EJC term 'sanctions of a criminal nature' refers to the same sanctions as the ECtHR term 'criminal charge'. According to Case C-489/10 *Bonda*, ECLI:EU:C:2012:319, the ECJ applies the ECtHR criteria, set in ECtHR 8 June 1976, *Engel*, no. 5100/71, to qualify a sanction as 'criminal charge' (or, in EJC terms, as a sanction of a criminal nature). On the ground of these criteria administrative fines generally qualify as 'criminal'.

[27] Case C-293/12 *Digital Rights Ireland*, ECLI:EU:C:2014:238.

Directive 2006/24/EC, which obliged providers of electronic communications services and public communications networks to retain, for a certain period, data relating to a person's private life, and to allow competent national authorities access to these data.

In its judgment the ECJ delivers a public lecture on the intensity of judicial review on proportionality to which interferences with fundamental rights in general, and with the right to respect for private life (Article 7 CFR) and the connected protection of personal data (Article 8 CFR) in particular, should be subjected. The Court states:[28]

> 46. In that regard, according to the settled case-law of the Court, the principle of proportionality requires that acts of the EU institutions be appropriate for attaining the legitimate objectives pursued by the legislation at issue and do not exceed the limits of what is appropriate and necessary in order to achieve those objectives.
>
> 47. With regard to judicial review of compliance with those conditions, where interferences with fundamental rights are at issue, the extent of the EU legislature's discretion may prove to be limited, depending on a number of factors, including, in particular, the area concerned, the nature of the right at issue guaranteed by the Charter, the nature and seriousness of the interference and the object pursued by the interference.
>
> 48. In the present case, in view of the important role played by the protection of personal data in the light of the fundamental right to respect for private life and the extent and seriousness of the interference with that right caused by Directive 2006/24, the EU legislature's discretion is reduced, with the result that review of that discretion should be strict.

In the remainder of the judgment it appears that the retention directive does not survive this strict review. Therefore it is declared invalid. *Digital Rights Ireland* is concerned with the validity of a Union directive. From the subsequent case of *Tele2 Sverige AB* it can be derived that the judicial assessment by the national court of a national act seriously interfering with the fundamental rights of Articles 7 and 8 CFR should be as strict as the judicial review of such interferences by the ECJ.[29] So, this assessment standard is indeed transported to the national courts. The principle of procedural autonomy does not apply.

According the ECJ in *Digital Right Ireland* the strictness of judicial review of interferences with fundamental rights generally depends on a number of factors, such as the area concerned, the nature of the right at issue, the nature and seriousness of the interference and the object pursued by it. As yet there is no case law, in which the ECJ has applied these factors to interferences with other fundamental Charter rights than Articles 7 and 8.

---

[28] *Digital Rights Ireland*, points 46–48, As regards this standard of judicial review the ECJ refers, by analogy, to ECtHR 4 December 2008, *S. and Marper v. the United Kingdom* [Grand Chamber], nos. 30562/04 and 30566/04, § 102.

[29] Case C-203/15 *Tele2 Sverige*, ECI:EU:C:2016:970.

### 3.4.2 Process Review in Fundamental Rights Cases?

In its case law the ECtHR increasingly applies a so-called process review when assessing national legislative interferences with fundamental rights. Under this review the ECtHR, when examining whether a national act limiting the exercise of a fundamental right can be justified by a general interest, takes into account the process by which the act has been adopted.[30] If it has been adopted with great care and after extensive deliberations in an open and transparent decision-making process, this is an (additional) argument for the ECtHR to arrive at a positive judgment as regards the act in question.[31] On the other hand, the lack of procedural care often constitutes an important reason to find a violation of the fundamental right.

In the ECJ's case law this approach is only applied in a limited number of cases.[32] The most clear example is the case of *Glatzel*, wherein the Court, when assessing whether a directive provision was in breach with Article 21 CFR (prohibition of non-discrimination), took into account the quality of the EU legislative process.[33] According to the Court this process had been good enough to uphold the directive provision. Whether the ECJ will apply a process review more often in the future, remains to be seen. In preliminary proceedings concerning possible violations of fundamental EU rights by the Member States, such review is not to be expected very often,[34] as it seems at odds with the purpose of the procedure, to develop uniform EU standards as regards the fundamental right in question. In the light of this purpose the judgment of the ECJ on the same limitation of a fundamental right in two Member States, obviously cannot depend on a possible differences in respect of the legislative process in which it has been adopted. However, in cases, concerning the fundamental right's consistency of secondary Union law, the ECJ might apply a more process-oriented approach more often.[35]

---

[30] Gerards 2018; Nussberger 2018.

[31] See for both sides of this process review, Gerards 2018, pp. 141 and 155.

[32] See for other ECJ cases in which procedural arguments played a (modest) role, Beijer 2018, pp. 190–193, and Lenaerts 2012. The ECJ applies—arguably increasingly—a process review in cases concerning national limitations of free movement rights, f.i. in Case C-320/03 *Commission v. Austria*, ECLI:EU:C:2005:684. See for other examples Van den Brink et al. 2015, pp. 201–202 and Zglinski 2018.

[33] Case C-356/12 *Glatzel*, ECLI:EU:C:2014:350. In the literature the process review in this case has been criticised, because the legislative process showed some serious flaws. See Beijer 2018, p. 206, with references to other critical literature, who qualifies the case as a 'bad' example of process review.

[34] To avoid misunderstandings, when reviewing if a EU or national measure limiting a fundamental right is proportionate to the purpose of the limitation the ECJ does take into account whether the act provides for sufficient procedural guarantees, in particular the possibility of judicial review. See Beijer 2018, pp. 196–197, for examples. However, these guarantees are not concerned with the legislative process of the act in question itself.

[35] Beijer 2018, pp. 207–208.

## 3.5 Differentiated Intensity of Judicial Review on the Basis of Article 47 CFR

In some cases the ECJ provides for guidance as regards the intensity of national judicial review on the basis of the right of effective judicial protection of Article 47 CFR. From the case law it can be derived that Article 47 does not require one uniform standard of judicial review in all cases, but that the precise intensity depends on the applicable Union rules. Depending on the rules in question, Article 47 CFR may require a thorough judicial review (*Samba Diouf*), a very restrained review only (*Berlioz*) or something in between (*Egenberger*).

Moreover, it can be noted that—with an exception of the requirement of unlimited jurisdiction, already discussed in Sect. 3.3—Article 47 CFR does as yet not set a standard of review of decisions of EU institutions by the Union Courts.

### *3.5.1 Thorough Review of the Statement of Reasons in Samba Diouf*

The case of *Samba Diouf* was concerned with intensity of judicial review in asylum cases.[36] In the case the ECJ obliges the national courts, on the basis of Article 47 CFR, to exercise in asylum cases a 'thorough review' of the legality of the decision and, in particular, of the reasons which led the competent authority to reject the application of asylum as unfounded.[37] In this respect the Court states that, in order for the right of an effective remedy to be exercised effectively,

> [t]he national court must be able to review the merits of the reasons which led the competent authority to hold the application for international protection to be unfounded or made in bad faith, there being no irrefutable presumption as to the legality of those reason.[38]

The case does not contain any reference to the principle of national procedural autonomy. Moreover, from the considerations it is clear that national judicial review of the merits of the reasons of an asylum decisions should be thorough and, thus, rather strict, although they leave some room as regards the precise level of strictness. The latter issue has not been clarified by the ECJ as yet, perhaps also because it is nowadays addressed in the Recast Directive on common procedures in asylum cases 2013/32.[39] Article 46, third paragraph of the directive prescribes a 'full and ex nunc examination of both facts and point of law' of asylum decisions by the national courts of first instance.

---

[36] Case 69/10 *Samba Diouf*, ECLI:EU:C:2011:524.

[37] *Samba Diouf*, point 56.

[38] *Samba Diouf*, point 61.

[39] Official Journal 2013, L 180/60.

In the Netherland there has been a lively debate as regards the question how strict ('full') the 'full examination of facts and law' should be. Some scholars argue that a full examination should be 'unlimited'. Therefore national courts should not conduct a legality review of the decisions taken by the asylum authorities only, but should substitute their own appraisal of the facts that might constitute a right to asylum for that of the authorities.[40] The Dutch Council of State has rejected this view and has determined that the authorities still enjoy some discretion as regards the appraisal of uncertain facts, more in particular in respect of whether the statements of person seeking asylum are plausible.[41] According to the Council of State this discretion—and the judicial deference resulting from it—is justified by the fact that the authorities have more expertise in assessing the plausibility of such statements, because they have an overview of all asylum decisions, including decisions granting asylum. As means of compensation the Council of State prescribes to the first instance courts a strict procedural test of the fact-finding process and of the statement of reasons. Whether this test is sufficient in the view of the ECJ remains to be seen. Whatever the outcome may be, it is clear that in the area of asylum law judicial deference in relation to national decisions is limited.

### *3.5.2 Restrained Review of the Statement of Review in Berlioz*

A second case in which Article 47 CFR determines the intensity of national judicial review is *Berlioz*.[42] The case was about a penalty imposed on Berlioz by the Luxembourg tax authority for failing to comply with the decision to provide the authority with information to enable it to respond to a request made by the French authorities on the basis of Directive 2011/16, on administrative cooperation in the field of taxation. In its judgment the ECJ stated first that, on the basis of Article 47 CFR, Berlioz was entitled to challenge the legality of this decision before the Luxembourg court.

In order to determine the intensity of judicial review to be conducted by this court, the ECJ observed that the cooperation between tax authorities on the basis of the directive is founded on the principle of mutual trust. Therefore, the requested Luxembourg authority must, in principle, trust the requesting French authority that the request for information complies with domestic law and is necessary for the purpose of the French tax investigation. Thus, the Luxemburg authority cannot substitute its own assessment of the possible usefulness of the information for that

[40] For instance by Reneman in her commentary on the judgments of the Dutch Council of State of 13 April 2016, ECLI:NL:RVS:2016:890 and ECLI:NL:RVS:2016:956, in AB 2016/195. Cf. more in-depth Reneman 2014, pp. 249–282.

[41] Dutch Council of State 13 April 2016, ECLI:NL:RVS:2016:890, and ECLI:NL:RVS:2016:956.

[42] Case C-682/15 *Berlioz*, ECLI:EU:C:2017:373.

of the French authority.[43] Nevertheless it must verify whether the information sought by the French authorities is not devoid of any foreseeable relevance to the investigation being carried out by the requesting French authority.[44] In order to facilitate this verification the requesting French authorities must provide an adequate statement of reasons explaining the purpose of the information sought.

After this preliminary statements, the ECJ determines as follows about the required intensity of judicial review by the Luxembourg court:

> 83. As regards [...], the review by a court seized of an action brought by a relevant person against a penalty imposed on him [...] that review may not only relate to the proportionality of that penalty and lead, where appropriate, to its being varied, but may also concern the legality of that information order [...].
>
> 84. If the judicial review guaranteed by Article 47 of the Charter is to be effective, the reasons given by the requesting authority must put the national court in a position in which it may carry out the review of the legality of the request for information.
>
> 85 In the light of what has been stated in [...] the present judgment concerning the requesting authority's discretion, it must be held that the limits that apply in respect of the requested authority's review are equally applicable to reviews carried out by the courts.
>
> 86. Consequently, the courts must merely verify that the information order is based on a sufficiently reasoned request by the requesting authority concerning information that is not— manifestly— devoid of any foreseeable relevance having regard, on the one hand, to the taxpayer concerned and to any third party who is being asked to provide the information and, on the other hand, to the tax purpose being pursued.

From these considerations it is quite clear that an Article 47 CFR consistent judicial review in the case at hand must be really restrained. This restraint is indirectly related to the principle of mutual trust from which it can be derived that the requested Luxembourg authorities are only allowed to verify whether the information sought by the French authorities 'is devoid of any foreseeable relevance' to the French investigation. In order to facilitate this verification, the French authorities should provide for an adequate statement of reasons for the request.

Because of the limited verification right of the Luxembourg authorities, the intensity of judicial review of the authorities' decision by the Luxembourg court is even more restricted. It is only allowed to verify whether the information order is based on a sufficiently reasoned request by the French authority that is not *manifestly* devoid of any foreseeable relevance to the investigation. In fact the Court, therefore, requires a double judicial restraint.

Moreover—and different from the autonomy approach, discussed in Sect. 3.2—the Court does not leave any room for the national courts to apply a (possible) more strict judicial standard on the basis of its national law.

---

[43] *Berlioz*, point 77.

[44] See for this and the following consideration, *Berlioz*, points 78 and 80.

### 3.5.3 Result-Driven Rather than Strict Review in Egenberger

Finally, the intensity of judicial review required by Article 47 CFR is at stake in the recent German case of *Egenberger*.[45] The case concerned a tension between two fundamental rights, the right of non-discrimination and the freedom of religion, more in particular between the right of workers not to be discriminated against on grounds of their religion or belief, and the right of churches and other organisations whose ethos is based on religion to reject an application for employment on the ground of their right of autonomy. At the end, the case boils down to the question whether judicial review as regards the scope of the right of autonomy should be deferential and limited to the plausibility of the viewpoint of the church in question—which is the point of view of the German Constitutional Court[46]—or whether it may or should go further than such a restricted control. In its judgment the ECJ refrains from explicitly prescribing a specific intensity of judicial review, but concentrates on the result that should be achieved by the national court by applying an Article 47 CFR consistent judicial review of the question concerned. It states:[47]

> In the light of the foregoing, it must be concluded that, where a church or other organisation whose ethos is based on religion or belief asserts, in support of an act or decision such as the rejection of an application for employment by it, that by reason of the nature of the activities concerned or the context in which the activities are to be carried out, religion constitutes a genuine, legitimate and justified occupational requirement, having regard to the ethos of the church or organisation, it must be possible for such an assertion to be the subject, if need be, of effective judicial review by which it can be ensured that the criteria set out in Article 4(2) of Directive 2000/78 [the afore-mentioned genuine, legitimate and justified requirement - RW] are satisfied in the particular case.

As already stated, the ECJ refrains from giving an explicit judgment on how intense national judicial review (marginal, strict, plausibility control) should be, arguably to avoid tensions with the German Constitutional Court. At the same time, it does set a standard as regards this intensity by stating that the question whether the church's rejection of an application for employment can be based on religion should be subjected to effective judicial protection by the national court, thus *ensuring* that the genuine, legitimate and justified requirement is fulfilled. Moreover, in the following considerations the ECJ clarifies in detail what these requirements should entail in the case at hand. Therefore the judicial test, required by the ECJ, seems not to be deferential at all. In addition, the Court does not make any reference to procedural autonomy, although the possible tensions with the German judicial approach to the freedom of religion is quite clear.

---

[45] Case C-414/16 *Egenberger*, ECLI:EU:C:2018:257.

[46] See for the view of the Constitutional Court (*Bundesverfassungsgericht*), the preliminary reference of the *Bundesarbeitsgericht* in *Egenberger*, point 31 of the judgment.

[47] *Egenberger*, point 55.

To some extent the approach in *Egenberger* resembles the approach in *East Sussex County Council*, discussed in Sect. 3.2.

In both cases the ECJ applies a 'result-driven' approach and prescribes in rather detail the result that should be achieved by a Union law consistent national judicial review, namely to determine whether an act or situation is in conformity with Union law requirements. A clear differences between both cases is, that in *East Sussex County Council* the ECJ still recognizes, as a matter of principle, the Member States' autonomy to apply its national concept regarding judicial review, while *Egenberger* makes no mention of this concept at all.

Nevertheless the message of both cases is similar, the Court steers on the result of national judicial review, while at the same time staying away from national sensitivities as regards their standard of judicial review.

## 3.6 Process Review of Margins of Appreciation and Discretion

### *3.6.1 Process Review Before the Union Courts*

A final situation in which the standard of judicial review by the Union courts is relatively clear concerns the situation in which authorities enjoy a margin of appreciation or discretion when laying down an act of general application or taking a decision. Conceptually margins of appreciation and of discretion can be distinguished.[48] The latter refers to the situation that the authority is empowered to balance different political considerations against each other, while in case of margins of appreciation the authorities' leeway emanates from the technical, scientific, economic or otherwise factual complexity of the matter under review. However, in the case law of the ECJ such distinction is generally not made and both terms are used interchangeably. Therefore both categories are examined together.

At the Union level the EU institutions enjoy a wide margin of discretion when laying down acts of general application, such as regulations and directives. From the landmark case of *Fedesa* and numerous subsequent case law it is clear that the Court exercises serious restraint when reviewing the substance of those acts.[49] Obviously the Court cannot substitute its own assessment for that of the Union legislator. To the contrary, it must confine itself to examining whether the legislator's assessment

> contains a manifest error or constitutes misuse of power, or whether the authority has manifestly exceeded the limits of its discretion.

---

[48] Schimmel and Widdershoven 2009, pp. 65–66.

[49] Case C-331/88 *Fedesa*, ECLI:EU:C:1990:391. Cf. Van den Brink et al. 2015, pp. 191–194.

As regards substance this standard requires quite some judicial deference. In addition, however, in several ECJ cases this judicial deference as regards substances is compensated to some extent by a procedural test. This process review is for instance applied in the case of *Spain v. Council*,[50] wherein the Council and Commission—according to the ECJ—had not taken into 'consideration all the relevant facts and circumstances of the case' and had therefore not been able to refute Spain's claim that the Regulation on cotton aid would make the production of cotton economically unfeasible.[51] Therefore 'the information submitted' by both institutions did not

> 'enable the Court to ascertain whether the Community legislator was able, without exceeding the bounds of the broad discretion it enjoys in the matter, to reach the conclusion' [it had reached in the Regulation – RW]'.[52] [...] 'Consequently it must be concluded that the principle of proportionality was infringed'.[53]

From this statement it is clear that the EU legislature is under a duty to examine all the facts and circumstances relevant to the act, and that serious deficiencies in respect of the examination may lead to the invalidity of the act contested.

The Court does not give precise guidelines as regards the content and depth of the examination required. It does for instance not prescribe an obligation to subject the act to an impact assessment of the various (alternative) options which could have been used to achieve the purpose of the act concerned. Moreover in its case law the ECJ has not recognized a formal right for the public or of those who will be affected by an act to participate in the legislative process. Then again, from the case of *Vodaphone*, it can be derived that the ECJ considers the fact that the institution subjected the proposal for a regulation to a public consultation and conducted a thorough impact assessment of the various options, to be a positive factor when reviewing a regulation in the light of the proportionality principle.[54] In the literature is has been argued that the Court should develop this test on 'procedural proportionality'[55] further into a test on evidence-based legislative rationality.[56]

In respect of decision-making in individual cases, EU institutions' discretion usually emanates from the technical, scientific, economic or otherwise factual complexity of the appraisal of facts concerned. As regards judicial review of the substance of such appraisal the ECJ's approach has always been, and still is, restraint. According to a long-standing case law, the Union Courts are not allowed to substitute their own appraisal of the facts for that of the institution and should

---

[50] Case C-310/04 *Spain v. Council*, ECLI:EU:C:2006:521. See for other relevant case law, Lenaerts 2012, and Van de Brink et al. 2015, p. 182.

[51] *Spain v. Council*, point 133.

[52] *Spain v. Council*, point 134.

[53] *Spain v. Council*, point 135.

[54] Case C-58/08 *Vodaphone*, ECLI:EU:C:2010:321. See on this case extensively, Lenaerts 2012, and Van Gestel and De Poorter 2016.

[55] See for this term Lenaerts 2012, p. 8.

[56] Cf. Van Gestel and De Poorter 2016. See also De Poorter's contribution to this volume.

limit their review to whether the decision at issue is 'not vitiated by a manifest error of a misuse of power, or that the institution did clearly exceed the bounds of its discretion'.[57] Since the nineties of the past century, this judicial defences as regards substance, however, is increasingly compensated by a process review of the fact-finding activities conducted by the institution, and of the adequateness of the statement reasons.

An important first step in this development was taken by the ECJ in *Technische Universität München*.[58] The case was concerned with the validity of a custom decision of the Commission, based on a technical evaluation, which was binding for the German authorities when deciding on a customs exemption. In his preliminary question the referring German court questioned the lawfulness of the very marginal judicial test of technical decisions by the Court, mentioned above, on manifest error or misuse of power only.[59] The ECJ declared:

> 13. It must be stated first of all that, since an administrative procedure entailing complex technical evaluations is involved, the Commission must have a power of appraisal in order to be able to fulfil its tasks.
>
> 14. However, where the Community institutions have such a power of appraisal, respect for the rights guaranteed by the Community legal order in administrative procedures is of even more fundamental importance.
>
> Those guarantees include, in particular, the duty of the competent institution to examine carefully and impartially all the relevant aspects of the individual case, the right of the person concerned to make his views known and to have an adequately reasoned decision. Only in this way can the Court verify whether the factual and legal elements upon which the exercise of the power of appraisal depends were present.
>
> 15. The Court must therefore examine whether the disputed decision was adopted in accordance with the principles mentioned above.

In the remainder of the judgment the Court established that the Commission had not complied with the principles mentioned. It had been advised by a group of experts which did not possess the technical knowledge required, it had not provide any opportunity to the person concerned to make his view known on the relevant circumstances and documents and, as a result, the decision did not contain a sufficient statement of reasons. Therefore the Commission's decision was declared invalid. So, in this case a strict review of the fact-funding process compensated the judicial deference as regards the substance of the decisions indeed.

The process review of *Technische Universität München* has been refined in *Tetra Laval*.[60] This case dealt with the intensity of judicial review of complex

---

[57] See already Case 55/75 *Balkan-Import Export*, ECLI:EU:C:1976; point 8; Case C-225/91 *Matra v. Commission*, ECLI:EU:C:1993:239, points 24 and 25; Case C-157/96 *National Framers' Union*, ECLI:EU:C:1998:191, point 39.

[58] Case C-269/90 *Technische Universität München*, ECLI:EU:C:1991:438.

[59] That this reference is made by a German court is no coincidence. As explained in Sect. 3.2, German courts do normally exercise a more intensive scrutiny of such decisions.

[60] Case C-12/03 P *Tetra Laval*, ECLI:EU:C:2005:87. See on this case extensively Essens et al. 2009, p. 209.

economic assessments in a merger case, but the standard developed in it is in a comparable way applied by the Union courts when reviewing scientific or technical complex decisions in other areas of EU law.[61] In *Tetra Laval* the ECJ distinguishes between the review of the establishment of the facts on one hand and the review of the appraisal of the facts in the light of the relevant legal framework, on the other.[62] As regards the establishment of the facts the intensity of judicial review is strict. In this respect the Union Courts have to:[63]

> establish, amongst other things, whether the evidence relied on is factually accurate, reliable and consistent and also whether it contains all the information which must be taken into account in order to assess a complex situation [...].

From this consideration it is apparent that the Union Courts scrutinize the establishment of the relevant facts by the Commission intensively. They have to establish whether the authority's fact-finding was accurate, reliable, consistent and complete. In addition, as can already been derived from *Technische Universität München*, in the fact-finding process the authorities should observe procedural safeguards, in particular the right to be heard of the persons concerned. This obligation was not addressed in *Tetra Laval*, because it had not been raised by the company. In other competition law cases the Court does conduct a strict assessment of whether the Commission complied with the Union rights of defence.[64]

The same applies for example to cases concerning EU sanction's decisions placing individuals or entities, suspected of financing terrorist activities, on the black list.[65] In these cases non-compliance with the rights of defence is the main reason for declaring such decisions invalid.[66]

As regards the appraisal of the facts in the light of the legal framework the authorities enjoy a wide margin of appreciation. Therefore the Union Courts are, as stated above, only allowed to assess whether the substance of the decision at issue is 'not vitiated by a manifest error of a misuse of power, or that the institution did clearly exceed the bounds of its discretion'. However, according to *Tetra Laval* this judicial deference in relation to the substance of the decision, is compensated to some extent by a strict review of the reasons of the decision. More in particular, the Courts should review whether the information produced is 'capable of substantiating the conclusions drawing from it'.[67]

---

[61] See in the area of public health, Joined cases T-74/00 *Artegodan*, ECLI:EU:T:2002:283; Case T-13/99 *Pfizer*, ECLI:EU:T:2002:209; and in the environmental law area, Case T-474/04 *Germany v. Commission*, ECLI:EU:T:2007:332.

[62] Schimmel and Widdershoven 2009, pp. 61–68; Caranta 2011, pp. 28–34.

[63] *Tetra Laval*, point 39. In the same vain Case C-413/06 P *Bertelmans AG and others*, ECLI:EU:C:2008:392.

[64] See for the different obligations resulting from the rights of defence in more detail Van de Brink et al. 2015, pp. 237–245.

[65] See f.i. Joined Case C-402/05 P and C-41/05 P *Kadi and Al Barakaat*, ECLI:EU:C:2008:461.

[66] For more details, Beijer 2018, pp. 188–190.

[67] *Tetra Laval*, point 39.

### 3.6.2 Process Review Before the National Courts

A final question is whether the European standard of judicial review of administrative discretion of Union institutions is transported by the ECJ to the national courts when reviewing discretion in cases within the scope of Union law. As regards the *Tetra Laval* standard there is as yet no clear ECJ case law, wherein the standard has been imposed on the national courts. Whether it is nevertheless applied in practice by the Dutch courts when reviewing complex economic assessments, is examined in the contributions to this volume of Lavrijssen and Kerkmeester.

The process review conducted in *Technische Universität München* has indeed been transported to the national courts in the recent case of *Sahar Fahimian.*[68] In this preliminary reference procedure the ECJ was asked whether under Directive 2004/14 national authorities enjoy a wide discretion which is subject to only limited judicial review in determining whether a third country national applying for a visa for the purpose of study, represents a threat to public security. According to the ECJ the assessment of the applicant's individual situation involves 'complex evaluations' based on multiple relevant factors. In this regard, the competent national authorities enjoy 'a wide discretion'.[69] Therefore, substantive judicial review of the appraisal of the facts should be limited 'to the absence of manifest errors'.[70] However, this judicial restraint as regards substance is counterbalanced by a strict process review. In this regard the national court must,[71]

> 'ascertain in particular whether the contested decision is based on a sufficiently solid factual basis'. [..] In addition, 'judicial review must also relate to compliance with procedural guarantees, which is of fundamental importance', and which include 'the obligation for those authorities to examine carefully and impartially all the relevant elements of the situation in question [...], and also the obligation to give a statement of reasons for their decision that is sufficient to enable the national court to ascertain [...] whether the factual and legal elements on which the exercise of the power of assessment depends were present.'

From this consideration—in which the Court explicitly refers to *Technische Universität München*—it is apparent that also the national courts are obliged to combine a very limited substantive review with a process oriented review. This review relates to both, the obligation of the authorities to examine carefully and impartially all relevant elements of the situation in question, and the statement of reasons.

It is intended by the Court as a means of compensation for the judicial deference as regards the substance of the appraisal of the facts. The judgment contains no

---

[68] Case C-544/15 *Fahimian*, ECLI:EU:C:2017:255.

[69] *Fahimian*, point 42.

[70] *Fahimian*, point 46.

[71] *Fahimian*, point 46.

reference to the principle of procedural autonomy.[72] Moreover, the judgment does not leave any room for the national court to apply a (possible) stricter national standard of judicial review.

## 3.7 Some Reflections

### *3.7.1 National Procedural Autonomy Is Vanishing*

From the foregoing it is clear that the ECJ in recent case law has strengthened its grip on the intensity of judicial review to be conducted by the national courts in cases within the scope of Union law.

National procedural autonomy in respect of the review standards is gradually but surely vanishing. As appears from the cases of *Berlioz* (Sect. 3.5.2) and *Fahimian* (Sect. 3.6.2), this implies in several areas of Union law that national courts are even not allowed to apply a possible stricter national standard of judicial review. This is in clear breach with the autonomy approach in the case of *Arcor* (Sect. 3.2). As regards several acts the Court limits national review autonomy by transporting its standards of review of EU acts to the review by the national courts of similar decisions or acts in the scope of Union law. Such transport has already occurred in relation to the strict substantive review of interferences with fundamental rights (Sect. 3.4) and to the process review of margins of discretion or appreciation (Sect. 3.6) and will probably also take place in respect of the unlimited jurisdiction standard applied to competition law sanctions and other administrative sanctions of a criminal nature (Sect. 3.3). In addition, the intensity of judicial review of the national courts is influenced by the right of effective judicial protection of Article 47 CFR (Sect. 3.5). From the relevant case law it can be derived that this provision does not require one uniform standard of judicial review in all cases, but that the precise intensity of review depends on the applicable EU rules. In asylum cases national review of the merits of the statement of reasons must be thorough, in cases concerning the cooperation between tax authorities the review must be restraint. However, in all cases wherein the required standard of judicial review is derived from Article 47 CFR alike, procedural autonomy no longer plays a role.

The only fairly recent case in which the Court has applied the autonomy approach is *East Sussex County Council* (Sect. 3.2). In this case the Court recognized as a matter of principle the autonomy of the UK courts to use their domestic *Wednesbury* test, but at the same time prescribed a judicial review of whether the

[72] The absence of such reference can—to my opinion—not be explained by the fact that Article 18(4) of Directive 2004/14, contains the right of persons concerned 'to mount a legal challenge' against a rejection of an application for a visa. After all, in *East Sussex County Council* (Sect. 3.2) a similar right of appeal was prescribed in Article 6 of the directive concerned. In that case the ECJ nevertheless did apply the autonomy approach, because the provision did not determine the extent of judicial review. The same goes for Article 18(4) of Directive 2004/14.

contested decision is compliant with the EU conditions, which seems to go further than this test. A similar 'result-driven' approach is used by the ECJ in the case of *Egenberger* (Sect. 3.5.3), in which a possible difference of vision with the German Constitutional Court was at stake. Arguably, this approach is applied when the Court wants to steer national judicial review, while avoiding at the same time tensions with the national courts. If this really is the ECJ's intention, this seems a prudent way of dealing with such tensions.

### 3.7.2 On Substantive, Procedural and Semi-Procedural Review

The final question is what this increasing interference by the Court with the national standards of judicial review exactly entails. As regards some national acts or decisions within the scope of EU law the Court imposes a substantive review.

This applies to the strict substantive review of national interferences with, in any event, Articles 7 and 8 of the Charter (Sect. 3.4.1), and will probably apply to the unlimited jurisdiction standard for assessing competition law sanctions and other administrative sanction of a criminal nature as well (Sect. 3.3.2).

As regards the large group of decisions which leave the authorities a margin of discretion or appreciation the Court prescribes a combination of a limited review on, in short, the absence of a manifest error of the substance of the decision and the appraisal of the relevant facts, with a strict review of the fact finding process (Sect. 3.6.2).

This process review is concerned with the authorities' examination of the establishment of the facts. This examination must be careful and impartial (*Fahimian*) and the evidence relied on must be accurate, reliable, consistent and complete (*Tetra Laval*). Moreover, the fact-finding process must comply with the applicable procedural safeguards, more in particular with the rights of defence. This seems self-evident as these safeguards are the tool *par excellence* for the parties alike to ensure that no relevant facts have been left out in the decision-making process.[73] If the procedural rights are not observed properly, it cannot be ruled out that important facts or circumstances have not been taken into account.

In addition, the Court requires the national courts to conduct a test of the authorities' statement of reasons for their decision and the appraisal of the facts on which it is based. This statement should enable the Court to ascertain that the factual and legal elements on which the decisions has been based were indeed present (*Fahimian*, Sect. 3.6.2). Moreover, as is apparent from Sects. 3.5.1 (*Samba Diouf*) and 3.5.2 (*Berlioz*), a review of the adequateness of the reasons of the decisions concerned may be required on the basis of Article 47 CFR as well. This judicial test of the statement of reasons can be situated between a substantive test

[73] Schimmel and Widdershoven 2009, pp. 63–65; Caranta 2011, pp. 25–26.

and a procedural test only. It is not substantive, as the court does not conduct an appraisal of the facts itself. Then again, is goes further than merely testing whether the examination of the facts has been careful, accurate et cetera. Therefore, in the literature this test has been qualified as 'semi-procedural'.[74] This qualification seems adequate to me, although the label 'semi-substantive' would have been adequate as well. Albeit, the combination of this semi-procedural test of the statement of reasons and the strict process review of the examination of the facts seem to me a sufficient compensation for the lack of substantive review of the appraisal of the facts.

Finally it can be noted that the ECJ sometimes applies a process-oriented review when assessing the fundamental right's consistency of secondary Union acts (Sect. 3.4.2), and when reviewing the proportionality of such Union acts in general (Sect. 3.6.1). This process review is a deliberate choice of the ECJ. According to Koen Lenaerts (now president of the ECJ) in 2012, process review enables the Court to increase 'judicial scrutiny over the decision-making process of the EU-institutions', while at the same time, preventing 'the ECJ from intruding into the realm of politics'.[75] In the literature is has been argued that the Court should apply this test more often in fundamental rights cases,[76] Whether the Court will honour this wish, remains to be seen. What I do not expect is that the Court will apply this approach very often in preliminary reference proceedings concerning violations of fundamental EU rights by the Member States. After all, this would seem at odds with the purpose of this procedure, to develop uniform EU standards as regards the fundamental right in question (Sect. 3.4.2).

## 3.8 Conclusion

This chapter has examined, in a comparative way, the standards of judicial review applied by the ECJ when assessing Union acts and decisions and the standards imposed by the ECJ on the national courts reviewing decisions within the scope of Union law. An important finding is that the ECJ has in recent case law strengthens its grip on the level of judicial review of those national decisions. The traditionally applied autonomy approach seems to a large extent and increasingly something of the past. This implies in some areas of Union law that the national courts are no longer allowed to apply a stricter national standard of review.

Furthermore, it has been shown that the ECJ has restricted national review autonomy *inter alia* by transporting its own standards of review of EU acts to the review by national courts of similar acts and decisions. In addition, EU influence on the intensity of national judicial review is sometimes exercised on the basis of the

[74] Bar-Siman-Tov 2012, 2016.

[75] Lenaerts 2012, p. 15.

[76] Beijer 2018, pp. 207–208.

right of effective judicial protection of Article 47 of the Charter, although this right does not provide for one uniform standard of judicial review in all cases.

The standards of judicial review transported to the national courts include the standard of strict substantive review (of interferences with fundamental rights), the process-oriented review standard (of margins of discretion or appreciation) and, probably, the standard of unlimited jurisdiction (of competition and other sanctions of a criminal nature).

The process-oriented review of margins of discretion combines a strict test of the authorities' establishment of the relevant facts and of their compliance with the rights of defence with a serious test of the statement of reasons related to the appraisal of the facts. Therefore, it could better be qualified as 'semi-procedural'. This semi-procedural review counterbalances the judicial restraint as regards the substance of the decisions concerned.

## References

Bar-Siman-Tov I (2012) Semiprocedural Judicial Review. Legisprudence 6:271–300

Bar-Siman-Tov I (2016) The dual meaning of evidence-based judicial review of legislation. The Theory and Practice of Legislation, 4(2):107–133

Beijer M (2018) Procedural Fundamental Rights Review by the Court of Justice of the European Union. In: Gerards J, Brems E (eds) Procedural Review in European Fundamental Right Cases. Cambridge University Press, Cambridge, pp 177–208

Besselink L F M (2007) A Composite European Constitution. Europa Law Publishing, Groningen

Broberg M, Fenger N (2014) Preliminary References to the European Court of Justice. Oxford University Press, Oxford

Caranta R (2011) Evolving Patterns and Change in the EU Governance and their Consequences on Judicial Protection. In: Caranta R, Gerbrandy A (eds) Traditions and Change in European Administrative Law. Europa Law Publishing, Groningen, pp 15–61

Eliantonio M, Grashof F (2016) C-71/14, East Sussex Country Council v. Information Commissioner, Property Search Group, Local Government Association (Judgment of 6 October 2015) – Case Note. Review of European Administrative Law 9(1):35–45

Essens O, Gerbrandy A, Lavrijssen S (eds) (2009) National Courts and the Standard of Review in Competition Law and Economic Regulation. Europa Law Publishing, Groningen

Gerards J (2018) Procedural Review by the ECtHR: A Typology. In: Gerards J, Brems E (eds) Procedural Review in European Fundamental Rights Cases. Cambridge University Press, Cambridge, pp 127–160

Lenaerts K (2012) The European Court of Justice and Process-Oriented Review. Yearbook of European Law 31(1):3–16

Lenaerts K, Maselis I, Gutman K (2014) EU Procedural Law. Oxford University Press, Oxford

Nussberger A (2018) Review by the ECHR: View from the Court. In: Gerards J, Brems E (eds) Procedural Review in European Fundamental Rights Cases. Cambridge University Press, Cambridge pp 161–208

Ortlep R, Widdershoven R (2015) Judicial Protection. In: Jans J et al (eds) Europeanisation of Public Law. Europa Law Publishing, Groningen, pp 333–435

Prechal S (2015) Europeanisation of National Administrative Law. In: Jans J et al (eds) Europeanisation of Public Law. Europa Law Publishing, Groningen, pp. 39–72

Prechal S, Widdershoven R J G M, Jans J H (2015) Introduction. In: Jans J et al (eds) Europeanisation of Public Law. Europa Law Publishing, Groningen, pp 3–38

Pünder H, Klafki A (2018) Administrative Law in Germany. In: Seerden R (ed) Comparative Administrative Law. Intersentia Publishing, Cambridge pp 49–108

Reneman M (2014) EU Asylum Procedures and the Right to an Effective Remedy. Hart Publishing, Oxford and Portland, Oregon

Schimmel M, Widdershoven R J G M (2009) Judicial Review after Tetra Laval: Some Observations from a European Administrative Law Point of View. In: Essens O et al (eds) National Court and the Standard of Review in Competition Law and Economic Regulation. Europa Law Publishing, pp 51–77

Scholten M, Luchtman M (eds) (2017) Law Enforcement by EU Authorities. Implications for Political and Judicial Accountability. Edward Elgar Publishing, Cheltenham-Northampton MA

Thompson K (2018) Administrative Law in the United Kingdom. In: Seerden R (ed) Comparative Administrative Law. Intersentia Publishing, Cambridge, pp 197–266

Van den Brink J, Den Ouden W, Prechal S, Widdershoven R, Jans J (2015) General Principles of Law. In: Jans J et al (eds) Europeanisation of Public Law. Europa Law Publishing, Groningen, pp 135–262

Van Gestel R A J, De Poorter J C A (2016) Putting evidence-based law making to the test: Judicial review of legislative rationality. The Theory and Practice of Legislation 4(2):155–185

Widdershoven R J G M, Craig P (2017) Pertinent issues of judicial accountability in EU shared enforcement. In: Scholten M, Luchtman M (eds) Law Enforcement by EU Authorities. Implications for Political and Judicial Accountability. Edward Elgar Publishing, Cheltenham-Northampton MA, pp 330–352

Zglinski J (2018) The Rise of Deference: The Margin of Appreciation and Decentralized Judicial Review in EU Free Movement Law. Common Market Law Review 55:1341–1386

# Chapter 4
# Judicial Scrutiny of Regulatory Decisions at the UK's Specialist Competition Appeal Tribunal

**Despoina Mantzari**

## Contents



**Abstract** This chapter explores the determinants of judicial scrutiny of regulatory decisions at the UK's specialist Competition Appeal Tribunal (CAT); a unique feature of the UK's regulatory and competition law landscape. Unlike ordinary courts, the CAT's bench combines legal and non-legal expertise in areas such as economics, business and accountancy. Despite its specialist nature, however, and contrary to what intuition would suggest, the CAT does not always afford a narrow margin of appreciation to the regulators' discretionary assessments. Rather, as the chapter demonstrates, the CAT's scrutiny of regulatory decisions is determined by a *tripartite* relationship between the *expert* regulators, the *expert* CAT and the generalist Court of Appeal. It is the interplay between the *specialist/specialist* relationship, which characterises judicial scrutiny of the regulators' decisions by the CAT and the *generalist/specialist* relationship, which in turn characterises judicial

Dr. D. Mantzari is a lecturer in Competition Law and Policy at University College London, Faculty of Laws (d.mantzari@ucl.ac.uk). Any views expressed, omissions or mistakes are mine.

D. Mantzari (✉)
University College London, London, UK
e-mail: d.mantzari@ucl.ac.uk



J. de Poorter et al. (eds.), *Judicial Review of Administrative Discretion in the Administrative State*, https://doi.org/10.1007/978-94-6265-307-8_4

scrutiny of the CAT's assessments by the Court of Appeal that determines the degree of deference to the regulators' discretionary assessments.

**Keywords** Competition Appeal Tribunal · sector-specific regulation · judicial review · intensity of review · competition law · specialised tribunals

Once thought to occupy the periphery of the emerging at the time regulatory state, courts have nowadays surged as one of its central actors.[1] In recent years, the UK, as well as other European countries, have experienced an enhancement of the role of courts (and other types of adjudicative body) in the regulatory process. The surge in the number of legal battles between the regulators and the regulated is a clear illustration of this trend.[2] Institutional and broader legal developments can explain the judiciary's involvement in regulating the regulators. On the institutional front, the number of actors involved in the production and application of the law has increased tremendously following the EU-driven liberalisation and market integration efforts. National regulatory bodies, supranational bodies, 'network agencies' as well as private actors all interact in what has become an institutionally fragmented regulatory process; often indicated with the term 'multi-level governance'.[3] As a result of such institutional complexity, rich incentives are presented to prospective litigants to challenge regulatory decisions before national courts, the European Court and even the Strasbourg Court.[4]

On the substantive front, broader constitutional and jurisprudential developments in several EU Member States have created new grounds for the review of regulators' decisions. Prominent amongst these is the UK, which is now said to enjoy a 'multi-streamed jurisdiction';[5] a term employed to denote that judicial review encompasses not only common law principles, but also relevant applications of EU law and of the European Convention of Human Rights (ECHR).[6] At the same time, the establishment of a specialist tribunal, the Competition Appeal Tribunal (CAT), possessing both statutory review jurisdiction (similar to common law judicial

[1] For example, scholars in the UK anticipated a limited role for the courts in the wake of the Conservative programme of privatisation. See Black and Muchlinksi 1998, p. 1.

[2] See e.g. 'Regulatory Appeals in Practice' in BIS, 'Streamlining Regulatory and Competition Appeals-Consultation on Options for Reform' (June 2013) available at https://assets.publishing.service.gov.uk/government/uploads/system/uploads/attachment_data/file/229758/bis-13-876-regulatory-and-competition-appeals-revised.pdf. Last accessed 17 September 2018.

[3] For a commentary see Tapia and Mantzari 2013, Chapter 14.

[4] See e.g. Judgment of the ECtHR, 27 September 2011, *A/Menarini Diagnostics S.R.L. v Italy*, Appl. No 43509/08.

[5] Rawlings 2008, pp. 95–96.

[6] See e.g. *Peter Marcic v Thames Water Utilities Limited* [2002] EWCA Civ 65 and *Marcic v Thames Water Utilities Ltd* [2003] UKHL 66. See further *BT v OFCOM* [2012] CAT 11.

review) and statutory appeal jurisdiction (where it engages with the factual merits of the case) represents a new, attractive venue to challenge regulatory decisions. This chapter will focus on the judicial scrutiny of regulatory decisions by the specialist CAT. It will specifically focus on appeals from the sector-specific regulators of water (OFWAT),[7] communications (OFCOM),[8] and energy (OFGEM).[9]

The advent of the CAT has given rise to 'a crude equation: review of experts by generalists—wide margin of appreciation; review of experts by other experts (potentially even "more experts") narrow margin of appreciation'.[10] The story, however, is more complicated than what this paradigmatic scheme might suggest. This chapter will demonstrate that the CAT's scrutiny of regulatory decisions is determined by a *tripartite* relationship between the expert regulators, the expert CAT and the generalist Court of Appeal. At the heart of this relationship lies the interplay between the *specialist/specialist* relationship that characterises judicial scrutiny of the regulators' decisions by the CAT and the *generalist/specialist* relationship that characterises judicial scrutiny of the CAT's assessments by the Court of Appeal. This *tripartite* relationship between the regulators, the CAT and the Court of Appeal gives rise to a varying intensity of review better understood as a continuum. On the one end of the continuum lie judgments over primary facts reached following the evaluation of evidence, and discretionary decisions over which the tribunal will exercise a profound and rigorous scrutiny. On the other end of the continuum lie multifaceted policy considerations, which depend on inferences drawn from the evidence. In such cases the CAT is prepared to afford a margin of appreciation to the discretionary assessments of regulators.

The chapter will first briefly discuss the institutional landscape of regulatory appeals (Sect. 4.1) before identifying those institutional features of the expert tribunal that enable it to exert a high intensity of review of the expert regulators' decisions (Sect. 4.2).

It will then explore the inter-institutional interactions between the CAT and the generalist Court of Appeal and highlight the latter's role in regulating the tribunal's decision-making process (Sect. 4.3). It will be shown that in a number of cases the Court of Appeal points to institutional competence considerations that ought to

[7] OFWAT was established by the Water Act 2003 and is responsible for the regulation of the water and sewerage industries in England and Wales.

[8] But only with respect to the regulation of telecommunications. OFCOM was established by the Communications Act 2002 and operates under a number of Acts of Parliament and other statutes. It is responsible for regulating the TV and radio sectors, fixed line telecoms, mobiles, postal services and the airwaves over which wireless devices operate.

[9] OFGEM was set up by the Utilities Act in 2000. It is charged with implementing the Gas Act 1986, the Electricity Act 1989, the Utilities Act 2000, the Competition Act 1998, the Enterprise Act 2002, the Energy Acts of 2004, 2008, 2010, 2011 and the relevant EU legislation as well as the administration of a number of environmental projects on behalf of the Department for Business, Energy and Industrial Strategy (BEIS).

[10] De la Mare 2007.

govern the CAT's scope of review of regulatory agencies' decisions.[11] Those primarily refer to the regulatory agency's superior institutional legitimacy in deciding cases involving multifaceted policy considerations. Section 4.4 offers some concluding remarks.

## 4.1 The Institutional Landscape of Regulatory Appeals in a Nutshell

For our purposes here, judicial review should be understood as the scrutiny by the judicial branch of administrative action. The traditional function of judicial review as commonly understood is to control the legality of administrative decisions.[12] In the UK a distinction exists between appeal and review. Appeal is understood to be concerned with the merits of the case and further entails the power to substitute the decision for that of the primary decision-maker. Appeal rights are statutory, meaning that the courts have no inherent appellate jurisdiction. Review is understood to be concerned not with the merits of the decision, but with its 'validity'. Unlike appeal, it is not based on a statute, but on an inherent jurisdiction within the superior courts.

The appeal routes against sector-specific regulatory agencies' decisions vary, as we shall see below, depending on the nature of the case and further, differ significantly for each of the regulated sectors. The existence of this complex institutional architecture for appeals can be explained historically. There were no precedents for the regulators to work with when the first industries were privatised back in the 1980s and the early 1990s and the whole policy process developed in an incremental fashion.[13] While in the original legislation establishing the utility regulators, regulatory decisions could only be challenged by way of judicial review before the generalist High Court and on limited grounds, namely illegality, irrationality or procedural impropriety, today the routes of both appeal and judicial review are available. In fact, the introduction of statutory rights of appeal in the late 1990s have gradually led to the marginalisation of judicial review as the primary means to challenge regulatory decisions. Furthermore, the establishment of the specialist CAT has largely replaced the High Court as the primary venue for hearing such challenges. As we shall see in greater detail below, contrary to the ordinary courts, the CAT's bench combines legal and non-legal expertise in areas such as economics, business and accountancy. The turn towards a closer supervision of regulatory agencies' decisions could also be interpreted in the light of the wider

[11] For an in-depth analysis of the role of institutional competence considerations in judicial scrutiny of economic evidence enshrined in the regulatory agencies' discretionary assessments, see Mantzari 2016.

[12] Wade 1961.

[13] To this effect, see Prosser 2005.

transformation of judicial review following the incorporation of the ECHR into domestic law via the Human Rights Act 1998. Potentially new grounds of review, such as that of proportionality, have blurred the boundaries between 'merits' review and judicial review.

Subsequently, the courts' review of the decisions of agencies is moving from a position of traditional reluctance to intervene in areas of policy to a position of more intense scrutiny.[14]

The processes for the review of regulatory decisions are largely inconsistent. Financially significant regulatory decisions for the investors and ultimately the consumers (e.g. price control decisions, licence modifications) can be appealed on the merits to the specialist Competition and Markets Authority (CMA). In contrast, OFCOM's licencing decisions under the Communications Act 2003 were, until very recently, subject to an appeal on the merits before the CAT by any party affected by the decision. Such an appeal can cover material errors of fact or of law and it can go beyond that to challenge the exercise of discretion. That said, Jacob LJ in *T-Mobile (UK) Limited v Office of Communications*[15] emphasized that such an appeal is not intended to duplicate, still less, usurp, the functions of the regulator:

> After all it is inconceivable that Article 4 [of the Framework Directive], in requiring an appeal which can duly take into account the merits, requires Member States to have in effect a fully equipped duplicate regulatory body waiting in the wings just for appeals. What is called for is an appeal body and no more, a body which can look into whether the regulator had got something materially wrong. That may be very difficult if all that is impugned is an overall value judgment based upon competing commercial considerations in the context of a public policy decision.[16]

But, Section 87 of the recently enacted Digital Economy Act 2017 has introduced a judicial review standard. It remains to be seen what will be the scope and intensity of review applied by the CAT under this new standard of review. A further appeal on point of law can be brought to the Court of Appeal on behalf of a party or anyone else with sufficient interest. However, in the case where an appeal raises a price control matter this is hived off by the CAT and referred to the CMA for determination 'on the merits'. Finally, where the sectoral regulators exercise concurrent powers with the CMA under the Competition Act 1998, there is a right of appeal on the merits to the CAT and then on a point of law to the Court of Appeal. In such cases, the CAT's powers extend to substituting the decision for that of the regulator. In contrast, challenges against penalties and companies' licence conditions are heard by the High Court on grounds similar to those of judicial review.

[14] To this effect, see Poole 2009.

[15] [2008] EWCA Civ 1373.

[16] Ibid., at para 31.

## 4.2 The Specialist/Specialist Interplay: CAT Versus Regulators

This section will discuss the implications of the specialist/specialist interplay for the judicial scrutiny of regulatory decisions. In doing so, it will identify which of the CAT's institutional characteristics allow the latter to exercise its self-proclaimed 'profound and rigorous scrutiny'[17] over all aspects of the regulators' decisions.

It will then explore how these institutional characteristics played out in a seminal competition law appeal against a non-prohibition decision of the water regulator, OFWAT; the so-called Albion saga.[18]

### *4.2.1 The Impact of the CAT's Institutional Features on the Intensity of Review*

The CAT epitomises the example of a hyper-specialised adjudicative body. A number of reasons are identified in support of this statement, including the tribunal's membership and composition, its limited jurisdiction over regulatory and competition law disputes and the judges' perception of their role. To the aforementioned features this section will add the CAT's dual—appellate and review—jurisdiction over regulatory disputes and the tribunal's procedural rules.

First, the CAT's membership coupled with its subject-matter expertise has a direct impact on the degree of deference afforded to regulatory agencies' discretionary economic assessments. The CAT itself has acknowledged that 'the relevant expertise in its disposal may render the tribunal a more demanding and/or less deferential tribunal than might otherwise be the case where a court is called upon to review a decision of a specialist regulator'.[19] The membership consists of two panels: a panel of chairmen and a panel of ordinary members. The majority on the panel of chairmen are judges of the Chancery Division of the High Court. Some chairmen and all the other members come from academia, private practice, the civil service, business and industry. Typically, a three-member tribunal (a chairman and two ordinary members) will be constituted by the President to hear a particular case. Because competition and regulatory law are areas of law heavily influenced by

---

[17] See *Hutchison 3G v OFCOM* [2008] CAT 11, at para 164; *Vodafone Ltd v OFCOM,* [2008] CAT 22, at para 46; and *TalkTalk Telecom Group Plc v OFCOM* [2012] CAT 1 (TalkTalk case), at para 71.

[18] The Albion saga is long and complicated. Emphasis is placed primarily upon the following judgments: [2008] CAT 31 (hereinafter, 'Albion unfair pricing judgment'); [2006] CAT 23 (hereinafter 'Albion Main Judgment') [2006] CAT 36 ('Albion Further Judgment'); 2008 EWCA Civ 536 (hereinafter 'Albion Court of Appeal judgment'); [2009] CAT 12 (hereinafter 'Albion remedies').

[19] *BSkyB v Competition Commission* [2008] CAT 25, at para 61.

economics and economic evidence and analysis, the specialist CAT does not suffer to the same extent from the 'epistemic deficit'[20] vis-à-vis the expert regulator as the one observed in generalist courts, such as the High Court or the Court of Appeal.

Secondly, the CAT's perception of its role also influences the intensity of the review. That is clearly illustrated in the early cases, where the CAT made a bold attempt to establish its image as a hyper-competent tribunal. For example, in the *IBA Health* case,[21] the Court attempted to disengage itself from the *Wednesbury* test of unreasonableness that required a decision 'to be so unreasonable that no reasonable authority would have ever come to it',[22] in favour of the 'ordinary' and 'natural meaning' of the word.[23] The ordinary meaning of unreasonableness would enable a more wide-ranging factual inquiry than that allowed under the restrictive *Wednesbury* test.

Thirdly, the CAT's statutorily defined standards of review allow the tribunal to review any error of law, fact and discretion.[24] In particular, the tribunal has interpreted the reference to an appeal 'on the merits' to mean that it has 'full jurisdiction to find facts, make its own appraisals of economic issues, apply the law to those facts and appraisals, and determine the amount of any penalty'.[25] These grounds of challenge are partly based on the need to avoid the Tribunal converting itself from an appellate tribunal to a first instance decision-maker. Its remedial powers are also very wide. The CAT may not only remit a decision to the CMA or to a sectoral regulator, but may also take any decision these bodies could themselves have taken. The following passage illustrates the expansive terms in which the CAT has expressed its approach to its appellate jurisdiction vis-à-vis the Office of Fair Trading (now CMA) and sector-specific regulators:

> It is in our view inevitable that matters will often be gone into in more detail on appeal than was possible at the administrative stage, particularly since at that stage the OFT has no power to compel witnesses or to cross-examine. As a matter of general approach, we do not think we should seek artificially to limit or inhibit a deeper development of the case at the appeal stage, always provided that the basic procedural framework, and the overriding principle of fairness, are respected.[26]

Fourthly, the CAT's expansionary review is greatly facilitated by the court's procedural rules, which favour a laborious examination in respect of each aspect of the regulators' findings of fact and expert analysis.[27] Crucially, the tribunal enjoys broad discretion to consider new evidence, which was not submitted to the regulator

[20] Brewer 1998, p. 1586.

[21] *IBA Health Ltd v OFT* [2003] CAT 27.

[22] *Associated Provincial Picture Houses Ltd. v Wednesbury Corporation* [1948] 1 K.B. 223, at para 230.

[23] Ibid., at para 225.

[24] See Competition Act 1998, schedule 8.

[25] *Freeserve v Director General of Telecommunications* [2003] CAT 5, at para 107.

[26] *Aberdeen Journals Ltd v DGFT* [2002] CAT 4, at para 61.

[27] See e.g. *Everything Everywhere Ltd v CC* [2012] CAT 11.

before it made the decision which is being appealed or, evidence that informed the regulator's decision during the administrative phase but that was made available to the parties either in the regulator's final decision or during the appeal process.[28] In contrast, a High Court judge will typically refuse to allow a decision-maker to adduce evidence to justify its original decision or to allow a party to challenge a decision on the basis of material that was not available to the decision-maker when the original decision was made. In such cases, the High Court will normally remit the decision for reconsideration by the original decision-maker on the basis of the new evidence.

Finally, although the CAT is first and foremost an appellate tribunal and not the primary fact-finder,[29] the information record is enhanced through its discretion to permit oral cross-examination of witnesses, especially when the primary facts are in dispute.

In fact, the tribunal has gone as far as to argue that a merits appeal 'provides…a right to call and cross examine witness[es]'[30] Most interestingly, the CAT recently implemented the 'hot tub' approach.[31] A 'hot tub' refers to the mechanism by which expert witness evidence is taken concurrently with the relevant tribunal taking the lead in questioning the experts, usually with counsel then having the opportunity to ask supplementary questions of the expert called by the other side. Hot tubs seek to identify areas where experts are in agreement and to flag up those where there is disagreement. In contrast, the High Court rarely hears witnesses or expert witnesses and it has never sat with an assessor in a judicial review case.

### *4.2.2 The Albion Saga*

The Albion saga stands out as a prime manifestation of the specialist/specialist interplay, as it offers an excellent example of the degree of intrusion of the appellate judge upon the discretionary economic assessments of the regulator. All the tools available to the CAT that enable it to perform an intensive review of economic evidence were put into play. The tribunal determined disputes over primary facts, held extensive case management conferences, cross-examined expert witnesses and

---

[28] See e.g. the *Tobacco litigation* where OFT did not disclose the report produced by Professor Schaffer until the appeal stage although this material was available to it during the administrative stage. See *Imperial Tobacco and others v OFT* [2011] CAT 41.

[29] In proceedings under the Competition Act 1998 Act the CAT acts both as an appellate review court and also as a court of first instance exercising the role of the primary decision-maker. See further *J J Burgess & Sons v OFT* [2005] CAT 25 where the CAT adopted its own decision, on the merits of the case, in which it disagreed with the OFT's analysis and substituted its finding of an abuse for that of the OFT.

[30] *VIP Communications Ltd v OFCOM* [2007] CAT 3, at para 43.

[31] *British Telecommunications Plc v Ofcom* [2017] CAT 4; *Socrates Training Limited v The Law Society of England and Wales* [2017] CAT 12.

finally substituted its decision for that of the authority on the appropriate pricing methodology.

The litigation concerned the lawfulness of the price offered by Dwr Cymru ('DC'), an incumbent water undertaker, for the partial treatment and transmission of non-potable water through a pipeline to a paper factory. Albion, a new entrant statutory water undertaker since the privatisation of the water industry in England and Wales, claimed that the price quoted to it by DC for 'common carriage' across part of DC's network (Ashgrove system) was excessive and gave rise to a margin squeeze in violation of Chapter II of the Competition Act 1998.[32]

No statutory provision for common carriage was in place at the time of the complaint, although both OFWAT and the Office of Fair Trading (OFT) recognised that if an undertaker refused a request for common carriage or imposed an unreasonable price this would constitute a breach of the Competition Act 1998 rules. Following an investigation, OFWAT found that the common carriage price was justified on their application of the retail-minus pricing methodology (Efficient Component Pricing Rule – ECPR methodology.) It further noted that the same result would have been achieved if the 'costs principle' inserted by the Water Act 2003 had been applied; a provision not yet in force at the time of the complaint.

Albion appealed to the CAT against OFWAT's non-prohibition decision, arguing that DC had abused its dominant position by (i) demanding excessive prices and (ii) by causing a margin squeeze. The CAT upheld the appeal founding that the undertaking had engaged in margin squeeze practices. The tribunal delivered a number of judgements on this matter, scrutinising several aspects of the regulatory decision in great detail. In determining whether OFWAT's decision on excessive pricing was correct, the CAT referred to the EU case law on the matter and held that the appropriate costs to consider were those 'actually' and 'efficiently' incurred. The CAT scrutinised the 'averaging accounting costs'[33] approach that OFWAT sanctioned. Although the CAT agreed that OFWAT was right to apply the 'average accounting costs' methodology, it disapproved of the regulator's 'regional averaging approach'. Lengthy arguments were held over the differences that exist in relation to the cost drivers of potable and non-potable water supply pipes. The CAT found that separate cost drivers exist in operation, and judged that DC erred in grouping the different types of pipe together for the purposes of common carriage price regulation.[34] The tribunal criticised DC sharply for the lack of 'any detailed or verifiable breakdown of the components of cost'.[35] Furthermore it did not accept the argument that the information provided was corresponding to that demanded by

[32] Albion was granted an inset appointed under Section 6 of the Water Industry Act 1991.

[33] This method calculates the price for common carriage on the basis of average revenue for all customers, apportioning those revenues between different classes of activity (in this case resources, treatment and distribution and then making adjustments for specific classes of customers).

[34] Albion Main Judgment, at para 628.

[35] Ibid., at para 464.

OFWAT.[36] It therefore, held that a regulated price does not necessarily reflect cost nor it is necessarily 'reasonable'.

With regard to the margin squeeze allegation, the CAT criticised OFWAT for failing to apply the guidance contained in its own paper on pricing issues for common carriage[37] as well as the guidance provided by the then Office of Fair Trading and the European Commission on the issue. The tribunal took the view that the margin between the first access price (23.2p/m3) and the retail price (26p/m3) gave rise to an abusive margin squeeze.

In doing so, the CAT, first of all, chose the relevant 'imputation test'. There are two main 'imputation tests' for the assessment of an abusive margin squeeze: the 'as efficient competitor' test (AEC) and the 'reasonable efficient competitor' test' (REC).[38] The AEC test focuses upon the costs of the dominant undertaking's own downstream operation, while the REC pays more attention to the costs of an actual or potential competitor, even one less efficient than the incumbent, in the downstream market. Both of them feature in the EU soft law. Nonetheless, the CAT followed the AEC test which has been adopted by the EU Courts.[39]

The Court further delved into the following three issues related to the application of the AEC test: (a) the way to assess access policies; (b) the form of cost-analysis and (c) the rule to determine margins. Each will be examined in turn.

First, the CAT ruled that in cases where the dominant undertaking is not separated at different levels of the supply chain, a correct analysis in order to establish whether there is a squeeze would require the assumption of a 'notional business'—i.e. a hypothetical downstream arm of the incumbent acting in competition with DC.[40] Then the costs must be allocated to that hypothetical retail arm of the incumbent, including an appropriate amount for profits. If the retail arm can trade profitably at the level of the upstream price charged to the competitors, there is no

---

[36] Ibid., at para 468.

[37] See Ofwat Reference MD 163, published 30 June 2000.

[38] See Commission's Notice on the Application of Competition Rules to Access Agreements in the Telecommunications Sector ('Access Notice') OJ [1998] C 265/2, at paras 117 and 118: the AEC implies 'that the dominant company's own downstream operations could not trade profitably on the basis of the upstream price charged to its competitors by the operating arm of the company.' Regarding the REC: 'In appropriate circumstances, a price squeeze could also be demonstrated by showing that the margin between the price charged to competitors on the downstream market (including the dominant company's own downstream operations, if any) for access and the price which the network operator charges in the downstream market is insufficient to allow a reasonably efficient service provider to obtain a normal profit (unless the dominant company can show that its downstream operation is exceptionally efficient).'

[39] The Commission has applied the AEC test since its 1998 decision in Napier; see 88/518/EEC: Commission Decision of 18 July 1988 relating to a proceeding under Article 86 of the EEC Treaty (Case No IV/30.178 Napier Brown—British Sugar). In 2000, the General Court reaffirmed the AEC test in Case T-2/95, *Industrie des Poudres Sphériques v Council* [1998] ECR II-3939 and in 2007 in case T-271/03, *Deutsche Telekom v Commission* [2008] ECR II-477.

[40] Albion Main Judgment, at para 900. The failure to consider the costs of a notional retail arm of the incumbent was in the CAT's view a 'central weakness' of the regulator's decision (at para 906).

squeeze. Hence, the endorsement of the AEC test led the CAT to reject the notion of 'avoided costs' as a 'satisfactory basis' for the margin squeeze test.[41] Because the avoided costs method does not take into account the incumbent's fixed costs or the entrant's total costs, the application of such a notion would imply that the competitor would need to be 'more efficient' than (as opposed to 'equally efficient' to) the incumbent in order to be able to compete in the market. Finally, the CAT ruled on the appropriateness of the ECPR test to determine margins and any alleged squeeze; hence signalling that pricing methodologies are not immune from strict scrutiny, nor do they form part of the margin of appreciation, as the EU Courts have ruled in a number of preliminary rulings delineating the NRA's arena of discretion.[42] The application of the ECPR rule was one of the choices lying in the regulator's arena of discretionary power. There was no legal constraint to applying the ECPR in support of OFWAT's application of an average accounting cost methodology. Whether it promotes more or less competition is a different story. However, the CAT felt confident to decide whether the application of such a controversial rule should be accepted or not. Engaging in an academic discussion on the ECPR and examining its application in different countries around the globe in a comparative manner,[43] it clearly rejected the use of the ECPR: 'it cannot be assumed that [the incumbent's] upstream price is reasonable…[t]he margin squeeze in question cannot be justified on the basis of an ECPR approach which is itself unsound'.[44]

It may be argued that the CAT sought to align the access-pricing regime with orthodox regulatory practice. Notwithstanding the value of the academic criticism advanced against the ECPR, the CAT advanced competition over any other objective that the regulator could have considered when deciding to apply the ECPR. The tribunal judged that an economic approach, which requires new entrants to be 'super-efficient' effectively eliminates the development of competition and is not consonant with the government's policy goal in regulated industries. At the same time, the CAT was unable to offer any alternative choice to the regulator as the other solution advanced in the economics literature to the issue of access pricing, known as the Ramsey pricing rule, had also been discarded.[45]

Having explored the impact of the CAT's institutional features on the intensity of review the next section will examine the influence of the Court of Appeal on the CAT's scope of review.

---

[41] Ibid., at para 910 (ruling out the 'avoided costs' principle as the basis of reasoning of some European decisions).

[42] See C-438/04, *Mobistar SA v Institut belge des services postaux et des télécommunications* (IBPT) [2006].

[43] The ECPR rule was banned in the New Zealand Telecommunications sector following the *Clear* case and it was rejected by the US Supreme Court in the *Verizon* case. See cases *Telecom Corporation of New Zealand v Clear Communications Ltd* [1995] 1 NZLR 385 and *Verizon v FCC*, 535 US 467 (2002).

[44] Albion Main Judgment, at para 873.

[45] See generally Laffont and Tirole 2000.

## 4.3 'Regulating' the CAT: The Court of Appeal's Influence on the CAT's Decision-Making Process

This section will discuss how the preferences of the generalist Court of Appeal shape and ultimately constrain the CAT's propensity towards a heightened review of multifactorial regulatory decisions. It will argue that the Court of Appeal 'regulates' the institutional interactions of the CAT with regulators on the basis of relative institutional competence considerations. Those primarily refer to the regulatory agency's superior institutional legitimacy in deciding cases involving multifaceted policy considerations. As will be shown, whilst in the early cases the Court of Appeal was primarily concerned with striking an institutional balance between the CAT and the regulators, it gradually emerged as the 'regulator' of the CAT's decision-making process. The discussion will begin with an overview of the Court of Appeal's early interaction with the specialist tribunal in the context of regulatory disputes, and will then move on to consider the CAT's exercise of self-restraint in the context of appeals from OFCOM. In particular, OFCOM's decisions related to the market review process in electronic communications represent the largest number of regulatory appeals before the CAT, rendering the authority a repeat player before the tribunal.

Institutional competence considerations were prominent in the Court of Appeal's reasoning in the early days of the CAT when the Court of Appeal sought to strike what it perceived to be as 'the right balance' between the CAT and the regulators. Hence in the *Floe I* case[46] the Court of Appeal considered that the tribunal had gone too far in requiring OFCOM to reach a conclusion, either finding an infringement or a decision to issue a statement of objections within five months.[47] In the opinion of Lloyd LJ, while it was entitled to 'express its own view as to how urgently the case should be dealt with', it is not 'able to give directions to the regulator in relation to the conduct of further investigation'.[48] In the same vein in the *Floe II* case,[49] the Court of Appeal remarked on the potential for specialist adjudicatory bodies to issue 'advisory opinions to litigants or potential litigants' and as such 'do things which they are not intended, qualified or equipped to do'.[50]

However, in subsequent case law the Court of Appeal makes more explicit the use of institutional competence considerations in cases involving the balancing of potentially conflicting considerations relevant to the regulator's objectives. The Court of Appeal's judgement in the 08 numbers case,[51] concerning the correctness or otherwise of OFCOM's dispute resolution between BT and a number of mobile

---

[46] *OFCOM v Floe Telecom Ltd* [2006] EWCA Civ 768, at para 35. See CAT judgment, *Floe Telecom Ltd (in liquidation) v OFCOM* [2005] CAT 14.

[47] Ibid.

[48] Ibid.

[49] *OFCOM and T-Mobile (UK) Ltd v Floe Telecom Ltd* [2009] EWCA Civ 47.

[50] Ibid., at para 20.

[51] *Telefónica O2 UK Ltd v BT* (the "*08 Numbers*" case) [2012] EWCA Civ 1002.

network operators in respect of calls to non-geographic numbers (i.e. numbers beginning with 080, 0845, 0871) is a case in point.

Dispute resolution is a form of ex post regulation in its own right, provided by the Communications Act whenever 'meaningful commercial negotiations' between the parties have failed.[52] In resolving a dispute, OFCOM has the power to 'give a direction fixing the terms or conditions of transactions between the parties to the dispute'[53] in a way that meets the public policy objectives as set out in article 8 of the Framework Directive of electronic communications.[54] OFCOM had to decide whether it was fair and reasonable for BT to apply new termination charges for calls to the relevant numbers hosted on its network, based on the level of retail charge made by originating communications providers for calls to these numbers. In doing so, Ofcom construed an analytical framework for assessing whether the changes made by BT were 'fair and reasonable' judged by three governing principles closely related to the objectives set out in Article 8.2 of the Framework Directive: (a) that mobile network operators should be able to recover their efficient costs of originating calls to the relevant numbers; (b) that the new charges should provide benefits to consumers and (c) that they should not entail a material distortion of competition. Ofcom found that the second principle, the so-called 'welfare test' was not sufficiently met. The regulator distinguished between three potential effects on consumers: the 'direct effect', that is the effect on consumer prices for calls to 08 numbers. The 'indirect effect', which referred to the possibility that revenue gains by BT would feed back to the consumer in the form of lower charge or higher standards of service by service providers who use 08 numbers and the 'mobile tariff package' effect, that is the potential for mobile network operators essentially deprived of one revenue stream to try to compensate themselves by seeking to raise prices elsewhere. Though Ofcom thought that the direct and indirect effect was likely to be positive, it thought that the mobile tariff package effect was likely to be negative because mobile network operators would probably try to recoup the higher termination charges by raising charges for other services. Despite these circumstances of profound uncertainty, the CAT directed the regulator to follow either of the two alternative routes it proposed:[55]

> If, therefore, the test to be applied is whether the NCCNs can be shown to provide benefits to consumers, then that test is not met. However, we do not consider this to be the correct test in the circumstances of the present case, because it places undue importance on Ofcom's policy preference, at the expense of the two other relevant factors that we have identified as forming a part of Principle 2 (namely Principle 2(ii) [the risk of a distortion to competition arising from restricting CP's commercial freedom to price] and BT's private law rights.

---

[52] See Communications Act 2003, s 185. See further OFCOM, *Dispute Resolution Guidelines-Ofcom's guidelines for the handling of regulatory disputes*, available at http://stakeholders.ofcom.org.uk/binaries/consultations/dispute-resolution-guidelines/summary/condoc.pdf.

[53] Communications Act 2003, s 190.

[54] See *Hutchison 3G UK Ltd v OFCOM* [2009] EWCA Civ 683.

[55] Ibid., at para 396.

> We consider that whilst Ofcom's welfare analysis could override these other factors, it should only do so where it can clearly and distinctly be demonstrated that the introduction of the NCCNs would act as material disbenefit to consumers. In short, given the presence of the two other factors that we have identified, it is not enough for the welfare analysis to be simply inconclusive. The welfare analysis must demonstrate, and demonstrate clearly, that the interests of consumers will be disadvantaged.[56]

The Court of Appeal overruled the CAT and restored Ofcom's decision. It highlighted the forward-looking nature of OFCOM's assessments by stressing that the regulator had come to its conclusion by way of a balancing exercise in the face of uncertainty as to whether the changes would produce benefit or harm to consumers, taking into account the likely effects on competition and having regard to their overriding statutory duties to further the interest of consumers. Hence, the CAT was not entitled to override OFCOM's conclusions. The Court of Appeal did not actually argue that the Tribunal had balanced the various regulatory objectives in a different way from that adopted by OFCOM. Nonetheless, in a critical tone, it pointed to OFCOM's superior institutional legitimacy and expertise in cases involving the balancing exercise of the various regulatory duties.[57] It hence reminded the tribunal that it could not reach its own 'different conclusion as to how the relevant considerations should be balanced against each other, unless Ofcom's conclusions could be shown to have been wrong in law'.[58]

Potentially conflicting considerations also arise in the imposition of regulatory remedies following the finding of Significant Market Power (SMP). In such cases, the Court of Appeal has repeatedly held that:

> any value judgement (of OFCOM) as between different considerations, must carry great "weight" - the weight to be attached to different considerations in forming a value judgement is a matter for Ofcom as the NRA charged with the duty of resolving disputes, and in the absence of any misdirection by Ofcom the court will normally respect its determination, whether or not the court would itself have balanced the considerations in the same way and reached the same conclusion.[59]

In remedies following the finding of a SMP, while the CAT declares that it will not simply consider whether the decision of the regulator to impose a price control is 'within the range of reasonable response' but whether the decision is the 'right one',[60] it simultaneously proclaims that 'it may be slower to overturn certain decisions where there may be a number of different approaches which OFCOM could reasonably adopt':[61]

---

[56] Ibid.

[57] *Telefónica O2 UK Ltd v BT* (the "*08 Numbers*" case) (n 51), at para 89.

[58] Ibid.

[59] *BT v OFCOM* (PPC) [2012] EWCA Civ 1051.

[60] *Vodafone & Others v OFCOM* [2008] CAT 22, at para 46.

[61] Ibid.

> It is (…) common ground that there may, in relation to any particular dispute, be a number of different approaches which OFCOM could reasonably adopt in arriving at its determination. There may be no "single right" answer to the dispute. To that extent, the Tribunal may, whilst still conducting a merits review of the decision, be slow to overturn a decision which is arrived at by an appropriate methodology even if the dissatisfied party can suggest other ways of approaching the case which would also have been reasonable and which might have resulted in resolution more favourable to its cause.[62]

The CAT's reasoning largely echoes the Court of Appeal's guidance to the Tribunal in cases involving the assessment of multifactorial regulatory decisions. In such cases, the tribunal maintains a respectful attitude in not substituting its own view for a tenable view of the regulator properly made on a sound factual foundation. In spite of its specialist nature and in spite of its appellate jurisdiction, the CAT is prepared to allow a margin of discretion to the initial decision-maker.[63] The 'margin of appreciation test,' which has recently entered English domestic jurisprudence,[64] features prominently in the European Court of Justice (CJEU) case law, involving review of complex economic[65] or technical[66] appraisals. Despite the calls to 'marginalise' its application,[67] this judge-made doctrine still survives as a doctrinal constraint upon the appreciation of economic evidence enshrined in the European Commission's decisions.

The concept of a margin of appreciation suggests an ambit of discretion, a 'latitude in the factual assessment'[68] left to the Commission by the Treaty or legislative provisions. However, its wide application renders its 'properties' uncertain. The Courts have applied the doctrine in areas as diverse as mergers[69] and

[62] *T-Mobile (UK) Ltd and Others v OFCOM* [2008] CAT 12, at paras 82 and 83; see further Telefónica *UK Ltd v Ofcom* [2012] CAT 28, at para 45.

[63] Rose 2009. For a more recent pronouncement see *BT v Ofcom* [2016] CAT 22.

[64] Ibid.

[65] See e.g. Case C-42/84, *Remia v Commission* [1985] ECR I-2545, at para 35; C-56/64 and 58/64, *Consten and Grundig* [1996] Rec. p. 279; Case C-194/99 P, *Thyssen Stahl v Commission* [2003] ECR I-10821, at para 78; Case T-170/06, *Alrosa v Commission* [2007] ECR II-2601, at para 108.

[66] See Case T-201/04, *Microsoft v Commission* [2007] ECR II-3601, at para 88; Case T-321/05, *AstraZeneka v Commission* [2010] ECR II-02805, at para 32; Case C-269/90, *Technische Universität v Hauptzollamt München-Mitte* [1991] ECR I-5469, at para 14.

[67] See e.g. Jaeger 2011.

[68] Bailey 2004; see further Kalintiri 2016.

[69] Joined Cases C-68/94 and C-30/95, *French Republic and Société commerciale des potasses et de l'azote* (SCPA) *and Enterprise minière et chimique (EMC) v Commission* [1998] ECR I-1375; T-342/99, *Airtours v Commission* [2002] ECR II 2585; Case T-351/03, *Schneider Electric v Commission* [2002] ECR II-4071; Case T-5/02, *Tetra Laval v Commission* [2002] ECR II-4381, at para 119; T-342/99, *Airtours v Commission*, at para 64.

abuse of dominance cases,[70] as well as in fields where the Commission enjoys discretion of a political nature, such as state aid,[71] when reviewing administrative or legislative acts of institutions required to balance different interests and policies,[72] and decisions of independent expert committees.[73] The courts' recognition of a margin of appreciation triggers, in turn, a limited standard of review (contrôle restraint).

Although, as a general rule, in actions for annulment the EU Courts exercise a comprehensive, full review of legality (contrôle normal)[74] of an allegation of error of fact or of procedural impropriety,[75] review is limited when faced with complex economic assessments. As a consequence, the EU judicature will limit itself to:

> verifying whether the rules on procedure and on statement of reasons have been complied with, whether the facts have been accurately stated and whether there has been any manifest error of appraisal or a misuse of powers.[76]

Despite the Courts' recognition of the existence of a margin of appreciation since the *Tetra Laval* case the CJEU has granted the General Court the power to exercise a deep review of the Commission's analysis. It can be argued that the CAT's control of regulatory agencies is very close to the EU courts' standard of review. The tribunal is prepared to test whether the regulators' findings withstand its 'profound and rigorous' scrutiny, while at the same time allowing a margin of appreciation in cases involving policy judgements.

Apart from institutional competence considerations, broader systemic considerations also affect the degree of judicial scrutiny at the CAT. The first one is enforcement-related. Regulatory disputes have never been tested before in a specialist adjudicatory body. By integrating institutional competence considerations into its reasoning, the CAT avoids institutional conflict with the regulatory agencies and ensures that its rulings will be carried out by the regulators. The second

---

[70] See e.g. Case T-65/96, *Kish Glass v Commission* [2000] ECR II-1885, at para 64 upheld by appeal by an order of the CJEU in Case C-241/00, *P Kish Glass v Commission* [2001] ECR I-7759; Case T-301/04, *Clearstream v Commission* [2009] ECR II 3155, at para 47; Case T-57/01, *Solvay v Commission* [2009] ECR II 4621, at para 250.

[71] Case C-333/07, *Société Régie Network v Direction de contrôle fiscal Rhône-Alpes Bourgogne* [2009] ECR I-10807, at para 78.

[72] See e.g. C-225/91, *Mantra SA v Commission* [1993] ECR-I 3203, at paras 24–25; C-372/97, *Italy v Commission* [2004] ECR I-3679.

[73] See e.g. cases T-13/99, *Pfizer Animal Health SA v Council of the European Union*, at paras 170–2; Case T-70/99, *Alpharma Inc. v Council of the European Union*, at paras 177–180; Joined Cases T-74/00, T-76/00, T-84/00, T-85/00, T-137/00 and T-141/00 *Artegodan GmbH a.o. v Commission* [2002] ECR II-4945.

[74] See Legal 2006.

[75] Case T-41/96, *Bayer AG v Commission* [2000] ECR II-3383, at paras 67, 69 and 71.

[76] GC, T-28/03 *Holcim v Commission*, [2005] ECR II-1357, at para 95. See also ECJ, Case C-7/05 P *John Deere v Commission*, [1998] ECR I-3111, at paras 34–36; Case 42/84 *Remia v Commission*, [1985] ECR I-2545, at paras 34–5; Case C-194/99 P, *Thyssen Stahl v Commission* [2003] ECR I-10821, at para 78.

consideration is related to the legitimacy of the CAT. Adherence to the Court of Appeal's guidance not only weakens the possibility of a costly reversal of its judgements, but further contributes to its legitimacy-building exercise vis-à-vis the regulators and the other actors of the regulatory space.

## 4.4 Conclusion

This chapter examined the determinants of judicial scrutiny of regulatory decisions at the specialist CAT. In doing so, it highlighted the interplay of two different interactions: the *specialist/specialist* interaction that is reflected in the tribunal's scrutiny of the regulatory agencies' discretionary assessments and the *generalist/specialist* interaction that manifests itself in the Court of Appeal's review of the CAT's determinations. The chapter showed that the *specialist/specialist* interplay mostly manifests itself in the context of appeals involving the assessment of liability for competition law infringements. In those cases, the CAT does not only exercise an intensive scrutiny of the merits of the regulatory agencies' decisions, but it also does not hesitate to substitute its decision for that of the authority on issues which have been traditionally considered as 'no-go' areas for generalist courts (e.g. pricing methodologies). The chapter attributed this intensity of review to a number of institutional features of the tribunal, such as its membership, its subject-matter expertise and its perception of its role.

Special attention was paid to the tribunal's rules of procedure, which, contrary to those of the High Court, favour an extensive examination of each aspect of the regulator's findings of fact and expert analysis. The chapter then turned to consider the *generalist/specialist* situation and the role of the Court of Appeal in constraining the CAT's propensity towards a more intensive review. It was shown that the Court of Appeal regulates the institutional interactions of the CAT with the regulatory agencies on the basis of considerations of relative institutional competence. Those primarily refer to the agency's superior institutional expertise and legitimacy in deciding cases involving multifaceted policy considerations. Thus, the CAT, in reviewing OFCOM's decisions involving the assessment of SMP remedies in electronic communications, essentially multifactorial disputes, exercises a measure of self-restraint predicated upon considerations of institutional competence. The chapter shows that there is scope for a specialist tribunal conducting a merits review of regulatory decisions to confer 'a margin of appreciation' to the discretionary assessments of the regulatory authority. It also pointed to a number of other micro-level considerations and broader systemic considerations that affect the degree of judicial scrutiny at the CAT (i.e. enforcement-related, legitimacy-building).

In conclusion, the status of the reviewing court and its access to epistemic competence is an important factor, but not a dispositive one, in determining the intensity of review of regulatory decisions. This is mostly attributable to nature of regulatory disputes.[77] Even specialist tribunals are limited in their ability to decide on regulatory remedies, which involve the representation of diverse interests, the balancing of a variety of goals, and prospective analysis.

## References

Bailey D (2004) The Scope of Judicial Review Under Article 81 EC. Common Market Law Review 41(5):1327–1360

Black J, Muchlinski P (1998) Introduction. In: Black J, Muchlinski P, Walker P (eds) Commercial Regulation and Judicial Review. Hart Publishing, Oxford, pp 1–17

Brewer S (1998) Scientific Expert Testimony and Intellectual Due Process. Yale Law Journal 107 (6):1535–1681

De la Mare T (2007) Regulatory Judicial Review: The Impact of Competition Law (paper presented at the 2007 ALBA conference)

Jaeger M (2011) The Standard of Review in Competition Cases Involving Complex Economic Assessments: Towards the Marginalisation of the Marginal Review? Journal of European Competition Law & Practice 2(4):295–314

Kalintiri A (2016) What's in a Name? The Marginal Standard of Review of "Complex Economic Evaluations". EU Competition Enforcement, Common Market Law Review 53(5):1283–1316

Laffont J J, Tirole J (2000) Competition in Telecommunications. MIT Press, Cambridge MA

Legal H (2006) Standards of Proof and Standards of Judicial Review in EU Competition Law. In: Hawk B (ed) Annual Proceedings of the Fordham Corporate Law Institute. Juris Publishing, Huntington, pp 111–116

Mantzari D (2016) Economic Evidence in Regulatory Disputes: Revisiting the Court-Regulatory Agency Relationship in the US and the UK. 36(3) Oxford Journal of Legal Studies 36(3): 565–594

Poole T (2009) The Reformation of English Administrative Law, Cambridge Law Journal 68 (1):142–168

Prosser T (2005) The Place of Appeals in Regulation-Continuity and Change. In: Vass P (ed) Centre for the Study of Regulated Industries. Regulatory Review 2004/2005, Bath, pp 195–212

Rawlings R (2008) Modelling Judicial Review. Current Legal Problems 61(1):95-123

Rose V (2009) Margins of Appreciation: Changing Contours in Community and Domestic Case Law. Competition Policy International 5(1):3–24

Tapia J, Mantzari D (2013) The Regulation/Competition Interaction. In: Géradin D, Lianos I (eds) Handbook on European Competition Law – Substantive Aspects. Edward Elgar Publishing, Cheltenham/Northampton, pp 588–627

Wade W (1961) Administrative Law. Clarendon Press, Oxford

[77] I have referred to such disputes as 'polycentric' in nature in a related piece referred to in n 11 above.

# Part II
# Judicial Review in the Administrative State and the Impact on Dutch Administrative Law

# Chapter 5
# A Future Perspective on Judicial Review of Generally Binding Regulations in the Netherlands: Towards a Substantive Three-Step Proportionality Test?

**Jurgen de Poorter**

## Contents




Jurgen de Poorter is professor of administrative law at Tilburg University and deputy judge in the District Court of The Hague. From 2005 until 2018 Jurgen de Poorter was a special advisor to the Dutch Council of State, in particular to the Administrative Jurisdiction Division of the Council of State. He recently published on methods of judicial lawmaking, judicial review of evidence based legislation and judicial dialogues in the European Union.

J. de Poorter (✉)
Tilburg University, Tilburg, The Netherlands
e-mail: j.c.a.depoorter@tilburguniversity.edu





J. de Poorter et al. (eds.), *Judicial Review of Administrative Discretion in the Administrative State*, https://doi.org/10.1007/978-94-6265-307-8_5

**Abstract** The traditional cautious approach of the Dutch courts when assessing the legality of generally binding regulations does not correspond with the actual role the administrative courts are supposed to play in the administrative state. A different approach seems possible if we look at the aim of judicial review from a different constitutional point of view and consider judicial review to be animated by the concern to ensure the non-disproportionate character of all exercises of administrative power, rather than by the concern to ensure the democratic accountability of the administrative decision-making process. This contribution elaborates on how the concept of proportionality can be operationalized as a standard for the review of secondary legislation by the Dutch administrative courts.

**Keywords** Administrative procedural law · judicial restraint · the administrative state · judicial review · generally binding regulations · proportionality test

## 5.1 Introduction

The Dutch political and constitutional tradition has always been characterized by a limited role of the judiciary when it comes to judicial review of legislation. Article 120 of the Dutch Constitution is a predominant expression of this limited role. The core of that rule includes a prohibition on procedural testing,[1] on substantive testing, and on the testing of preparatory actions of primary legislation in the light of our Dutch Constitution.[2] In 1989 the Supreme Court ruled that the Dutch constitution even prohibits courts from testing a statutory provision in the light of fundamental principles of law.[3] The aforementioned political and constitutional tradition has also been reflected in Article 8:3 of the General Administrative Law Act that prohibits the administrative courts from reviewing secondary legislation. Although the administrative courts are not allowed to assess the legality of generally binding regulations directly, litigants may indirectly question the legality of the underlying legislation when appealing for example an individual administrative order.[4] Furthermore residual legal protection is provided by the Dutch civil courts. The Dutch Supreme Court set the standard for the review of secondary legislation in its landmark ruling *Landbouwvliegers*.[5] In this case, it decided that civil courts might review secondary legislation but in a restrained way, e.g. applying the

[1] Dutch Supreme Court 27 January 1961, ECLI:NL:PHR:1961:AG2059 (Prof. Van den Bergh).

[2] Dutch Supreme Court 19 November 1999, ECLI:NL:PHR:1999:AA1056 (Tegelen/Limburg).

[3] Dutch Supreme Court 14 April 1989, ECLI:NL:PHR:1989:AD5725 (Harmonisatiewet).

[4] Bok 1991.

[5] See recently Dutch Supreme Court 22 May 2015, ECLI:NL:HR:2015:1296 (Privacy First). This residual protection is only possible in case of a lack of sufficient legal protection in the proceedings before the administrative courts.

standard of unreasonableness or of a manifest error.[6] Both the civil and the administrative courts have adopted this so-called Landbouwvliegers-standard.

In this chapter I want to elaborate on the judicial review of generally binding regulations by the administrative courts in the Netherlands. There are several reasons for that. The first reason is that in the academic literature the discussion about the appropriateness of the prohibition for the administrative courts to review secondary legislation in a direct way, seems to be revitalized. In this respect I point at the discussions during the conference of the Dutch Association of Administrative Law in 2017.[7] Secondly, it is apparent from the case-law of the supreme administrative courts that the way these courts assess the legality of generally binding regulations, seems to be subject to change. See for example the *Alcohol lock case*, in which the Administrative Jurisdiction Division of the Council of State (AJD) invalidated the regulation because of an infringement of Article 3:4 of the General Administrative Law Act, e.g. on the basis of a proportionality test that seems to go beyond the traditional Landbouwvliegers-standard.[8] This might have to do with the question that has been raised in the academic literature lately if and to what extent the traditional constitutional frame of mind underlying the doctrinal judicial restraint corresponds with the actual relationship between different actors in what is called 'the administrative state'.[9] The role of the administrative courts is traditionally thought from the principle of separation of powers and our view on judicial review is thus largely animated by the concern for democratic accountability. But is that what one might expect the administrative courts to do in the administrative state? A different approach seems to be possible if we look at the aim of judicial review from a different constitutional point of view and consider judicial review to be animated by the concern to ensure the non-disproportionate character of all exercises of administrative power, rather than by the concern to ensure the democratic accountability of the administrative decision-making process.[10] My hypothesis is that the traditional cautious approach of the Dutch courts when assessing the legality of secondary legislation does not correspond with the actual role the administrative courts are supposed to play in the administrative state. The question I want to explore here is how the concept of proportionality can be operationalized as a standard for the review of secondary legislation by the Dutch administrative courts.

[6] Dutch Supreme Court 16 May 1986, ECLI:NL:PHR:1986:AC9354.

[7] Hirsch Ballin et al. 2015.

[8] The Administrative Jurisdiction Division of the Council of State: 4 March 2015, ECLI:NL:RVS:2015:622.

[9] Hirsch Ballin 2015, pp. 19–30 and De Poorter and Capkurt 2017.

[10] Carolan 2009, p. 106.

## 5.2 Changes in the Constitutional Framework

As mentioned earlier the constitutional design of administrative law has been strongly related to the concept of the *trias politica* in which the executive power was somehow considered to be a form of execution of what had been decided by the legislator supplemented by a permanent political control and a political accountability to a democratically elected body.[11] In this presumed mechanism of political control and accountability the executive branch found its legitimacy. This constitutional design also affected the way we used to perceive the interrelationship between the executive branch and the judiciary. Our view on judicial review is traditionally largely animated by this concern for democratic accountability. In this approach the judicial review was placed in the traditional scheme of a *transmission belt theory* in which the role of the administration consisted of applying the instructions that were set by the legislature. The administrative court's insistence on a statutory basis for any delegation of administrative power was designed to link these bodies to the consent-based legitimacy of the elected organ, and also to ensure that the powers ultimately exercised were dealt with by reference to clear statutory instructions or policy rules.

As mentioned earlier the question arises as to what extent this traditional constitutional framework corresponds with the actual relationship between the different actors in what is called 'the administrative state'. As a result of the development of the modern administrative state, as described by Jenet McLean and Mark Tushnet, we have seen the rise of independent agencies as a fourth branch within the overall scheme of government.[12] We could also see this in the Netherlands, where we had these 'authorities': agencies that are expected to be independent.[13] Take for example the Market and Consumer Authority that has gained stronger political independence and broader political powers at the same time. As Hirsch Ballin had rightfully argued earlier similar remarks could be made with respect to the bureaucracies that work under political accountability. An example of the latter is the so-called IND (Immigration and Naturalisation Service) that in practice takes the decisions in the field of asylum law, but in legal reality it is the Minister of Justice or his Secretary of State that takes the decisions. The large majority of administrative decisions are not taken under direct political control. The same applies to decisions of administrative authorities laying down generally binding regulations. What we have seen is a development whereby the level on which policy choices have been made has shifted increasingly. In the past those choices were often made on the level of democratically elected authorities, whereas nowadays—as a result of delegation and sub delegation by the legislature—these policy choices are made by administrative authorities. This means that in the

[11] Hirsch Ballin 2015, p. 22.

[12] McLean and Tushnet 2015, pp. 121–130.

[13] It should be noted that in this context the term independency is used in a sense that must not be confused with the term independency usually used in relation to the judiciary.

majority of the cases those who are politically responsible may only set the broader policy goals that are relevant for this bureaucratic decision-making process, but at the same time should refrain from giving direct instructions. In our modern state the administration has an ordering and correcting role. This role cannot be understood solely as the application of rules that have been developed by the legislator. Sometimes these rules have been developed by the administration herself—the regulating agencies—or there are policy rules that give the administration leeway to manoeuvre. This makes a trias-approach of administrative law with the supposed democratic legitimacy problematic in a certain way. It doesn't seem to be right to identify these 'bureaucrats' as the executors of the political will, or as 'alter egos of the political actors'. Their expertise must be recognized in some degree of independence from political control.[14] Therefore special forms of accountability are developed especially for this fourth branch. The legitimacy of this kind of agencies with the power to regulate and take administrative decisions is not based on a constitutional basis of political control, rather than on indirect democratic legitimacy by means of external transparency.[15]

## 5.3 The Role of the Courts in the Administrative State: The Courts as Regulatory Watchdogs?

What does all this tell us about the role of the courts in assessing the legality of generally binding regulations? The role of the administrative courts has always been linked to the concern for democratic accountability. The basic thought seemed to be that to the extent the legislator does not set instructions there appeared to be a corresponding rule-free environment for the administration which justifies a judicial restraint. A different approach though seems to be possible and more in line with the changing constitutional framework, if we look at the aim of judicial review from a different constitutional point of view and consider judicial review to be animated by the concern to ensure the proportionate character of all exercises of administrative power, rather than by the concern to ensure the democratic accountability of the administrative decision-making process. Legal protection by the courts should primarily be aimed at guarding the integrity and integrality of the balancing of interests as is structured by the principle of proportionality. In the context of administrative law, this principle of proportionality ensures that administrative authorities show proper respect for individuals and that relationships of powers between the state and individuals are understood as clear relationships of law.[16]

The importance of a judicial proportionality test of legislation and regulation seem to be growing ever since in legislative policy in the EU as well as in the

[14]McLean and Tushnet 2015, pp. 121–130.
[15]Lindseth 2010, p. 90.
[16]Thomas 2000.

Netherlands more emphasis is being put on the attempts to make regulation more rational, predictable and evidence-based. Antokolskaia describes this move towards 'evidence-based legislation' as: "the legislator in his choices for legislative interventions takes a rational and focused approach and does not let himself be guided by just political and ideological reasoning, but also by relevant results of scientific inquiry assessing the (expected) effectiveness of those interventions".[17] As a result of the growing importance of designing rules that can actually work, more emphasis is being put on questions like a. is a certain measure *suitable* to achieve the goal(s) set out by the legislature, b. is it *necessary* in the sense that there are no less intrusive alternatives available to reach the policy goals and c. are the costs *not excessive* in comparison to the benefits of the selected measure?[18] Therefore the proportionality principle seem to be the most obvious lens to look at the quality of this evidence-based legislation and regulation. Although much has been written about the virtues of this tendency toward evidence based-law-making, sceptics have argued that one should not overestimate the advantages of an evidence-based approach because policy makers and politicians are not always willing to take scientific insights into account.[19] Taking a critical look at current practices, the question arises as to how evidence-based law-making actually is. Impact assessments, for example, rarely lead to a choice for alternatives to legislation, consultations seldom result in significant changes to legislative drafts and the results of legislative experiments are sometimes simply neglected. In other words, how relevant and reliable are existing procedures that should make our laws and regulations more evidence-based? At the same time regulatory oversight seem to be relatively weak. Supervisory institutions are usually not capable of blocking bad legislative drafts from passing through. As I have argued earlier with my colleague Van Gestel little attention has been paid so far to the role of the courts as regulatory watchdogs.[20] In a way this is understandable from the aforementioned traditional constitutional point of view: the idea that each branch of government has its own constitutional role to play explains why courts have always been reluctant to invade the legislative domain. But to what extent this doctrine is still useful as a model to understand the relationships between the actors involved in the law-making process in the modern administrative state, is up for debate.[21]

[17] Antokolskaia 2013, p. 174.

[18] This paragraph is mainly derived from earlier work, see Van Gestel and De Poorter 2016.

[19] House of Commons Science and Technology Committee, Scientific advice, risk and evidence based policy making, Seventh report of session 2005–2006, House of Commons, London November 2006, p. 47.

[20] For an exception see Popelier 2012, pp. 257–270.

[21] See Ackerman 2010, pp. 128–133 and Ackerman 2000.

## 5.4 Proportionality in a Legislative Context

### *5.4.1 The Proportionality Principle as a Standard of Conduct in Administrative Rulemaking*

In the Netherlands, subsidiarity and proportionality are important indicators for legislative quality.[22] The subsidiarity principle requires that regulatory decisions should as much as possible be left to local authorities and non-governmental organisations.[23] The Dutch legislature prefers self-regulation to governmental regulation, whenever this is possible.[24] Consequently, the guidelines for legislative drafting introduce a number of issues that should be taken into account before new laws are introduced. Instruction 7 of these guidelines determines that:

> Before deciding to introduce a regulation, the following steps shall be taken: a. knowledge of the relevant facts and circumstances shall be acquired; b. the objectives being aimed at shall be defined in the most specific, accurate terms possible; c. it shall be investigated whether the objectives selected can be achieved using the capacity for self-regulation in the sector or sectors concerned or whether government intervention is required; d. if government intervention is necessary, it shall be investigated whether the objectives in view could be achieved by amending or making better use of existing instruments, or, if this proves impossible, what other options are available; e. the various options shall be compared and considered with care.

Dutch legislators should refrain from direct intervention as much as possible and instead provide a general framework for self-regulation where possible. In practice, however, the explanation why non-regulation or self-regulation has not been preferred over governmental regulation is often absent or weak.[25,26] Although proportionality is usually mentioned in the same breath with subsidiarity, it has a different meaning. Proportionality depends on other norms because it can only function in relation to legislative or constitutional provisions that leave a certain margin of discretion. It requires a balancing of interests in which thc composite weight of the disadvantages of a regulatory decision for the addressees may not

[22] An extensive explanation of these (and other) quality indicators can be found in: Ministry of Justice, Legislation in perspective, The Hague 1991.

[23] The principles of subsidiarity and proportionality as legislative quality indicators can be found in the Dutch Guidelines for legislative drafting. See: http://wetten.overheid.nl/BWBR0005730/2011-05-11.

[24] The ideas behind the Dutch emphasis on self-regulation are heavily influenced by the ideas of Niklas Luhmann and Gunter Teubner as can be witnessed in the Green paper: Zicht op wetgeving, Parliamentary Papers II, 1990–1991, 22008, nr 2.

[25] Instruction 212, under b, of the guidelines on legislative drafting requires that the necessity of regulatory intervention and the consideration of alternative modes of regulation are always presented in the explanatory memorandum of a proposed bill.

[26] Van Gestel and Menting 2011.

outweigh the advantages to the general interest.[27] Although the guidelines for legislative drafting do not contain a direct codification of the proportionality principle, we do recognize some elements of proportionality in it. The exact significance and the practical implications of the guidelines remain unclear though due to the fact that these instructions have not been accepted by Dutch courts as a statutory basis for judicial review of legislation.

For other reasons too, the significance of these guidelines is somehow limited: they only apply to the drafting of regulation by the central government. These guidelines are thus not applicable to secondary legislation drafted by administrative authorities that have not been part of the central government. That does not mean that there exists no legal basis for a proportionality standard in this regulatory context. The Dutch General Administrative Law Act (GALA), actually requires administrative authorities in the sense of GALA to comply with the principle of proportionality. Article 3:4, Section 2 of the GALA reads as follows: 'The adverse consequences of an order for one or more interested parties may not be disproportionate to the purposes to be served by the order'. The provision had two objectives: on the one hand, it created a statutory basis for the case law on 'arbitrariness' and on the other, it established a standard of conduct for the administration.[28] The term proportionality could very well serve both purposes. However the case law of the administrative courts gives us little guidance as to the exact meaning of Article 3:4, Section 2 of the GALA as a standard of conduct for the rulemaking process. In the first place this has, of course, to do with the fact that general rules cannot be the object of a *direct* appeal before an administrative court. Secondly, the fact that Dutch case law is in the main strictly about individual decisions entails that the step-by-step approach of the proportionality principle is often not appropriate. This has to do with the fact that these individual decisions are mostly taken as a reaction to a demand or a request and therefore the question of whether the decision is necessary or suitable is hardly ever opportune.[29] Therefore the most relevant question in Dutch case law seem to be the question about proportionality stricto sensu, which standard has for the first time recently also been applied to a general rule in the so-called Alcohol-lock case.[30] The only cases though in which all steps of the proportionality principle are being applied are those whereby EU-law or human rights laid down in the European Convention on Human Rights are involved. In these cases the Dutch administrative courts follow the case law of the Luxembourg and Strasbourg courts.

The interim conclusion can be that the exact meaning of the proportionality principle as a standard of conduct in the Dutch rulemaking process is quite unclear. The legal basis of this standard is somehow fragmented. On the one hand there are the guidelines for legislative drafting including some elements of the principle of

[27] De Moor-van Vugt 1995, p. 16.
[28] De Waard 2016, p. 114.
[29] Ibid., p. 135.
[30] AJD 4 March 2015, ECLI:NL:RVS:2015:622.

proportionality only applying to regulatory decisions of the central government, whereas on the other hand the GALA includes a standard of conduct for administrative decision-making—including the drafting of generally binding regulations—that looks very much like a proportionality principle but that has not been operationalized in the case law due to the fact that these generally binding regulations cannot be object of a direct appeal before an administrative court.

### 5.4.2 *Proportionality in Dutch Legislative Practice: The Case of the Alcohol Lock*

A beautiful example about things going wrong in the process of rulemaking from a proportionality perspective is the case of the alcohol lock. On the basis of the alcohol lock legislation the administrative authority responsible for driver safety (*Centraal Bureau Rijvaardigheid*) could require someone arrested for drunken driving to participate in a so-called alcohol lock programme in which the offender gets a special license for driving a car that contains an alcohol lock which prevents the car from starting before taking a breathalyser test. The offender needs to bear the costs for the installation of an alcohol lock in his car. Refusing to participate in the programme results in an invalidation of ones license for five years. This so-called alcohol lock program has been introduced by the Dutch government as a means to reduce the number of victims of road accidents due to drunken driving.

Van Gestel and Van Lochem have critically analysed the alcohol lock measure from a proportionality perspective.[31] These scholars have scrutinized the legislative draft of the alcohol lock legislation and focused on how empirical research had been used to justify normative decisions concerning the proportionality of the proposed regulatory measures.[32] Taking a closer look at the alcohol lock legislation the first thing they noticed is that the text of the explanatory memorandum on the exact goals of the alcohol lock program is rather vague. Specific targets have been presented in terms of an estimated decrease in the number of (fatal) casualties and teaching heavy drinkers how to separate the use of alcohol from the driving of a motor vehicle. The evidence on how these targets are going to be accomplished is rather weak. As Van Gestel and Van Lochem have argued problematic is the lack of clarity on the relationship between the introduction of alcohol lock programs in other legal systems and the estimated drop in (fatal) accidents in the Netherlands. There is no necessary causal relationship between the introduction of alcohol lock programs abroad and the effects the introduction of an alcohol lock could have on road accidents in the Netherlands.[33] What is striking is that no comprehensive impact assessment or study of potential regulatory alternatives, such as mandatory

[31] Van Gestel and Van Lochem 2018.

[32] Ibid.

[33] Ibid.

medical treatment and targeted rehab programs—has been undertaken. The Advisory Division of the Council of State also pointed to weaknesses in the effectiveness of the program due to: (1) the lack of a parallel mandatory addiction treatment program aimed to take away the root cause of the problems of the group of heavy drinkers on which the alcohol lock program is focused; (2) the susceptibility to fraud of the program, shown for example by the refusal to introduce additional sobriety inspections (e.g. think of people with an alcohol lock notification on their driving license who might keep driving with borrowed cars); (3) potential overlap with criminal law measures, which can make that offenders cannot be submitted to the alcohol lock program due to, among other things, the need to avoid ne bis in idem problems. This not only delays the implementation of the program, but could also increase the uncertainty among drunken drivers about what lies in wait for them which could negatively affect the willingness to participate.[34] The legislature has disregarded this critical advice of the Council of State and the lack of sufficient evidence with regard to the necessity and the suitability of the alcohol lock program.

The alcohol lock legislation has finally been invalidated by the Administrative Jurisdiction Division of the Dutch Council of State (AJD) but only because of an infringement of Article 3:4 of the General Administrative Law Act. This had to do with the fact that certain categories of offenders, who could not afford the installation of an alcohol lock in their cars, were automatically confronted with an invalidation of their driver's license for five years. Among those offenders were people who needed their license to make a living. The invalidation by the AJD was based on an assessment into the proportionality stricto sensu. The AJD remained silent though on the point of the necessity and suitability of the alcohol lock program.

### *5.4.3 The Need for a Notice and Comment Procedure in Dutch Administrative Law?*

As is shown in para 9.4.1 the subject of administrative rulemaking is a relatively blind spot in Dutch administrative law.[35] This raises the question if we don't need to pay more attention to rulemaking as an element of administrative law and to the standardization of the rulemaking process.[36] The traditional assumption that the legitimacy of the rulemaking procedure can be fully based on the electoral-representative control and accountability seems to be too narrow in the administrative state. The lack of political control and accountability urges us to think of other means to strengthen the legitimacy of the rulemaking process. As

[34] Parliamentary Papers II 2008–2009, 31 896, nr. 4, pp. 4–7.

[35] Scheltema 2014, pp. 6–8.

[36] See earlier De Poorter and Capkurt 2017.

Popelier has rightfully argued strengthening the elements of participation and rationalization of the law-making process is a useful strategy to compensate for democratic deficit problems of traditional law-making.[37] In this respect we can learn a lot of the so-called notice and comment procedure from the American Administrative Procedure Act which provides the administrative authorities with rules on the process of rulemaking and the judiciary with guidance as to the judicial review of legislation and regulation. The development of rules concerning the process of rulemaking should not be left to the judiciary. It is up to the legislature to take the lead. Inspiration could also be found in the ReNEUAL Model Rules on EU Administrative Procedure, especially those concerning Administrative Rulemaking. A new Division in the GALA could contain rules on the publication of an initiative or a draft regulation including a description of the objectives or the measure. It should also contain rules on the preparation of the regulation, like for example about the examination of the relevant facts, the prescription of an impact assessment and the explanation of the reasons for the choices made and their alternatives and the naming of the interest groups that have been heard in the preparatory phase of drafting the act and publish their documents. Finally it could also contain rules on the consultation and participation of stakeholders.

Such a notice and comment procedure does not only establish a standard of conduct for the administration but it could also contribute to the operationalization of the judicial proportionality test of generally binding regulations in Dutch administrative law. A proportionality test presupposes a means-end test. At present this proportionality test is often hampered due to the fact that the regulatory body is not very transparent about the aims that are being pursued by this regulation. The more general these aims are, the more difficult it is for the court to assess the proportionality of the chosen measure. Another complicating factor at this moment is that in case the regulatory body is transparent about the aims of the measure, it is most of the time rather unclear what exactly the evidence is on which the presumption is based that these goals will be reached best by exactly this measure. In order to conduct a true proportionality test it seems to be important that regulations meets certain minimum standards of administrative law-making. A notice and comment procedure in the GALA will therefore contribute to a mature judicial review of generally binding regulations in Dutch administrative law.

## 5.5 Current Developments on Proportionality in Dutch Case Law

The principle of proportionality plays a vital role in the judicial review of administrative decisions in most western jurisdictions, but its significance and practical implementation differs in most jurisdictions. There is for example the 'original'

[37] Popelier 2011, pp. 555–568.

Wednesbury test according to which a disproportionate act 'is only that act which is so unreasonable that no reasonable person' could have adopted it.[38] At the other end of the spectrum we find the three-, or four-step proportionality test as developed in Germany and in a slightly reshaped version adopted by the Court of Justice of the European Union and the European Court of Human Rights.[39] In the Netherlands proportionality is not a stranger to the legal system. However, it is rarely applied by the Dutch courts. In this regard some legal scholars speak of Dutch sobriety: Dutch courts employing the concept of reasonableness instead of proportionality to test the legality of an administrative decision.[40]

### 5.5.1 From Arbitrariness to Proportionality Stricto Sensu

Since *Landbouwvliegers* the main rule in Dutch administrative law is that courts, when examining the balancing of interests, should confine itself to a marginal control on arbitrariness. Typical for this marginal control is that the court does not give its own appreciation of what is reasonable or unreasonable. Instead the court focuses on the outcome of the balancing of interests the administration has performed and only if there is an apparent imbalance, the court will assess a violation of the legal standards. Recently a development seems to have taken place in the case law of the AJD in the sense that a more intense test is applied on the reasonableness of the balancing of interests. This test is directly based on Article 3:4, Section 2 GALA and goes beyond the traditional standard of prohibition of arbitrariness. In this respect the ruling on the alcohol lock can be seen as the landmark case.[41] Interesting is that the AJD collected evidence for its decision from past and pending cases. Based on the experience in these cases it noticed that the costs of the alcohol lock measure for citizens were in practice much higher than anticipated by the legislature. Offenders, who could not afford the installation of an alcohol lock in their cars, were automatically confronted with an invalidation of their drivers-license for five years. Among those offenders are people who need their license to make a living. Even for those who can afford to pay for the alcohol lock in their car, the consequences may be disproportionate. Just think of the case in which the offender needs to drive other cars than his own (e.g. the taxi driver). In such a case, the offender runs the risk of losing his job. The AJD found the consequences of the alcohol lock regulation in the individual case disproportionate and ruled that the alcohol lock legislation was in breach of Article 3:4, Section 2, GALA.

[38] Davies and Williams 2016, pp. 75–77.

[39] Marsch and Tünsmeyer 2016, pp. 13–43.

[40] See De Waard 2016, pp. 109–141.

[41] AJD 4 March 2015, ECLI:NL:RVS:2015:622.

Although this test carried out by the AJD seems to be more intense than the traditional control on arbitrariness, it is in a certain way limited as well. The test still essentially holds an assessment on proportionality stricto sensu: are the chosen means proportional to the goal that is pursued, regarding the nature of the interests involved and the extent to which these interests will be harmed. However, as mentioned above, the AJD refused to decide over the necessity and suitability of the alcohol lock program to achieve the legislature's aims.[42] This is a pity because exactly on these points the Advisory Division of the same Council of State (AD) had criticized the alcohol lock programme. As mentioned before the AD, for example, noticed that the regulation was not linked with an intensive treatment programme for offenders to overcome their addiction, which left the underlying (addiction) problems intact. Moreover, the AD casted doubts about the susceptibility of the programme to fraud. Hence, there were previous doubts as to how effective the programme was going to be and whether there were no less intrusive alternative measures available to achieve the same goals.[43]

### *5.5.2 Recent Developments: Towards a Process-Oriented Three-Step Proportionality Test?*

Judicial review of generally binding regulations in Dutch administrative law does not (yet) take the form of a three step approach or a real means-ends test. In his recent opinion to the AJD advocate-general Widdershoven argues that the supreme administrative courts in the Netherlands should give more structure to a three step proportionality test resembling what for example the CJEU performs.[44] If we read the opinion of the advocate-general very closely it seems that what he proposes can best be qualified as a process-oriented three-step proportionality test. According to the advocate-general the court can very well focus on formal principles of good administration like the obligation to gather the necessary information concerning the relevant facts and the interests to be weighed (Article 3:2 GALA) and the obligation that an administrative decision shall be based on proper reasons, both as permeated and coloured by the proportionality principle. Until now the supreme administrative courts in the Netherlands have not assessed the legality of a generally binding regulation directly in the light of these formal principles of good administration. A generally binding regulation has only been invalidated because it is considered to be in breach of a formal principle of good administration if this defect in the regulation leads to the conclusion that the regulation is apparently

[42] See also Van Gestel and De Poorter 2016, pp. 155–185.

[43] Advisory opinion W09.08.0371/IV. See: https://www.raadvanstate.nl/adviezen/zoeken-in-adviezen/tekst-advies.html?id=8501&summary_only=&q=alcoholslot.

[44] Opinion of 22 December 2017, ECLI:NL:RVS:2017:3557.

unreasonable. We might say that this will only be the case if any research into the question of suitability or necessity appears to be absent.

As advocate-general Widdershoven has argued an assessment of a generally binding regulation in the light of Article 3:2 GALA can in theory include a more intense test. This means that the regulatory authority is obliged to gather the necessary information concerning the relevant facts and the interests to be weighted. According to Widdershoven this also means that the court is obliged to assess whether the regulatory authority has conducted proper research into the necessity and the suitability of the measure. To what extent this exactly goes beyond simple box-ticking does not become quite clear from his opinion. With regard to the alcohol lock case one could imagine the court to assess whether the regulatory authority has conducted any research at all into the necessity and suitability. Since the alcohol lock legislation was based on research into the introduction of alcohol lock programs in other legal systems in relation to the estimated drop in (fatal) accidents, it might very well be that the court would conclude that the regulatory authority cannot be said to have been acting in breach of the obligation to gather necessary information concerning the relevant facts and the interests concerned. But a more intense judicial review on the obligation to gather information is at least in theory conceivable as well. One could imagine the court to assess whether the evidence concerning the necessity and suitability is complete, unequivocal and consistent to the extent that it can sustain the legislative measure. What would have happened if the AJD would have applied such a three step proportionality test in the alcohol lock case? One could imagine that the AJD would have ruled that since no comprehensive impact assessment or study of potential regulatory alternatives has been undertaken the necessity of the measure is rather questionable, moreover since there seems to be no direct causal relationship between the introduction of an alcohol lock abroad and the effects the introduction could have on road accidents in the Netherlands also the suitability of the measure seems to be doubtful. Although advocate-general Widdershoven tends to a more intense three-step proportionality test, it remains rather unclear how this three-step proportionality test will turn out in practice. First it is to be seen what the AJD will decide in relation to the opinion of the advocate-general.

## 5.6 Future Step: Towards a More Substantive Plausibility Test of the Proportionality Claim?

As soon as a more intense judicial proportionality test is being advocated, this calls the expertise of the courts into question. Can the courts be expected to scrutinize the validity and the truth-value of the evidence underlying the proportionality claim of the generally binding regulation? On the surface, courts face some hurdles with respect to scientific evidence that legislatures can avoid. Although this argument is frequently used as a rationale for judicial restraint, there seems to be little empirical evidence that legislators and regulatory agencies are better fact finders than courts.[45] As I have argued with Van Gestel earlier:

> Of course, the latter usually have more time, facilities and resources than courts. However, the fact that legislatures and regulatory agencies have better tools at their disposal does not lead to the conclusion that these tools are always used effectively. The legislative process suffers from some weaknesses that are different to those of the judicial procedure. Legislators and regulatory agencies may, for instance, have an incentive to present science in a way that fits best a particular political decision because the initiators of a certain law have an interest in the outcome. (…) Courts usually do not have this problem since they are supposed to take an independent position. Furthermore, courts normally have the advantage of being able to decide with hindsight, which makes it much easier to look at the effects of regulatory decisions and the strengths of the evidence on which these are based.

The question though remains how courts can actually carry out a more substantive proportionality test.

The Dutch courts are not yet willing to include ex ante evaluations or empirical data in a proportionality test of legislation at all. But if we take a look at for example the CJEU we see that this court does find it necessary to conduct a procedural review of legislation in which it takes ex ante evaluations into account.[46] At the same time it does not go as far yet as to scrutinize the underlying data or the scientific evidence on which consultations and impact assessments rest. Is that the approach advocate-general Widdershoven suggests to take where he refers to the case law of the CJEU? The problem with this remains that in case ex ante evaluations are of poor quality because the underlying data or scientific evidence is corrupted, this will negatively affect the court's judgment and support the idea the pre-legislative scrutiny is a matter of box-ticking.[47] Would there be a possible way forward? To a large extent, I would say, this depends on whether the legislature is willing or obliged to collaborate on this. The fact is, that courts have more opportunities to function as regulatory watchdogs and intensify their proportionality review in case legislators and regulators are prepared to provide more specific information about the aims of the drafts, the choice of regulatory instruments, and the methods of ex ante evaluations they apply. Here the development of a notice and comment procedure can be helpful. I believe that courts could demand more clarity as to how legislators and regulators use facts, empirical data, and scientific evidence as a basis for regulatory decisions with regard to the necessity, suitability and proportionality of the measures being taken. Judicial review of the substantive truth-value or validity of the empirical basis on which laws and regulations rest however does not mean that the courts should duplicate the work of the legislator. A court may require though that the underpinning of legislative drafts rely on independent research that is carried out according to accepted methods in the field,

---

45 See also Van Gestel and De Poorter 2016, pp. 155–185.

46 See for example Lenaerts 2012, pp. 3–16.

47 See Van Gestel and De Poorter 2016, pp. 155–185.

while avoiding cherry picking or otherwise trying to steer the outcomes.[48] Against this background the judicial assessment of the plausibility of the proportionality claim can include two dimensions. First the courts could develop criteria as to *the person or the institution* that acts as an expert carrying out the research necessary for the regulatory authority to assess the necessity, suitability and the proportionality stricto sensu. Secondly, the courts should develop criteria as to the assessment of *the validity and reliability of the evidence itself* underlying the proportionality claim by the regulatory authority.

With regard to the criteria as to the person or institution that acts as an expert providing the regulatory authority with evidence for the proportionality claim we could distinguish between at least two elements: a. the expert should be independent and impartial and b. he needs to have considerable expertise on the subject. As to the first element it is important for the court to know if there exists a hierarchical relationship between the regulatory authority and the expert; if there is a financial relationship between the expert and the regulatory authority; or if the expert has some personal interests in a certain outcome of the research. If this is the case this might be a sign of a lack of independency or impartiality. With regard to the expertise on the subject we are facing a serious question in the courtroom: judges often need experts because of the fact that they themselves lack expertise in other areas but the law, but how then do they assess the expertise of the expert? What does the judge know about the education, the experience and the competency of the expert? In other words, we are looking for criteria on how you measure what makes someone an expert. Here we might learn from for example the UK and ask the expert to provide us with a disclosure statement on the specific expertise of the expert. A disclosure statement might provide tools in order to assess the plausibility of the evidence underlying the regulatory measure.

As regards the evidence itself the judicial review should not only be aimed at assessing if this evidence is complete, unequivocal and consistent but also if the validity and reliability of the evidence underlying the proportionality claim is plausible. Even if the evidence provided by the legislative authority is complete in the sense that it captures all relevant aspects of the proposed measure, unequivocally and consistently, we may want to ensure that cherry picking has been avoided or that the conducted research cannot draw on a certain degree of acceptance in the scientific community in a certain field. On this point we could possibly learn from the evidentiary standard announced in *Daubert v. Merrell Dow Pharmaceuticals*, which governs the admissibility of expert evidence in federal courts and state courts in the U.S.[49] In Daubert, the U.S. Supreme Court made clear that courts need to ensure that expert testimony is both relevant and reliable. In essence, Daubert aims to ensure that scientific evidence brought before courts by litigating parties meets the same standards of reliability that the relevant scientific field itself would require.

[48] Ibid.

[49] 509 U.S. 579 (1993). Not every state court is always very strict in applying the US Supreme Court Daubert doctrine.

In such a more substantive model of judicial review it is still up to the regulatory authority to examine the relevant aspects and to undertake an impact assessment. The task of the administrative courts is to assess whether the outcome of this research into the proportionality of the measure sounds plausible. Testing the plausibility of the evidence-base of generally binding regulations means filtering out the cases in which the provided evidence is questionable, rather than duplicating the process of collecting evidence. As Breyer has rightfully argued: "One could not hope to replicate the subtleties and uncertainties that characterize good scientific work. A judge is not a scientist and a courtroom is not a laboratory. (…) Rather, the law must seek decisions that fall within the outer boundaries that mark the scientifically sound decisions that, *roughly* speaking, *approximately* reflect the scientific 'state of the art'."[50]

## 5.7 Conclusions

Returning to the research problem, I departed from the hypothesis that the traditional cautious approach of the Dutch courts when assessing the legality of secondary legislation does not correspond with the actual role the administrative courts are supposed to play in the administrative state. I have claimed that a different approach seems to be possible if we look at the aim of judicial review from a different constitutional point of view and consider judicial review to be animated by the concern to ensure the non-disproportionate character of all exercises of administrative power, rather than by the concern to ensure the democratic accountability of the administrative decision-making process. The research question I asked myself in this contribution was how the concept of proportionality can be operationalized as a standard for the review of secondary legislation by the Dutch administrative courts.

My overall conclusion is that the administrative courts should demand more clarity as to how legislators and regulators use facts, empirical data, and scientific evidence as a basis for regulatory decisions with regard to the necessity, suitability and proportionality of the measures being taken. That means a substantive proportionality test in order to scrutinize the underlying data or the scientific evidence on which consultations and impact assessments rest. The problem with a process-oriented proportionality test is that in case ex ante evaluations are of poor quality because the underlying data or scientific evidence is corrupted, this will negatively affect the CJEU's judgment and support the idea that the pre-legislative scrutiny is a matter of box-ticking. A judicial assessment of the plausibility of the proportionality claim can include two dimensions. First the courts could develop criteria as to *the person or the institution* that acts as an expert carrying out the research necessary for the regulatory authority to assess the necessity, suitability

[50] Breyer 1998, pp. 537–538.

and the proportionality stricto sensu. Secondly, the courts should develop criteria as to the assessment of *the validity and reliability of the evidence itself* underlying the proportionality claim by the regulatory authority.

Courts will have more opportunities to function as regulatory watchdogs and intensify their proportionality review in case legislators and regulators are prepared to provide more specific information about the aims of the drafts, the choice of regulatory instruments, and the methods of ex ante evaluation they apply. The need for standards on rulemaking in Dutch administrative law is apparent. Introducing a notice and comment procedure in Dutch administrative law would therefore not only establish a standard of conduct for the administration but it will also contribute to the operationalization of the judicial proportionality test of generally binding regulations in Dutch administrative law.

## References

Ackerman B (2000) Good-bye Montesquieu. In: Rose-Ackerman S, Lindseth P, Emerson B (eds) Comparative Administrative Law. Edward Elgar, Cheltenham, pp 128–133

Ackerman B (2010) The New Separation of Powers. Harvard Law Review 113(3):663–729

Antokolskaia M (2013) Van politiek gestuurde wetgeving naar evidence based wetgeving: Nog een lange weg te gaan [From Politically Controlled Legislation to Evidence Based Legislation: Still a long way to go]. In: Van Boom W, Giesen I, Veheij A (eds) Capita Civilologie: Handboek Empirie en Privaatrecht [Capita Civilology: Handbook Empiricism and Private Law]. Boom Juridische Uitgevers, The Hague pp 173–203

Bok A (1991) Rechterlijke toetsing van Regelgeving [Judicial Review of Generally Binding Regulations]. Kluwer, Alphen a/d Rijn

Breyer S (1998) The Interdependence of Science and Law. Science 280:537–538

Carolan E (2009) The New Separation of Powers: A Theory for the Modern State. Oxford University Press, Oxford

Davies A, Williams J (2016) Proportionality in English Law. In: Ranchordas S, de Waard B (eds) The Judge and the Proportionate Use of Discretion: A Comparative Study. Routledge, New York, pp 73–108

De Moor-van Vugt D (1995) Maten en Gewichten: Het evenredigheidsbeginsel in Europees perspectief [Sizes and Weights: The Proportionality Principle in European Perspective]. Proefschrift [Thesis] Tilburg University, Tilburg

De Poorter J, Capkurt F (2017) Rechterlijke toetsing van algemeen verbindende voorschriften: over de indringendheid van de rechterlijke toetsing in een toekomstig direct beroep tegen algemeen verbindende voorschriften [Judicial Review of Generally Binding Regulations: About the Intensity of Judicial Review in a Future Direct Appeal against Generally Binding Regulations]. NTB [Dutch Journal for Administrative Law] 2017/10

De Waard B (2016) Proportionality in Dutch Administrative Law. In: Ranchordas S, de Waard B (eds) The Judge and the Proportionate Use of Discretion: A Comparative Study. Routledge, New York, pp 109–141

Hirsch Ballin E (2015) De Constitutie van het Bestuursprocesrecht [The Constitution of Administrative Procedural Law]. In: Marseille A T, Meuwese A C M, Michiels F M C A, De Poorter J C A (eds) Behoorlijk Bestuursprocesrecht [Proper Administrative Procedural Law]. Boom Juridische Uitgevers, The Hague, pp 19–30

Hirsch Ballin E, Ortlep R, Tollenaar A (2015) Rechtsontwikkeling door de bestuursrechter [Legal Development by the Administrative Court]. Boom Juridische Uitgevers, The Hague.

Lenaerts K (2012) The European Court of Justice and Process-oriented Review. Yearbook of European Law 31(1):3–16
Lindseth P (2010) Power and Legitimacy: Reconciling Europe and the Nation State. Oxford University Press, Oxford
Marsch N, Tünsmeyer V (2016) The Principle of Proportionality in German Administrative Law. In: Ranchordas S, de Waard B (eds) The Judge and the Proportionate Use of Discretion: A Comparative Study. Routledge, New York, pp 13–42
Mclean J, Tushnet M (2015) Administrative bureaucracy. In: Tushnet M, Fleiner T, Saunders C (eds) Routledge Handbook of Constitutional Law. Routledge, Abingdon, pp 121–130
Popelier P (2011) Governance and better regulation: dealing with the legitimacy paradox. European Public Law 17(3):555–569
Popelier P (2012) Preliminary Comments on the Role of Courts as Regulatory Watchdogs. Legisprudence 6(3):257–270
Scheltema M (2014) Internationale regelgeving buiten de staten om: de behoefte aan bestuursrechtelijke beginselen over regelgeving [International regulations outside the states: the need for administrative principles on regulations]. NTB [Dutch Journal for Administrative Law] 2014/28
Thomas R (2000) Legitimate Expectations and Proportionality in Administrative Law. Hart Publishing, Oxford
Van Gestel R, Menting M (2011) Ex Ante Evaluation and Alternatives to Legislation: Going Dutch? Statute Law Review 32(3):1–18
Van Gestel R, de Poorter J (2016) Putting evidence based lawmaking to the test: judicial review of legislative rationality. The Theory and Practice of Legislation 4(2):155–185
Van Gestel R, van Lochem P (2018) Evidence based regulation and the translation from empirical data to normative choices. Erasmus Law Journal (upcoming)

# Chapter 6
# Judicial Review in Dutch Environmental Law: General Observations

**Tom Barkhuysen and Michiel van Emmerik**

## Contents



**Abstract** In the Netherlands as elsewhere, the topic of deference to the administration is an important doctrine that continues to provoke much debate. This doctrine, which is also referred to as the limited judicial review of administrative

---

Prof. Dr. T. Barkhuysen is professor of constitutional and administrative law at Leiden University, the Netherlands and partner at Stibbe (t.barkhuysen@law.leidenuniv.nl). Dr. M. L. van Emmerik is associate professor of constitutional and administrative law at Leiden University and deputy judge at the District Court Midden-Nederland (administrative cases; m.l.vanemmerik@law.leidenuniv.nl). This chapter was also presented as a national report at the IACL congress 2018 in Fukuoka, Japan and will be published in this context.

---

T. Barkhuysen (✉) · M. van Emmerik
Leiden University, Leiden, The Netherlands
e-mail: t.barkhuysen@law.leidenuniv.nl

M. van Emmerik
e-mail: m.l.vanemmerik@law.leidenuniv.nl



J. de Poorter et al. (eds.), *Judicial Review of Administrative Discretion in the Administrative State*, https://doi.org/10.1007/978-94-6265-307-8_6

actions, is the subject of dynamic developments. The exact role that the court should play in the review of administrative actions remains a contentious issue. The focus of this contribution is the relationship between the judiciary and the administration. How has this relationship developed and what are the expectations for the future? It is concluded that the review of administrative acts by the judiciary has been intensified in several cases in recent years. There is, however, no uniform approach. The judiciary differentiates with a greater focus on proportionality. Clear limits for the judicial review can be found where specific expertise of the administration is at stake.

**Keywords** Judicial review · administrative actions · deference · proportionality · environmental law · fundamental rights

## 6.1 Introduction

In the Netherlands as elsewhere, the topic of deference to the administration is an important doctrine that continues to provoke much debate. This doctrine, which is also referred to as the limited judicial review of administrative actions, is the subject of dynamic developments. The exact role that the court should play in the review of administrative actions remains a contentious issue. If the court engages in an in-depth, intensive review, it may be accused of wrongly encroaching on the administration's territory and thus failing to observe the division of duties desired under constitutional law—in doing so, it would usurp the function of the administration. On the other hand, if it acts with restraint, it may be accused of offering inadequate legal protection. Thus, the development of this doctrine reflects a continuous search for a proper balance. In the Netherlands, additional factors include the structure of the system of legal protection, the influence of the European Convention on Human Rights (ECHR) and the law of the European Union (EU law), as will become clear in this contribution.

The focus of this contribution is the relationship between the judiciary and the administration. How has this relationship developed and what are the expectations for the future? Consequently, another important aspect of the judiciary's role—its relationship with the legislature and legislation—will not be addressed.[1] Still, the legislature does have a key role in determining the judiciary's position in relation to the administration. After all, when powers are being conferred to administrative bodies, it is often the legislature that defines the scope those bodies have to exercise the powers in question. For example, the legislature may confer policy-making discretion on an administrative body, meaning that this body itself may, in principle, decide whether or not to make use of a particular power. Or, it may confer assessment discretion, enabling the administrative body itself to determine whether

[1] See in this regard Uzman et al. 2010.

a jurisdiction requirement has been met,[2] for instance in cases where the existence of a 'threat to public order' is a prerequisite for the use of a certain power.

For our discussion of 'deference', we have opted for a chronological approach that is preceded by a brief outline of the development of the system of legal protection against the government in the Netherlands. The following topics will be addressed in sequence: an introduction to the Dutch system of legal protection against the government (Sect. 6.2), the development of the doctrine on the basis of the 1949 Supreme Court judgment in *Doetinchem* (Sect. 6.3), the requirements for judicial legal protection against government decisions set in 1985 by the European Court of Human Rights in *Benthem* (Sect. 6.4), the General Administrative Law Act as the green light for further development of the doctrine with harmonising effect on various subareas of administrative law (Sect. 6.5), and the conclusion, with an outlook for the future (Sect. 6.6). It should be noted at the outset that this is an outline discussion.

## 6.2 The Dutch Context: The System of Legal Protection Against the Government[3]

In the Netherlands, the early twentieth century was marked by debate on the issue of who could best offer legal protection: the administration or the judiciary. In 1905, Minister of Justice Loeff submitted legislative proposals aimed at introducing a general administrative law Act. These proposals met with fierce opposition, notably from the famous constitutional law scholar Struycken. In his classic essay '*Administratie of rechter?*' [Administration or Judiciary?],[4] he argued that the control of administrative actions by an independent judiciary was fairly pointless. In this 'modern' time of parliamentary democracy, primary control of the administration had to be exercised by Parliament, not by a judge appointed for life. Moreover, he was of the opinion that the judiciary could not control administrative actions in an in-depth manner, asserting that the court lacked the expertise to do so. Due to the many, broad discretionary powers at the administration's disposal, a review based 'on the law' would have little significance. After all, the law attached few specific requirements to those discretionary powers which decisions had to satisfy. If the court were to review beyond the law, it would encroach on the duties of the administration and disrupt the separation of powers. 'The court may not

[2] Cf. J. R. Angeren, F. Groenewegen and A. Klap, *Toetsing aan vage normen in het Nederlandse, Duitse, Engelse en Franse recht (preadviezen NVvR)* [Review against vague standards in Dutch, English and French law (preliminary advice Netherlands Association for the Judiciary)], Oisterwijk: Wolf 2014. Klap draws a distinction between various vague standards: those that entail a weighing of interests, those that demand an evaluation of future events, those that require specific expertise and those with a supranational character, as well as combinations thereof.

[3] Parts of this section have been extracted from Barkhuysen et al. 2014b.

[4] Struycken 1910.

usurp the function of the administration.' In Struycken's view, society would be better off if the actions of administrative bodies were to be reviewed by the administration itself, in the form of an administrative appeal. Such an appeal involves the dispute being resolved by the administration itself, often by a higher administrative body. Conversely, Loeff took the view that the administration should not be responsible for approving its own actions. Rather, in a state under the rule of law, the administration had to be subject to control by an independent judiciary. In order to strengthen that independence, he proposed increasing judges' salaries and bringing jurisdiction under the ordinary court (and not a separate administrative court).

To date, this discussion has not resulted in the Netherlands making a choice of principle between an administrative appeal and an independent judiciary. This means that the debate regarding the division of duties between the administration and the judiciary is long-standing and still ongoing, and that general administrative adjudication did not get off the ground until a relatively late stage. As regards individual Acts, Parliament did venture to take the step of appointing a special administrative court as the competent adjudicating body as regards certain types of decision, but the step towards an administrative court that could rule on all administrative decisions was only taken at a late stage (and has still not been taken completely). Although a few special administrative law tribunals were established as from around 1900, administrative appeal (legal protection within the administrative pillar) remained an important form of legal protection.

Appeal to the Crown was a special form of administrative appeal, which ultimately involved the dispute being resolved by Royal Decree (signed by the King and countersigned by a Minister). Appeal to the Crown was applied in many different types of dispute, including environmental disputes. The Council of State played a key role in appeals to the Crown, because the entire process took place before the Administrative Dispute Department of the Council of State. While the Crown had the power to depart from the Council of State's advice, it did so only sporadically. Furthermore, there were additional conditions attached to this so-called 'contrarian approach'. These matters were regulated in legislation such as the Administrative Decisions Appeal Act (*Wet Beroep administratieve beschikkingen*).

Compared with other European countries, the appeal to the Crown formed an exceptional remedy. The Netherlands was firmly convinced that an appeal to the Crown offered a unique and valuable form of legal protection. However, as evident from the *Benthem* case (to be discussed below in Sect. 6.3), the Netherlands was ultimately corrected on this point by the European Court of Human Rights.

And so, the Dutch system of administrative adjudication developed step by step. In the beginning, the main rule was legal protection by the administration. However, over the course of time it became increasingly common to set up and appoint adjudicating tribunals that were competent to adjudicate on particular legislation, resulting in a system of numerous special adjudicating tribunals. A few tribunals were allocated so many duties that they became large, guiding courts. The Appeals Tribunals adjudicated on many areas of social security law. Subsequently, citizens could appeal to the Central Appeal Tribunal, a tribunal that also acquired public service jurisdiction and that has now existed for over a century. After the Second World War, the Trade and Industry Appeals Tribunal was established to deal with economic administrative law. In due course, this tribunal also acquired an important function as appeal court. In tax disputes, the competent court is traditionally the ordinary court (the tax divisions at the District Courts, Courts of Appeal and the Supreme Court). With the implementation of the Administrative Decisions (Appeals) Act (*Wet administratieve rechtspraak overheidsbeschikkingen*) in 1976, the Council of State was designated as the 'general' administrative court. As a result, in addition to the appeal to the Crown, the Council of State also acquired a process in which it was to act as a court, and thus did have jurisdiction to render the final judgment in a dispute. If a citizen could not submit his *decision* to a special administrative court, the Council of State's Jurisdiction Division heard the appeal as the general administrative court. This court was thus presented with all manner of disputes, regarding decisions by, for instance, the Municipal Executive, Provincial Executive and the Minister.

The civil court has continued to play a supplemental role in this fragmented system. In the early twentieth century, the Supreme Court held that the State, provinces, municipalities, water authorities, etc., as (public law) legal entities, could act unlawfully (Article 6:162 of the Dutch Civil Code). The civil court has jurisdiction to take cognisance of proceedings based on unlawful act *in the absence of a judicial process under administrative law with sufficient safeguards*.[5] If there was a judicial process under administrative law in which the citizen could present his complaint regarding unlawful act, the civil court acknowledged that it had no role to play and declared the citizen's claim inadmissible. If the citizen could not avail himself of the administrative court (because, for example, his litigation did not concern a 'decision'), the civil court took on the case. In this way, the civil court began to provide supplementary legal protection, and case law emerged on the division of duties between the civil and administrative courts. And, with all the different judicial processes and case law on the allocation of jurisdiction, a varied patchwork of forms of legal protection against the government arose.

Notably, in light of all of the above, the Netherlands does not have any constitutional court. Indeed, the courts are prohibited from assessing primary legislation against the Constitution. However, this is largely compensated by the fact that the courts—more specifically, all courts regardless of their position in the judicial structure—can and must assess against convention provisions such as those from the ECHR and EU law.[6]

For more than a decade now, administrative adjudication in the Netherlands has been increasingly focused on final dispute resolution.[7] As a rule, the court can no longer limit itself to merely annulling an administrative decision; it must use all

[5] Cf. Supreme Court 31 December 1915, *NJ* 1916, p. 407 (*Guldemond-Noordwijkerhout*).

[6] See further Uzman et al. 2010.

[7] See, in particular, Polak et al. 2014.

available means to resolve the dispute as definitively as possible. For example, administrative courts are increasingly inclined to consider whether a new decision by the administration is still necessary. If that *is* the case, the courts attempt to elaborate on what the parties will have to do after the judgment, before the administration renders a new decision replacing the annulled decision. This, too, means looking for a proper balance between definitive judicial dispute resolution on the one hand and respecting administrative discretion (in terms of policy-making and assessment) on the other. In the Explanatory Memorandum to the article in the General Administrative Law Act that urges the court to resolve the dispute before it as definitively as possible (Article 8:41a of that Act), consideration is also given to the limits of constitutional law in this regard. It states that the court will settle the case and does not have to confine itself to annulment and referral to the administrative body: "if and in so far as its constitutional position and the available information permit this."[8] Here too, then, in a sense it concerns an issue in the area of deference.

## 6.3 The Development of the Doctrine on the Basis of the Supreme Court Judgment in *Doetinchem*

Having sketched the context of the Dutch system of legal protection against the government, we can now focus in more detail on the development of the doctrine of deference. Before 1949, there was no clarity in Dutch case law regarding the issue of whether, and if so to what extent, a court is entitled to review the administration's policy choices. Some argued that courts should not be permitted to concern themselves with this area at all due to their respective constitutional positions and that legal protection in this respect would only be possible within the administrative pillar (administrative appeal). Others took the view that the court—being independent from the administration—should indeed be able to play a role. This in fact echoes the old discussion between Loeff and Struycken as described above.

In a case prompted by a housing requisition by a municipality based on an emergency law designed to solve the most acute housing shortage after the Second World War, the Supreme Court got the opportunity to clarify the matter. A mentally ill married couple was confronted with such a requisition for the billeting of their house. They lodged an objection to this before the court, based on their mental vulnerability. The municipality defended itself with the argument that the legislature had given it full discretion to requisition a house and that such a decision was deemed to be efficient. The couple argued that in their case, partly in view of their special position, the decision would have entirely disproportionate effects. The lower courts found for the couple and accepted that there had been abuse of the law in the case in hand. The municipality appealed to the Supreme Court, taking the

[8] *Kamerstukken* [Parliamentary Documents] II 2009/10, 32450, no. 3, p. 55.

position that, in making such a finding, the lower courts had wrongly encroached on its discretionary policy-making powers. The Supreme Court overruled the judgments of the lower courts and introduced the arbitrariness formula. This means that the court must respect the administration's discretionary powers in terms of its policy-making and assessment, and permits the court to intervene only if there is an "arbitrary act". According to the Supreme Court, this is the case if "the requisitioning authority, when weighing the relevant interests, could not reasonably have arrived at a requisition, and no weighing of those interests must therefore be deemed to have been made."[9] Thus, loosely translated, the Supreme Court held that the court is not permitted to intervene if it *itself* is of the opinion that a decision is not reasonable or is disproportionate, but may only do so if a reasonable man could never have reached the decision in question. The background to this approach is the relationship between the judiciary, the legislature and the administration, in which the judiciary is considered to have the least democratic legitimacy. Incidentally, the Supreme Court ultimately decided in this case that the prohibition against arbitrariness had not been infringed and thus found for the municipality.

The origin of this approach is not absolutely certain. However, it is assumed that the Supreme Court partly drew its inspiration from the English *Wednesbury* case law that began in 1948.[10] In *Wednesbury*, the English court introduced a test of reasonableness with regard to administrative decisions.

Based on the *Doetinchem*-judgment, it subsequently became established case law of the civil courts and the administrative courts[11] that courts must perform a limited review of government decisions if the issue at hand is whether the administration made a policy choice that is legally acceptable when weighing the relevant interests, or has correctly interpreted vague standards.[12]

## 6.4 Intermezzo: The European Court of Human Rights Demands Judicial Legal Protection Against Government Decisions in *Benthem*

As stated, the Netherlands was firmly convinced that an appeal to the Crown referred to in Sect. 6.2 offered a unique and valuable form of legal protection. Mr. *Benthem* contested this and lodged a complaint with the European Court of Human Rights to the effect that the Crown was not an independent and impartial tribunal established by law within the meaning of Article 6 ECHR. The European Court of

---

[9] Supreme Court 25 February 1949, *NJ* 1949/558 (Doetinchem housing requisition).

[10] Associated Provincial Picture Ltd. v Wednesbury Corp. [1948] 1 K.B. 223. Cf. Groenewegen 2014.

[11] Council of State's Jurisdiction Division, 23 October 1979, AB 1980/198 (St. Bavo).

[12] Cf. Van Wijk et al. 2014, pp. 332–337; De Waard 2016; Schlössels and Zijlstra 2017, pp. 374–375.

Human Rights found in favour of *Benthem* in 1985.[13] That was a remarkable judgment in two respects. Firstly, it transpired that a dispute regarding an environmental permit (in those days a 'Nuisance Act Licence', fell within the concept of 'civil rights and obligations' from Article 6 ECHR. Whether the national system qualifies a certain act as coming under 'administrative law' or 'private law' is thus not decisive. The European Court of Human Rights gave its own interpretation to the concept 'civil rights and obligations', resulting in administrative law largely falling under the safeguard of Article 6 ECHR. Consequently, a form of independent and impartial administration of justice in accordance with Article 6 ECHR had to be introduced to deal with the acts of administrative bodies. Secondly, it emerged that the Dutch appeal to the Crown did not meet the European requirements for independent and impartial administration of justice, because the Crown is part of the administration. Following this judgment, the appeal to the Crown was abolished and appeal to the independent (administrative) court was ultimately made available in all cases.

It may be concluded that the *Benthem* judgment profoundly changed legal protection against the government in the Netherlands. This judgment also offers a safeguard against the judicial control of administrative actions being abolished or restricted once again. The fact that this is necessary became evident, for example, from the proposals made by a working group of administrators who opposed the juridification of public administration.[14] Since then, there have been increasing calls for restriction of judicial control, in particular with regard to infrastructural projects that are said to suffer too much delay as a result of this control.[15] However, thanks to *Benthem*, it is established that this control must be maintained and that solutions for any resulting problems must be sought within that framework.[16] A committee that considered the future of legal protection against the government, commissioned by the Administrative Law Association (*Vereniging voor Bestuursrecht*) fully endorsed this principle and made proposals for enhancing this legal protection within the Benthem preconditions. They paid a great deal of attention in this regard to improving the dispute resolution capacity of administrative procedural law and argued that the court itself should more often resolve the matter, whether or not after the administration has been given the opportunity via a so-called administrative loop to rectify any shortcomings in a decision.[17] This report formed the prelude to the amendments to administrative procedural law that have meanwhile been implemented. As the appeal to the Crown in fact performed outstandingly in terms of its dispute resolution capacity, it proved a source of inspiration for the

[13]European Court of Human Rights 23 October 1985, *AB* 1986/1, annotated by E. M. H. Hirsch Ballin, *NJ* 1986, 102, annotated by EAA (*Benthem t. Nederland*); see also Barkhuysen and Van Emmerik 2016.

[14]*Bestuur in geding* [Judging the Administration], Haarlem 1997.

[15]Cf. Koeman 2008.

[16]Cf. Van Angeren 2009, pp. 1–11.

[17]Administrative Law Association Committee on Legal Protection 2004.

report and the amendments. However, it must be avoided that the administrative court is in fact increasingly forced to usurp the administration's function. However, the Strasbourg case law also offers a safeguard in this respect, with Albert Benthem as a 'standard bearer'.

## 6.5 The General Administrative Law Act as the Green Light for Further Development of the Doctrine with Harmonising Effect on Various Subareas of Administrative Law

With the implementation of the General Administrative Law Act in 1994, the Supreme Court's adoption of limited judicial review in *Doetinchem* came briefly under scrutiny once again. That was triggered by the codification of the principle of proportionality in Article 3:4(2) of the General Administrative Law Act, which provides that "the adverse consequences of a decision for one or more interested parties may not be disproportionate to the objects to be served by the decision". The District Court of Roermond construed this to mean a standard directed to the court whereby it had to review itself the proportionality of the decision placed before it, for the grant of consent for the construction of a store. According to the District Court, the new Article 3:4(2) of the General Administrative Law Act was intended to break with the established case law on limited review. However, the Administrative Jurisdiction Division immediately corrected this on appeal in 1996: "this provision, directed to the administration, was not intended by the legislature to intensify judicial review (…)" and "(…) the aim was to prompt restraint by the court when reviewing the weighing of interests by the administration". And furthermore: "the District Court should have limited itself to the question of whether the weighing of the relevant interests was so disproportionate that it must be concluded that the appellants (…) could not reasonably have come to the decision to grant the exemption requested."[18]

In other words, a return to *Doetinchem*, albeit with an exception, by reason of Article 6 ECHR, for punitive administrative sanctions on which the court itself *is* required to rule without restraint on proportionality.[19] As regards punitive administrative sanctions, the Administrative Jurisdiction Division held as follows: "Article 6 of the Convention for the Protection of Human Rights and Fundamental

[18] Administrative Jurisdiction Division of the Council of State, *AB* [Judgments in Administrative Law] 1997/93, *AB-Klassiek* [Classic Judgments in Administrative Law] 2016/22, annotated by B. W. N. de Waard (Deventer: Kluwer 2016) (*Maxis and Praxis*).

[19] Administrative Jurisdiction Division of the Council of State, 4 June 1996, JB 1997/172, (*Huisman/APK*). See further Van Emmerik and Saris 2014.

Freedoms, which applies to the imposition of a penalty such as the once concerned here, entails that the court must review, without restraint, whether the penalty imposed by the Minister in the specific case is in accordance with the principle of proportionality."[20]

Another period then commenced in which this line of case law encountered relatively little resistance and in which the administrative court made particular efforts not to encroach on the administration's territory in situations involving discretionary powers with regard to policy-making and assessment. This approach even gained an additional (theoretical) basis in the literature.[21]

Remarkably, in environmental-law matters the Administrative Jurisdiction Division of the Council of State still performed a full review up to 1998. This was a legacy from the time of the appeal to the Crown, a form of administrative appeal to a higher administrative body where the problem with constitutional relationships that was encountered by the independent court did not apply. Even after the abolition of this appeal to the Crown as a result of the *Benthem* judgment discussed above, and appeal to the administrative court was made available in environmental disputes, the practice of intensive review remained guiding for quite some time. Until that time the Administrative Jurisdiction Division effectively determined what was in the interest of a good living environment, which was at odds with the practice in other legal areas such as planning and zoning law. The Administrative Jurisdiction Division finally put an end to this untenable special position in a judgment that was dubbed *Die Wende* by analogy with the developments in Germany around the fall of the Berlin Wall.[22] The Division held: "The respondent has a certain assessment discretion, which is limited, inter alia, by what ensues from the most recent generally accepted environmental insights".

The judicial review of the acts or omissions of supervisory authorities under administrative law is restrained in accordance with the points outlined above as well. According to the Supreme Court, bearing in mind the extensive discretionary powers in terms of its policy-making and assessment that are vested in those supervisory authorities, and given the risk in question and the circumstances of which the supervisory authority was aware, the question to be answered by the court is whether the supervisory authority could reasonably have adopted the policy as regards control and supervision (in the event of general supervisory failures), or could have arrived at the acts in question (in the event of specific supervisory failures). According to the Supreme Court, courts must conduct a limited review of

[20] Administrative Jurisdiction Division 27 January 2010, *AB* [Judgments in Administrative Law] 2010/48, annotated by O. J. D. M. L. Jansen.

[21] By Daalder and Schreuder-Vlasblom 2000, pp. 214–221.

[22] Administrative Jurisdiction Division of the Council of State, 21 April 1998, *AB* [Judgments in Administrative Law] 1998/199, annotated by G. Jurgens (*Die Wende*). See on this topic Leemans 2008.

such matters, with due observance of all interests, the circumstances at the time in question and the knowledge at that time. In other words, it is not about determining in hindsight whether a different decision would have been better.[23]

## 6.6 Conclusion, with an Outlook for the Future: After Harmonisation, Moving Towards Differentiation and a Greater Focus on Proportionality, but with Limits due to the Specific Expertise of the Administration

### *6.6.1 Moving Towards Differentiation and a Focus on Proportionality*

It is only in recent years that this established case law has been seriously called into question once again, but this time the arguments seem to resonate more than before. It has been argued that, based on the requirement of effective legal protection, it is necessary for the administrative court to conduct a more intensive review, certainly when fundamental rights are at issue.[24] A court that exercises too much restraint would also create the risk of an administration devoid of responsibility and lax in its exercise of due care in the knowledge that the court allows much leeway.

These signals have been cautiously picked up in the case law, but only as regards non-punitive administrative sanctions with a major impact, such as in the context of integrity screening that could lead to the refusal and/or withdrawal of permits.[25] In addition, reference may be made to a judgment of the Administrative Jurisdiction Division regarding a decision on the maximum amount of natural gas to be extracted in Noord-Nederland, which decision was taken by the Minister on the basis of a discretionary power. In view of the possible earthquake risks and the associated dangers for residents, the Division intensified its review in comparison with previous judgments. It did so primarily by giving additional focus to the proportionality and proper substantiation of the decision.[26] Under the influence of the ECHR and EU law (the Procedure Directive), immigration law has seen review intensify as well. The Administrative Jurisdiction Division held as follows: "It

[23] Cf. Supreme Court 13 October 2006, ECLI:NL:HR:2006:AW2077 (*Vie d'Or*); Supreme Court 21 November 2014, ECLI:NL:HR:2014:3349 (*AFM-DSB*); Supreme Court 2 June 2017, ECLI:NL:HR:2017:987 (*Zalco*).

[24] Barkhuysen et al. 2014a.

[25] Administrative Jurisdiction Division of the Council of State, 25 April 2012, *AB* [Judgments in Administrative Law] 2012/207 (Public Administration (Probity Screening) Act [*Wet bevordering integriteitsbeoordelingen door het openbaar bestuur*].

[26] Administrative Jurisdiction Division of the Council of State, 18 November 2015, *AB* [Judgments in Administrative Law] 2016/82, annotated by Bröring and Brouwer.

follows from the above that the administrative review of the State Secretary's position regarding the credibility of an account of the reasons for requesting asylum has a mixed character if a foreign national's account of the reasons for requesting asylum rests partly on statements and suppositions that are not substantiated with evidence. Most aspects and elements of a decision can be reviewed by the administrative court in terms of whether the State Secretary correctly took the position he adopted. If the State Secretary has decision-making discretion on aspects and elements of a decision, specifically when assessing the credibility of a foreign national's statements and suppositions that are not substantiated with evidence, the administrative court will have to review whether the State Secretary did not wrongly take the position that the account of the reasons for requesting asylum lacked credibility, albeit that in that case too the administrative court must review the care taken in and reasons given for the decision-making of the State Secretary when exercising that decision-making discretion. Consequently, the judicial review of a position of the State Secretary regarding the credibility of an account of the reasons for requesting asylum will be more intensive than before the entry into force of Article 46(3) of the Procedure Directive."[27]

However, for the time being there has not been a fundamental change of course across the full spectrum of administrative law. Such change may be at hand, though: Hirsch Ballin—former President of the Administrative Jurisdiction Division—received much support for his preliminary advice, issued as a publication of the Administrative Law Association, entitled '*Dynamiek in de bestuursrechtspraak*' [Dynamics in Administrative Adjudication], which he defended in 2015 and in which he pleaded for a more active role for the administrative court in a broad sense. Hirsch Ballin advocated abandoning the *Doetinchem* approach whereby discretionary powers conferred in terms of its policy-making and assessment automatically imply limited discretion by the court. Instead, he propounded a more balanced approach in which the intensity of the review is determined by considering the nature of the legal relationship and the weight of the relevant interests (including fundamental rights) of the parties involved. In his view, contemporary changes in constitutional relationships—particularly the insufficient democratic legitimacy of the administration as a result of the reticent, sometimes careless legislature, as well as the need for an administrative court that solves those disputes and keeps the legislature on its toes—require the judicial attitude to be adjusted accordingly. Otherwise, the administration actually operates too much within a 'legal lacuna', according to Hirsch Ballin. In the debate with Hirsch Ballin, Polak (the then President of the Administrative Jurisdiction Division) stated that the present formulation of limited discretion may require amendment in light of these points.

Hirsch Ballin's oral arguments, which were revolutionary in a sense, deserve to be followed-up. In so far as possible, administrative courts should have to render their own ruling on the question of whether a decision is reasonable and

---

[27] Administrative Jurisdiction Division of the Council of State, 13 April 2016, *AB* [Judgments in Administrative Law] 2016/195, annotated by M. Reneman.

proportionate. Furthermore, it is important to ensure that this does not only take place in a semantic sense. The administrative court will have to actually understand the substance of a dispute before rendering its own ruling and definitively resolving the dispute. In this way, an important boost is given to the quality of administrative adjudication in terms of workmanship, justice and effectiveness, thus increasing its legitimacy. As for the intensity of review, a tailored approach will be required, depending on the interests involved, and the assessment of proportionality will become more prominent. Depending on the circumstances of the case, a proper balance must thus be found between the respect that the court should have for the administration's discretionary powers in terms of policy and assessment on the one hand, and the interest of the interested parties in not having their interests affected to a disproportionate degree on the other.[28]

Inspiration may be drawn in this respect from EU law, in which there has been a differentiated approach regarding the intensity of review for quite some time. Determining intensity is not a matter of 'all or nothing' (full review or limited review) but entails a tailored approach depending on the nature of the legal relationship and the weight of the relevant interests of the parties involved.[29]

Reference may be made once more at this point to a new issue in the area of deference, namely where the limits lie as regards the administrative court's power, once a decision has been annulled, to settle the dispute itself without referring the matter back to the administration. In this respect, too, the limits relate to the constitutional position of the administration and the judiciary. But here, too, it is noticeable that in recent years the judiciary has become more inclined to deem itself able to do so.[30]

The recent advisory opinion of Advocate General Widdershoven in the so called *Purmerend*-case (that also deals with liquefied petroleum gas) is a further step in this direction. This opinion argues that a more intensive review of generally binding regulations is necessary to provide effective legal protection. According to this conclusion the intensity of the review should depend on the (personal) impact of the application of the regulation at hand. Especially when fundamental rights are at stake there is less room for deference.[31] Also within the area of the EU free movement of services based on the Services Directive, recent case law has led to a stricter review.[32] A higher level of scrutiny is thus required when restricting the free movement of services. Important to consider is the broad interpretation of the

[28] Cf. Administrative Jurisdiction Division of the Council of State, 26 October 2016, *AB* [Judgments in Administrative Law] 2016/447, annotated by Bröring (proportionality of the application of policy rules).

[29] Cf. Gerards 2007, pp. 73–113; Ortlep and Zorg 2016. See further, in the vein of comparative law, Ranchordás and De Waard 2016.

[30] Cf. Verheij 2013.

[31] ECLI:NL:RVS:2017:3557; a request for a preliminary ruling from the CJEU has been made by the the Administrative Jurisdiction Division of the Council of State Cf. De Poorter and Capkurt 2017.

[32] Court of Justice of the European Union 30 January 2018, ECLI:EU:C:2018:44.

concept of "services" used by the CJEU when determining the scope of the Directive, also extending to, for example, the restriction of retail trade through municipal zoning plans. This case law has been elicited by the Administrative Judicial Division of the Council of State with a request for a preliminary ruling concerning the *Appingedam* case.[33] Any such restrictions have to be non-discriminatory, necessary (meaning justifiable on the ground of an overriding reason relating to the public interest) and proportional (meaning the measures are suitable for securing the attainment of the objective pursued, they do not go beyond what is necessary to attain that objective and that this objective cannot be attained through other, less restrictive measures with the same result). These conditions go beyond what was previously required under Dutch law and this ruling is expected to also have a consequential effect outside of environmental and planning law.

### 6.6.2 But with Limits, Due to the Necessary Expertise

At the same time, there is another reason why—apart from the constitutional position of the judiciary and its tenuous democratic legitimacy—it may be necessary to exercise restraint in judicial review: namely, where the court lacks sufficient expertise. The ever-increasing complexity of the administration's duties is reflected in growing professionalization within government, and it is becoming more and more difficult for the judiciary to keep abreast of these developments.[34] These matters also have implications for the extensive case law of the European Court of Human Rights on 'full jurisdiction', which is also highly relevant for Dutch legal practice in this respect. Based on this right of 'full jurisdiction' acknowledged in the case law of the European Court of Human Rights (referred to as 'organe judiciaire de pleine juridiction' in the judgments (also) rendered in French), the national court must have jurisdiction to examine all issues of fact and of law that are relevant to the dispute. In this respect, expressly no distinction is drawn between questions of law and questions of fact, both of which may be equally crucial to the outcome of the dispute.[35] The court must be able to form its own opinion on both issues, and must not automatically rely on their valuation by other authorities (in particular the administration), let alone be bound by such. For example, in the Dutch *Terra Woningen* case, the European Court of Human Rights held that the fact that the

[33] Administrative Jurisdiction Division of the Council of State 20 June 2018, ECLI:NL:RVS:2018:2062.

[34] Scheltema 2015, pp. 803–818.

[35] See, for example, European Court of Human Rights 23 June 1981, *NJ* 1982/602 (*Le Compte, Van Leuven & De Meyere v Belgium*), para 51. The following passages are partially extracted from Barkhuysen and Van Emmerik 2016.

sub-district court in the case in hand had not formed an opinion of its own regarding possible soil pollution but had relied solely on the decision of the Provincial Executive in this regard was contrary to this aspect of the law on access to a tribunal from Article 6 ECHR.[36] According to the case law of the European Court of Human Rights, this right to 'full jurisdiction' forms an essential characteristic of the right of access to a tribunal from Article 6(1) ECHR and applies to *all* proceedings falling within the scope of Article 6 ECHR, in other words to all proceedings that entail the determination of civil rights and obligations or of any criminal charge.

While the court is thus not permitted to blindly follow the administrative decision, in the case law the question often concerns *the extent to which* the court may rely on the decision of the administration. Although restrictions on judicial control of the administrative finding of fact may be at odds with Article 6 ECHR,[37] they are not automatically impermissible.[38] There does have to be a convincing ground that justifies such restrictions, such as the nature of the substantive area of law and the administrative discretion associated with it, and the specialised nature of the finding of fact. It is important in this respect that the administrative finding of fact took place in—quasi-judicial—specialist administrative preparatory proceedings with sufficient safeguards.[39] Therefore, the restrictions on judicial control of the administrative finding of fact must in any case never be so far-reaching that the court relies entirely on the decision of the administration. After all, that would mean in fact that the interested party would have no access to the court on that point. In the context of the judicial proceedings, it must be possible to conduct a debate regarding the correctness of the administrative finding of fact and the manner in which it was reached. As evident from the case law of the European Court of Human Rights, the complete exclusion of such is unacceptable.[40]

Pursuant to the right to a fair trial protected by Article 6 ECHR, the court will have to take an active approach as regards calling witnesses who can shed light on

[36] European Court of Human Rights 17 December 1996, *NJCM-Bulletin* 1997, pp. 617 et seq., annotated by M. L. W. M. Viering (*Terra Woningen BV v the Netherlands*). See also, for example, European Court of Human Rights 13 February 2003, *AB* [Judgments in Administrative Law] 2004/52, annotated by B. W. N. de Waard (*Chevrol v France*).

[37] Widdershoven et al. 2001, p. 37. Cf. Barkhuysen et al. 2007, p. 104 and the case law there cited.

[38] See, in particular, European Court of Human Rights 22 November 1995, Series A. vol. 335A (*Bryan v United Kingdom*), and for confirmation of the Bryan line: European Court of Human Rights 7 November 2000, *AB* [Judgments in Administrative Law] 2003/25, annotated by L. F. M. Verhey (*Kingsley v United Kingdom*), confirmed in European Court of Human Rights 28 May 2002 (judgment of the Grand Chamber).

[39] European Court of Human Rights 22 November 1995, Series A vol. 335-A (*Bryan v United Kingdom*); Widdershoven et al. 2001, pp. 34–38.

[40] Cf. Schuurmans 2005, pp. 290–292 and Kuipers 1996, pp. 97–112. See the judgments European Court of Human Rights 17 December 1996, *NJCM-Bulletin* 1997, pp. 617 et seq., annotated by M. L. W. M. Viering (*Terra Woningen BV v the Netherlands*) and European Court of Human Rights 13 February 2003, *AB* [Judgments in Administrative Law] 2004/52, annotated by B. W. N. de Waard (*Chevrol v France*).

the crucial facts for the resolution of the dispute.[41] In addition, the court cannot automatically rely on an expert engaged by the administrative body. It must attempt to restore the balance (in the context of the 'equality of arms') between the parties in some other way, for example by enabling the interested party to enter expert evidence to the contrary, or, if that is not possible for financial or other reasons, by engaging an expert itself.[42] In this way, the court can keep a 'finger in the pie' as regards the specialised finding of fact by the administration and safeguard the principle of equality of arms between the parties as required by Article 6 ECHR.

Thus, the division of duties between the administration and the court as regards findings of fact for which a certain expertise is required also involves the search for a good balance and an approach that is tailored to the situation. Here, too, there seems to be a growing inclination amongst the judiciary to take a more active role than in the past, particularly under the influence of EU law and the ECHR. In view of all these dynamics, it may be concluded that, for the Netherlands in any event, the decision to put the doctrine of deference on the agenda was a fortunate one.

## References

Barkhuysen T, Van Emmerik M L (2016) AB-Klassiek [Classic Judgments in Administrative Law]. Kluwer, Deventer

Barkhuysen T, Damen L J A, De Graaf K J, Marseille A T, Den Ouden W, Schuurmans Y E, Tollenaar A (2007) Feitenvaststelling in beroep, (derde evaluatie van de Awb) [Fact Finding on Appeal (Third Evaluation of the General Administrative Law Act)]. Boom Juridische Uitgevers, The Hague

Barkhuysen T, Van Emmerik M L, Van Ettekoven B J, Mul V, Stijnen R, De Werd M F J M (2014a) Adequate rechtsbescherming bij grondrechtenbeperkend overheidsingrijpen [Adequate Legal Protection regarding Government Intervention Restricting Fundamental Rights]. Kluwer, Deventer

Barkhuysen T, De Kruif C, Schuurmans Y E, Den Ouden W (2014b) Bestuursrecht in het Awb-tijdperk [Administrative Law in the Era of the General Administrative Law Act]. Kluwer, Deventer

Daalder E J, Schreuder-Vlasblom M (2000) Balanceren boven nul [Balancing above Zero]. NTB [Dutch Journal for Administrative Law] 2000, 4:214–221

De Poorter J C A, Capkurt F (2017) Rechterlijke toetsing van algemeen verbindende voorschriften [Judicial Review of generally binding regultions]. NTB [Dutch Journal for Administrative Law] 10:1–15

De Waard B W N (2016) Leerstukken van bestuursprocesrecht [Principles of Administrative Procedural Law].Wolters Kluwer, Deventer

Gerards J H (2007) Het evenredigheidsbeginsel van art. 3:4 lid 2 Awb en het Europese recht [The Principle of Proportionality from Article 3:4(2) of the General Administrative Law Act and

[41] European Court of Human Rights 15 March 2016, *AB* [Judgments in Administrative Law] 2016/132, annotated by T. Barkhuysen and M. L. van Emmerik (*Gillissen v the Netherlands*).

[42] European Court of Human Rights 8 October 2015, *AB* [Judgments in Administrative Law] 2016/167, annotated by T. Barkhuysen and M. L. van Emmerik (*Korosec v Slovenia*).

European Law]. In: Barkhuysen T et al (ed) Europees recht effectueren [Effectuating European law]. Kluwer, Alphen aan den Rijn, pp 73–113

Groenewegen F T (2014) De intensiteit van de rechterlijke toets in Engelse Judicial Review procedures. In: Klap A P, Groenwegen F T, Van Angeren J R (eds) Toetsing aan vage normen door de bestuursrechter in het Nederlandse, Duitse, Engelse, en Franse recht: preadvies voor de Nederlandse Vereniging voor Rechtsvergelijking. Wolf Legal Publishers, Oisterwijk

Klap A P (2014) Rechterlijke toetsing aan vage normen in Nederland en Duitsland. In: Klap A P, Groenwegen F T, Van Angeren J R (eds) Toetsing aan vage normen in het Nederlandse, Duitse en Franse recht: preadvies voor de Nederlandse Vereniging voor Rechtsvergelijking. Wolf Legal Publishers, Oisterwijk

Koeman N S J (2008) Versnelling in het bestuursprocesrecht [Acceleration in Administrative Procedural Law]. M en R [Environment and Law] 35:227–230

Kuipers A J (1996) Het recht op 'full jurisdiction' [The Right to Full Jurisdiction]. In: Vucsán R L (ed) De Awb-mens: boeman of underdog? [The General Administrative Law Act Man: Bogeyman or Underdog?]. Damen bundle, Ars Aequi Libri, Nijmegen

Leemans T C (2008) De toetsing door de bestuursrechter in milieugeschillen [Review by the Administrative Court in Environmental Disputes] (diss. Leiden). Boom Juridische Uitgevers, The Hague

Ortlep R, Zorg W (2016) Marginale rechterlijke toetsing onder druk: een voortgaande tred vooruit? [Limited Review under Pressure: Continuous Steps Forward?]. In: Ortlep et al (eds) De rechter onder vuur [The Judge under Fire]. Wolf, Oisterwijk, pp 1–18

Polak J E M, Moor-Van Vugt A de, Schlössels R J N, Verheij N, Widdershoven R J G M (2014) VAR-Commissie rechtsbescherming, De toekomst van de rechtsbescherming tegen de overheid, Van toetsing naar geschilbeslechting [Administrative Law Association Committee on Legal Protection, The Future of Legal Protection against the Government]. Boom Juridische Uitgevers, The Hague

Ranchordás S, De Waard B W N (eds) (2016) The Judge and the Proportionate Use of Discretion, A Comparative Study. Routledge Abingdon-Oxon-New York

Scheltema M (2015) De Hoge Raad en het algemeen belang [The Supreme Court and the Public Interest]. In: R.J.N. Schlössels et al (eds) De burgerlijke rechter in het publiekrecht [The Civil Court in Public Law]. Kluwer, Deventer, pp 803–818

Schlössels R J N, Zijlstra S E (2017) Bestuursrecht in de sociale rechtsstaat [Administrative Law in the Social State under the Rule of Law]. Kluwer, Deventer

Schuurmans Y E (2005) Bewijslastverdeling in het bestuursrecht, Zorgvuldigheid en bewijsvoering bij beschikkingen [Division of the Burden of Proof in Administrative Law, Due Care and the Provision of Evidence in respect of Decisions], (diss. VU). Kluwer, Deventer

Struycken A H (1910) Administratie of rechter [Administration or Judiciary]. Gouda Quint, Arnhem

Uzman J, Barkhuysen T, Van Emmerik M L (2010) The Dutch Supreme Court: A Reluctant Positive Legislator? In: Van Erp S, Van Vliet L (eds) Netherlands Reports to the Eighteenth International Congress of Comparative Law. Intersentia, Antwerpen-Oxford-Portland, pp 423–468

Van Angeren J A M (2009) Mensenrechten en onafhankelijke bestuursrechtspraak [Human Rights and Independent Administrative Adjudication]. In: Barkhuysen T, Van Emmerik M L, Loof J P (eds) Geschakeld recht [Linked Law]. Kluwer, Alphen aan den Rijn

Van Angeren J R, Groenewegen F T, Klap A P (2014) Toetsing aan vage normen in het Nederlandse, Duitse en Franse recht: preadvies voor de Nederlandse Vereniging voor Rechtsvergelijking. [Review against vague standards in Dutch, English and French law: preliminary advice Netherlands Association for the Judiciary]. Wolf Legal Publishers, Oisterwijk

Van Emmerik M L, Saris C M (2014) Evenredige bestuurlijke boetes [Proportionate administrative penalties], (Preliminary advice VAR). Boom, The Hague

Van Wijk H D, Konijnenbelt W, Van Male R (2014) Hoofdstukken van bestuursrecht [Chapters on Administrative Law]. Kluwer, Deventer

Verheij N (2013) Van grensrechter naar geschilbeslechter, een evolutie in de Nederlandse bestuursrechtspraak (preadvies voor de Vereniging voor de Vergelijkende Studie van het recht van België en Nederland) [From Linesman to Dispute Adjudicator, An Evolution in Dutch Administrative Jurisdiction (preliminary advice for the Association for the Comparative Study of the Law of Belgium and the Netherlands)]. Boom, The Hague

Widdershoven R J G M, Willemsen P A, Schlössels R J N, Stroink F A M, Ten Berge J B J M, Bok A J, Voermans W J M, De Waard B W N (2001) Algemeen bestuursrecht 2001: hoger beroep [General Administrative Law 2001: Appeal]. Bju, The Hague

# Chapter 7
# Judicial Review in Dutch Environmental Law; from the Judge's Perspective

**Bart Jan van Ettekoven**

**Contents**



**Abstract** In this chapter the traditional constitutional framework for judicial review, which is based on the assumption that the exercise of administrative powers must be seen as a way of implementing the legislature's decisions is criticized. The model for judicial review has been reanalysed as part of the Administrative Jurisdiction Division of the Council of State (AJD)'s project on a more comprehensive form of judicial review. The reason for this is the fact that performing a limited judicial review of decisions taken by administrative authorities can no longer be justified, especially if it concerns decisions which have far-reaching consequences for citizens. The development in the direction of considering fuller judicial review is therefore one of the developments in the field of judicial review within the administrative courts in the Netherlands, which this chapter discusses.

Prof. mr. Bart Jan van Ettekoven is chair of the Administrative Jurisdiction Division of the Council of State in the Netherlands and professor of administrative law at the University of Amsterdam. This chapter is the written version of the introduction held by the author at the Conference on 19 January 2018.

B. J. van Ettekoven (✉)
University of Amsterdam, Amsterdam, The Netherlands
e-mail: B.J.vanEttekove@uva.nl



J. de Poorter et al. (eds.), *Judicial Review of Administrative Discretion in the Administrative State*, https://doi.org/10.1007/978-94-6265-307-8_7

This development can be seen from the fact that case law indicates that the AJD has reviewed more stringently government decisions, that concern punitive sanctions and decisions with disproportionate consequences. Another development which this chapter examines is the digitalisation of society and the associated digitalisation of government processes. Due to this development, administrative courts are faced with the challenge of how they should exercise their traditional powers of review in relation to administrative decision making which is dependent on operating systems based on big data technologies and algorithms. It is thus important for the administrative courts to ensure that the general principles of law such as 'fair trial' and 'equality of arms' are sufficiently safeguarded and to apply them in a way that is relevant to the modern (digital) world.

**Keywords** Judicial review · the Administrative Jurisdiction Division of the Council of State (AJD) · administrative courts · fundamental rights · exceptional review · digitalisation of government processes · fair trial · equality of arms · punitive sanctions · disproportionate consequences

## 7.1 Introduction

The organisation chose 'Judicial Review in the Administrative State' as the subject of this conference. An excellent choice because there are some exciting developments to discuss in the field of judicial review within the administrative courts in the Netherlands. Below I would like to share a few observations based on judicial practice, more specifically recent cases heard by the highest general administrative court. But first I would like to take you back to 2015.

On 22 May 2015 Professor Ernst Hirsch Ballin presented a paper to the Association for Administrative Law in the Netherlands (VAR) entitled 'Dynamics in the work of the administrative law courts'.[1] The paper itself created certain dynamics, for example at the Administrative Jurisdiction Division of the Council of State (henceforth abbreviated as: AJD). The reason for this is that Hirsch Ballin clearly charted the changes that have taken place in the domain where the administrative courts do their work. From this perspective he questioned—correctly, in my view—a number of established judicial practices. The issues he raised included the following. How logical is it to perform a limited review of decisions taken by administrative authorities, especially where the decisions in question have far-reaching consequences for citizens? Shouldn't the administrative courts themselves play a more active role in establishing the facts, assessing expert testimony and drawing legal conclusions on the basis of them?

Hirsch Ballin correctly points out that the traditional constitutional framework for judicial review is, to a degree, less convincing than it used to be. The framework

[1] Hirsch Ballin et al. 2015.

is based on the premise that the exercise of administrative powers must be seen as a way of implementing the legislature's decisions: this exercise of powers is subject to the political accountability and scrutiny of a democratically elected body. It is this presumed mechanism of political accountability and scrutiny that gives the executive its legitimacy. Nevertheless, this model based on the trias politica principle no longer fits well with the way in which administrative decisions are made in a democracy based on the rule of law. Or in any event, it no longer fits well with every single decision and decision-making process. Connected with this is the fact that the restraint long exercised by the courts in applying a limited form of review to certain administrative decisions can no longer be justified. That is also the reason why the model for judicial review has been revisited as part of the AJD's project on a more comprehensive form of judicial review. The need to reflect on the scope of judicial review is all the more pressing now that government action is perceptible in practically every aspect of people's daily lives and often has far-reaching effects on those lives. Just think for example of premises closure orders for cafes or private homes, orders closing down businesses, banning orders, domestic exclusion orders, emergency powers and denials of certificates of conduct, which can more or less temporarily prevent an individual from practising their profession.[2] These examples of the authorities' exercise of their powers quite frequently have implications for fundamental rights.

A more detailed study of the case law of the AJD shows a clear development in the direction of considering fuller judicial review. This development can be illustrated by a case heard by a grand chamber involving what in the Netherlands is known as 'exceptional review' of a generally binding regulation, a case in which State Councillor Advocate General Rob Widdershoven very recently gave an advisory opinion.[3] Comprehensive judicial review in the area of discretionary decision making—as in the case of legislation—is one thing, but it cannot be seen in isolation from the establishment of the facts and the role of the administrative courts in establishing those facts. On this issue too, developments can be seen in the case law.

We are also compelled to reflect further on the current model in connection with another development: the digitalisation of society and the associated digitalisation of government processes. Both have their advantages, but they also make it difficult for people to keep abreast of these developments. That is why it is important for the administrative courts to apply general principles of law such as 'fair trial' and 'equality of arms' in a way that is relevant to the modern (digital) world. I will return to this point later in the context of the AJD's judgment in the nitrogen deposition programme (or: PAS) case.

---

[2] Schreuder-Vlasblom 2016.

[3] Council of State, Administrative Jurisdiction Division (ABRvS), Advocate General; ECLI:NL:RVS:2017:3557.

## 7.2 The Project on Developing a More Comprehensive Form of Judicial Review

### 7.2.1 *First Steps in Reviewing Punitive Sanctions*

The project on developing a more comprehensive form of judicial review was set in motion at a meeting of the entire AJD in September 2016. Ideas were exchanged on a varied selection of cases. Following this meeting, a working group composed of state councillors and lawyers was set up to formulate initial proposals for adjustments to judicial practice. Many of these proposals ultimately met with Division-wide approval and are gradually being implemented. And now the first results of their implementation are visible in the case law.

Punitive sanctions form an important category of disputes in which the impact of decisions on individuals prompted the AJD to amend judicial practice. An administrative authority has a duty to ensure that the amount of a fine is proportionate to the seriousness of the contravention. The courts conduct a full review of whether a specific fine meets this criterion. In recent years the AJD has started to conduct a more intensive review of administrative fines. This is partly because, on the basis of ever stricter legislation, administrative authorities have been imposing larger fines—which have a greater effect on the person concerned—without taking sufficient account of whether the larger fines are justified or proportionate in specific cases. Administrative authorities tend to determine the amount of fines in accordance with their own fixed policies. The first step in reviewing punitive administrative sanctions is to ascertain whether the administrative rule in question is reasonable.

A good example of how this can go wrong for the administrative authority at this initial stage is the AJD's judgment of 6 May 2015.[4] The Minister of Social Affairs and Employment had imposed a fine of €2,160 on a company because two of its employees had been placing reinforcing rods above shoulder height. The trestles and scaffolding that had been provided were too low. The Minister concluded that the working methods of the two employees did not minimise the danger of excessive physical strain as much as reasonably possible. The company considered the fine to be unjustified, since it had done everything that was reasonably possible to limit the risks. In imposing fines under the Working Conditions Act, the Minister applies administrative rules, which contain grounds for reducing a fine. However, all three grounds for reduction must be fully complied with; if that is not the case, the fine will not be reduced. This administrative rule can lead to disproportionately large fines, and the AJD ruled that this had occurred in the case at hand. In carrying out the measures referred to in the judgment the company had largely complied with the second and third grounds for reduction and to a significant extent with the

[4] Council of State, Administrative Jurisdiction Division (ABRvS) 6 May 2015, ECLI:NL:RVS:2015:1421.

first. The AJD therefore found a diminished degree of culpability which constituted grounds for reducing the fine by 75%.

If the administrative rule is not considered to be unreasonable in itself, the specific circumstances of the case often determine whether or not the fine is found proportionate. This is illustrated by a judgment of 31 August 2016.[5] The Utrecht municipal executive imposed a fine of €7,500 on the owner of a building for contravening provisions of the Housing Allocation Act and the Regional Housing Allocation Bye-Law laid down by Utrecht Metropolitan Region Authority. On inspection, six women were found in the building who, online, offered sexual services to be provided on the premises. Also found in the building was one client who stated that he wanted to make use of these services. The women were renting the building from an estate agent. The owner of the premises challenged the fine on the grounds that he did not know, nor could he have known, that the estate agent was renting the building out as a brothel, and that as soon as he became aware of the situation he had done everything in his power to end it. Given the circumstances of the case, the AJD was satisfied that the owner had brought the offending behaviour to an end as soon as he was aware of it, and before he was informed of the inspection. The district court had wrongly failed to consider this as a special circumstance within the meaning of Section 5:46, Subsection 3 of the General Administrative Law Act (GALA). The AJD therefore decided to reduce the fine by 25% itself.

## 7.2.2 *More Comprehensive Review in Other Areas*

The trends with regard to punitive sanctions ultimately had an impact on the review of other types of decisions. Let me give you two examples. First, I would like to touch on developments relating to administrative rules and second on developments connected with generally binding regulations. I'm confident that you will understand that—in connection with the latter—no speculations can be made on the ruling in the grand chamber case which is specifically concerned with the comprehensiveness with which generally binding regulations are reviewed.

### 7.2.2.1 Reviewing Policy

In a case decided on 26 October 2016[6] the AJD expanded the scope for departing from an administrative rule pursuant to Section 4:84 of the GALA. In this case, the

[5] Council of State, Administrative Jurisdiction Division (ABRvS) 22 June 2016, ECLI:NL:RVS:2016:1751.

[6] Council of State, Administrative Jurisdiction Division (ABRvS) 26 October 2016, ECLI:NL:RVS:2016:2840.

police found a total of 721 XTC pills in a shed belonging to a private home. The house was occupied by a woman and her three young children. It was established that her ex-partner, who did not live in the house but was present on the night in question, had hidden the pills in the shed. The mayor acted in accordance with the relevant policy and ordered the house to be shut down for three months. This left the woman and her children homeless. She was also put on a 'blacklist' of people who would not be eligible for social housing for several years. The dispute centred on the question of whether there were special circumstances as referred to in Section 4:84 of the GALA. Section 4:84 states that administrative authorities must act in accordance with the administrative policy rule in question, unless this would lead to consequences for one or more interested parties which, due to special circumstances, would be disproportionate to the aims served by the policy rule. Until the end of 2016, the AJD took the line that circumstances that were taken into account when an administrative policy rule was drafted, or should be deemed to have been taken into account, are not 'special circumstances' within the meaning of Section 4:84. In its judgment of 26 October 2016 in this case, the Division departed from previous practice and ruled that circumstances that were taken into account in drafting an administrative policy rule, or should be deemed to have been taken into account, cannot be disregarded simply for that reason. Practice shows that even if the administrative authority took such circumstances into account in drawing up the policy rule, it could not have foreseen whether circumstances alone or in combination would lead to disproportionate consequences in a specific case. In the AJD's view administrative authorities must take all the circumstances of a case into account in reaching a decision. In the case at hand, the mayor had not taken all the relevant circumstances into account in his assessment under Section 4:84 of the GALA. The district court was therefore right to overturn the contested decision. The AJD concluded that there were grounds for giving a definitive decision on the dispute. This was because the mayor indicated at the hearing that he would confine himself to issuing a warning in the context of a new decision on an objection, given the time that had elapsed and the fact that no problems had arisen in the intervening period. The AJD therefore settled the matter itself by replacing the quashed decision with an administrative warning as referred to in the administrative policy rules.

#### 7.2.2.2 Reviewing Legislation

In the Netherlands, the courts exercise restraint when it comes to reviewing legislation. This restraint is prescribed by the Constitution, in particular Article 120 which states: 'The constitutionality of Acts of Parliament and treaties shall not be reviewed by the courts'. Secondary legislation is a different matter, although even here there seem to be reservations about judicial review. Section 8:3 of the GALA, for example, states that an order introducing a generally binding regulation cannot be challenged in the administrative courts. This does not mean that such generally binding regulations are totally outside the purview of judicial review. It is possible to challenge their lawfulness by bringing an action before the civil courts on the grounds of a wrongful act. In addition, their lawfulness can also be raised in proceedings before the administrative courts relating to a decision which is eligible for judicial review. The latter is known as exceptional review of legislation. And it is precisely in this area that judicial practice is evolving.

A good example of this is the judgment regarding the statutory alcolock, or alcohol activated vehicle immobiliser. In its judgment of 4 March 2015 the AJD declared certain provisions of the order regulating the alcolock programme non-binding.[7] The case concerned a car mechanic who was pulled over by the police at a drink-driving checkpoint. The results were such that the CBR, the administrative authority responsible for issuing driving licences, declared his licence invalid and ordered that he take part in the alcolock programme. The car mechanic considered this unreasonable. He argued that the alcohol level measured was only 1.3 parts per thousand. Furthermore, the impact of the decision on his work was substantial, since he had to drive the vehicles sent to him for repair. He was afraid of being fired if his participation in the alcolock programme meant he could not do his job properly. The case prompted the AJD to examine the order establishing the alcolock programme. A large number of cases were pending before the Division which similarly claimed that the consequences of the programme were disproportionate. Some drivers argued that they could not afford the cost of the programme—around €5,000 over a period of two years. Others claimed that participation in the programme put their jobs at risk (car mechanics and taxi drivers, for example). The order did not allow for the personal circumstances of the driver to be taken into account. It obliged the CBR to impose the programme if the conditions laid down in the order were fulfilled. The CBR had no leeway to make an individual assessment, even in situations where the programme had far-reaching consequences. In practice therefore, the obligation to impose an alcolock programme led to inequality and arbitrariness, since it had much more serious consequences for some than for others. For these reasons the AJD ruled that the provision containing that obligation was non-binding because it was incompatible with Section 3:4, Subsection 2 of the GALA. In a judgment given one day earlier the Supreme Court had concluded that the prosecution of a person for drunk driving is incompatible with the principles of due process if the defendant has already, on the basis of the same offence, been obliged to participate in the alcolock programme and that obligation can no longer be challenged.[8]

Another striking example of exceptional review of legislation is a case regarding the revocation of a market stall licence. In this case the AJD concluded that the municipal executive of The Hague should have disregarded the provision in the

[7] Council of State, Administrative Jurisdiction Division (ABRvS) 4 March 2015, ECLI:NL:RVS:2015:622.

[8] Supreme Court (Hoge Raad) 3 March 2015, ECLI:NL:HR:2015:434.

municipal Markets Bye-law which compelled it to revoke the licence.[9] The market trader whose licence was revoked ran two stalls on The Hague market. The Minister of Social Affairs and Employment had imposed on him a fine of €6,000 for contravening the Foreign Nationals Employment Act by employing a third-country national without a work permit to sell articles at one of his stalls. The market trader paid the fine. The municipal executive revoked the man's licence because of the contravention, as required by the Markets Bye-Law. The AJD ruled that the provision governing revocation of licences should have been disregarded in the case at hand because of the disproportionately adverse consequences for the trader. It therefore considered the contested decision to be incompatible with Section 3:4, Subsection 2 of the GALA, taking into account the fact that the financial consequences of losing his licence were substantial for the market trader, who had already paid a large fine for contravening the Act. Another factor was that the revocation of the licence made it impossible for the trader ever to return to the market in question.

### 7.2.3 *More Comprehensive Review Demands a Different Attitude on the Part of the Courts to the Establishment of the Facts*

As Professor Hirsch Ballin remarked, the administrative courts hold a mirror up to the executive, in line with the constitutional concept in which the executive implements laws and by those laws is obliged and empowered to establish the facts, to assess them and to exercise its discretionary decision-making powers accordingly. Consequently, according to the dominant interpretation of Dutch administrative procedural law, determining the facts is part of the executive's responsibility. The task of the courts in this context is to examine whether the executive has taken the steps necessary for this process in a correct and careful manner.

The consequence of the desire to review more fully the way in which administrative authorities make use of their discretionary powers is that the courts—if necessary—take a more active role with regard to establishing the facts. Such developments can also be seen in the AJD's case law. Obvious examples of this include the cases regarding gas extraction in Groningen. These show that despite the administrative authority's discretion in this respect, judicial review in these cases was not limited. At the same time, there is an acknowledgement that the administrative court must not replace the administrative authority's exercise of its discretionary powers with its own decision. In making that decision the administrative authorities can ask for advice from experts and can be called to account for their decisions by Parliament. Judicial review is concerned with answering the

[9] Council of State, Administrative Jurisdiction Division (ABRvS) 29 March 2017, ECLI:NL:RVS:2015:864.

question of whether the decision and the underlying assessment is in accordance with the statutory framework, is based on sufficient knowledge of the relevant facts and is properly substantiated. In addition, the court examines whether the adverse consequences of the decision for one or more interested parties are not disproportionate in relation to the aims the decision is meant to serve. In the first gas extraction case (2015) the AJD set aside the decision of the Minister of Economic Affairs in which he approved the extraction plans of the Dutch oil and gas company NAM on the grounds that the decision was not based on sufficient knowledge of the relevant facts and was not properly substantiated. With regard to the relevant facts, the Minister had wrongly assumed in his assessment of the interests concerned that the risks in the earthquake zone were comparable with the risks present in certain parts of the areas around Dutch rivers. In fact, risk assessments have shown that the risks in the earthquake zone are greater. And although, given his latitude for assessment, the Minister was entitled to attach great importance to security of supply, he had not sufficiently substantiated his reasons for permitting a higher level of production than is on average necessary to guarantee such security. The Minister should have provided better grounds to justify his decision.[10]

> (16.2) Many appellants have argued that in weighing interests fundamental rights are at stake, such as the right to life (security), privacy (encroachment of living environment), and the undisturbed enjoyment of the property, as referred to in articles 2 and 8 of the European Convention for the Protection of Human Rights and Fundamental Freedoms (ECHR) and the First Protocol to this Convention. (…) appellants have rightly argued that the nature and scale of the consequences associated with gas extraction are such that the said fundamental rights are applicable. This applicability has - in general - consequences for the requirements that can be imposed on the legislation applicable to gas extraction. For the specific consideration of the Minister (…) the applicability also has consequences. In brief, the Minister's consideration must demonstrate a reasonable balance between, on the one hand, the interests of citizens protected by fundamental rights and, on the other hand, the general interests involved. Admittedly, the minister has a margin of appreciation in that decision, but the applicability of the fundamental rights means that in this case high demands must be made on the grounds for the Minister's decision.

In its judgment of 15 November 2017 the AJD set aside the Minister's decisions in which he approved the 2016 production plan for the Groningen gas field submitted by NAM.[11] The Minister had agreed that the company could extract 21.6 billion cubic meters of gas annually in the next five years. The AJD ruled that the Minister had failed to substantiate his decisions properly. It found that the Minister's decision to set levels for gas production for the next five years without first assessing the risks was unacceptable. If it was true that these risks could not be assessed, the Minister could at the very least be expected to investigate and explain how alternative ways of protecting the safety of persons living in the earthquake zone would be included in decision making. The Minister should also have

[10]Council of State, Administrative Jurisdiction Division (ABRvS) 18 November 2015, ECLI:NL:RVS:2015:3578.

[11]Council of State, Administrative Jurisdiction Division (ABRvS) 15 November 2017, ECLI:NL:RVS:2017:3156.

explained why, in view of the risks involved, he continued to take security of supply as the lower limit for determining the volume of gas to be extracted.

A good illustration of a more comprehensive review of the establishment of the facts is the Amersfoort planning blight case. A company running a bed and breakfast in Amersfoort discovered that a 'urilift' (a pop-up public urinal) had been installed 10 m away from the façade of their building. The company had opened a pavement café in front of the building. They claimed compensation for planning blight, since they had suffered a loss of revenue as a result of the presence of the urilift. The municipal executive dismissed this claim on the basis of advice it had obtained. The AJD took a critical view of the advice, concluding that its shortcomings were such that the municipal executive was wrong to use it as the basis for its decision. It found that the company had demonstrated that it had suffered a loss of profits as a result of the decision granting an exemption from the land-use plan. The AJD then asked an advisory body on administrative law in environmental and land-use planning cases (the StAB) to take responsibility for commissioning an independent financial expert to assess the loss of revenue caused by the exemption decision. On the basis of that report, the AJD disposed of the case itself by granting the company's application for compensation for planning blight, setting the amount at €45,050 plus statutory interest.[12]

### 7.2.4 *Judicial Review and the Digitalisation of Government Processes*

The judicial review model does indeed need rethinking in light of the changes in the constitutional framework within which the courts function. But I would like to draw to your attention to another development the judiciary will have to respond to. That is the digitalisation, in society in general, and within the field of (administrative) law, in law-making, decision-making, and within the (administrative) courts. One of the main challenges for the next decade will be how to deal with the use of artificial intelligence. What will be the role in law practise of algorithms and Big Data, machine learning and natural language processing, predictive coding and (judge) profiling, blockchain and smart contracts and whatever comes next. Since 2012 the US Federal Courts not only allow technology assisted research (TAR), but even stimulate the use of it. Law firms in the USA, the United Kingdom and in the Netherlands already use legal tech for drafting and examining (standard) contracts, due diligence, text-analysis, and text-mining in combination with machine-learning. Administrative decision making relies increasingly on operating systems based on big data technologies and algorithms. This confronts the courts with the question of how they should exercise their traditional powers of review in relation to this type

[12]Council of State, Administrative Jurisdiction Division (ABRvS) 16 December 2015, ECLI:NL:RVS:2015:3819.

of decision making. But it also means that they have to be very aware of their duty to ensure that the principles of fair trial and equality of arms are sufficiently safeguarded during proceedings. A fine example is the judgment in the nitrogen deposition programme, also known as the PAS-case.

On 17 May 2017[13] the AJD gave judgment in ten cases involving the government's nitrogen deposition programme. The proceedings were brought by multiple environmental organisations, including one dedicated to the conservation of the Peel area in North Brabant. These organisations are working towards reductions in the nitrogen deposition burden on nitrogen-susceptible habitat types and the habitats of protected species, in Natura 2000 areas. The largest source of nitrogen emissions in the Netherlands is livestock farming, or more precisely, manure. The AJD submitted requests for a preliminary ruling to the Court of Justice of the European Union concerning the compatibility of the programme with Article 6 of the Habitats Directive. Although the CJEU's response to these questions will be partly decisive for the judgments to follow, the AJD has already reviewed a number of the grounds. An important aspect is the compulsory use by the competent authorities of the AERIUS software programme, provided for by the central government, which enables partially automated decision making. The AJD has conducted a full review of whether this undermines legal protection. The disadvantage of partially automated decision making is that it is neither transparent nor verifiable. This can be disadvantageous for interested parties seeking to challenge decisions based on use of the AERIUS-programme. To prevent such situations arising, the AJD finds that ministers and state secretaries have the duty to publish the choices made as well as the data and hypotheses on which they are based. They must do so in time, in full, of their own volition and in an appropriate form so that these choices, data and hypotheses are accessible to third parties. Otherwise, judicial review and meaningful legal protection against decisions based on these factors is impossible. The AJD quashed the decision of the local administrative authorities and introduced the concept of the need for transparency as a specific application of the duty of care (Article 3:2 GALA), one of the most important general principles of fair administration. The principle of transparency in relation to the use of legal technology in government processes is to be explored further. Is has potential and can be a useful instrument for the administrative courts to make judicial review effective. Like in the Amersfoort case the AJD appointed courts experts to investigate the facts. In the PAS case fact-finding meant the disclosure of the programme and algorithms used. The AJD felt the need to do so in order to guarantee a fair trial and to compensate the (potential) inequality in the position of the interested parties. Such situations should be avoided. Administrative authorities should be open and transparent about the quality and origin of the data used for their decision-making and the workings of Big Data programmes and algorithms.

[13] Council of State, Administrative Jurisdiction Division (ABRvS) 17 May 2017, including ECLI:NL:RVS:2017:1259 and ECLI:NL:RVS:2017:1260.

## 7.3 Some Conclusions

The review by the administrative courts is under development. At the AJD, the above mentioned project led to a debate about which government decisions require a more intrusive judicial review. It can be inferred from case law that the AJD has reviewed more stringently in a number of areas. Not in all areas and not with all government decisions. First and foremost, it concerns punitive sanctions. Furthermore, decisions with disproportionate consequences. It is of great importance whether fundamental rights are to be jeopardized. But also if the procedural position of the parties is at risk of being eroded, this is a reason for the AJD to ensure an effective remedy, for example by appointing court experts to investigate the facts and merits. The (administrative) judge faces a challenge when it comes to digitalisation of the law. More than basic knowledge of digital developments is needed to continue to guarantee meaningful judicial review. The general principles of law and the general principles of good governance may need to be reassessed in order to continue meaningful judicial review. The first steps on that road have been taken.

## References

Hirsch Ballin E, Ortlep R, Tollenaar A (2015) Rechtsontwikkeling door de bestuursrechter [Legal Development by the Administrative Judge]. Boom Juridische Uitgevers, The Hague

Schreuder-Vlasblom M (2016) De identiteit van het bestuursrecht [The Identity of Administrative Law]. NTB (Dutch Journal of Administrative Law) 53:1–8

# Chapter 8
# Who Guards the Guardians? Judicial Oversight of the Authority Consumer and Market's Energy Regulations in the Netherlands

**Saskia Lavrijssen and Fatma Çapkurt**

## Contents



Saskia Lavrijssen is professor of Economic Regulation and Market Governance of Network Industries at Tilburg University (s.a.c.m.lavrijssen@tilburguniversity.edu). Fatma Çapkurt is a researcher at the department of Constitutional- and Administrative law at Leiden University (f.capkurt@law.leidenuniv.nl). This chapter is an updated and elaborated version of the following article: S. A. C. M. Lavrijssen, J. Eijkens and F. Capkurt, 'Rechterlijke toetsing van energieregulering door het CBb en het recht op effectieve rechtsbescherming' (2016) 4 Tijdschrift voor Europees en economisch recht 142–161.

S. Lavrijssen (✉)
Tilburg University, Tilburg, The Netherlands
e-mail: s.a.c.m.lavrijssen@tilburguniversity.edu

F. Çapkurt
Leiden University, Leiden, The Netherlands
e-mail: f.capkurt@law.leidenuniv.nl



J. de Poorter et al. (eds.), *Judicial Review of Administrative Discretion in the Administrative State*, https://doi.org/10.1007/978-94-6265-307-8_8

**Abstract** Independent National Regulatory Authorities (NRAs) play an important role in the implementation and enforcement of European energy directives and regulation. The Dutch *Autoriteit Consument en Markt* (Authority for Consumers and Markets, hereafter: ACM) has been provided broad discretionary powers to regulate the energy market. This chapter examines the way in which the Dutch *College van Beroep voor het bedrijfsleven* (Appeals Tribunal for Trade and Industry, hereafter: CBB) has reviewed energy regulations. This chapter concludes that initially the CBB was very hesitant in reviewing the ACM's energy regulation, since it scrutinized administrative energy decisions of the ACM based on its discretionary powers very marginally in the period between 2002 and 2013. As a result of this marginal judicial review of the ACM's energy regulations, it has been extremely hard for appellants to realise effective judicial protection in the period between 2002 and 2013. However, in more recent judgements from 2014 and onwards, the CBB has become stricter in reviewing the ACM's energy regulations. The CBB has done this by reviewing the substance of decisions more intensely on procedural grounds. This chapter suggests that the CBB, when reviewing the ACM's energy regulations, should continue its recent intensification of the judicial review of regulatory decisions and favour the adoption of a procedural-proportionality review. By applying a procedural-proportionality review, courts will be given more instruments to ensure that energy regulations are made in a fair, well-informed, proportional and transparent way, which could enhance both the democratic legitimacy of energy regulations and the democratic accountability of the ACM.

**Keywords** Judicial review · energy sector · national regulatory authorities · discretion · marginal review · procedural-proportionality review

## 8.1 Introduction

In *The Spirit of Law*, Montesquieu introduced the separation of state powers into three branches of government: the legislator, the executive and the judiciary. However, the development of the modern administrative state gave rise to a new, fourth branch of government: the administrative bureaucracy.[1] Independent national regulatory authorities (NRAs),[2] such as the Dutch Authority Consumers and Markets (ACM), form a new, but highly important part of the administration.[3]

---

[1] McLean and Tushnet 2015, pp. 121–130.

[2] Independent national regulatory authorities are defined by Coen and Thatcher as "an unelected body that is organizationally separated from government and has powers over regulation of markets through endorsement or formal delegation by public bodies." Coen and Thatcher 2005, pp. 329–346.

[3] Directive 2009/72/EC of the European Parliament and of the Council of 13 July 2009 concerning common rules for the internal market in electricity and repealing Directive 2003/54/EC (OJ 2009, L211/55); Directive 2009/73/EC of the European Parliament and of the Council of the European

The ACM was created due to a merger of three independent administrative authorities; the Netherlands Competition Authority (NMA), the Independent Telecommunications Regulator (OPTA) and the Consumer Authority (CA). The energy sector is a highly technical and rapidly changing field. The past decade, the use of complex economic evidence in energy regulation partly increased due to the introduction of method decisions to regulate the natural monopolies, the distribution and transmission networks, in the energy sector. This complexity of energy regulation, combined with the legislator's inability to ex ante anticipate on all regulatory issues that arrive in the complex regulation of the energy sector, has led to the rise of administrative rulemaking by the ACM in the energy sector. This shift in rulemaking competences from the legislator to the administration is usually justified with the claim that independent administrative agencies have several institutional advantages over the legislator. Administrative rulemaking by independent national regulatory authorities such as the ACM is claimed to be more efficient and effective, due to the ACM's expertise and experience in the energy sector.[4] The European legislator delegated significant regulatory powers directly to the ACM for the implementation of European energy regulations and directives.[5] Those regulatory powers are largely exercised by the ACM through the adoption of generally binding regulations:[6] the ACM can set the maximum price of network tariffs, the method of calculating network tariffs, and the rules for access to energy networks through

Parliament and of the Council of 13 July 2009 concerning common rules for the internal market in natural gas and repealing Directive 2003/55/EC (OJ 2009, L211/94); Regulation 714/2009 of the European Parliament and of the Council of 13 July 2009 on conditions for access to the network for cross-border exchanges in electricity and repealing Regulation 1228/2003 (OJ 2009, L211/15); Regulation 715/2009 of the European Parliament and of the Council of 13 July 2009 on conditions for access to the natural gas transmission networks and repealing Regulation 1775/2005 (OJ 2009, L211/36) and Regulation 713/2009 of the European Parliament and of the Council of 13 July 2009 establishing an Agency for Cooperation of Energy Regulators (OJ 2009, L211/1).

[4] Gilardi and Maggetti 2011, pp. 201–214.

[5] Rose-Ackerman and Jordao 2014, pp. 1–73.

[6] Generally binding regulations are rules issued by competent public bodies that have external effect and are binding on those to who it relates to. Generally binding regulations contain general, abstract rules that are suitable for repeated application in practice without further specification. Article 8:3 GALA prohibits administrative courts to directly examine the legality of generally binding regulations. The administrative judge can only indirectly scrutinize generally binding regulations: the applicant can indirectly challenge the legality of generally binding regulations when litigants question the administrative decision that has been taken by a public body on the basis of that generally binding regulation (exceptive judicial review). The underlying structural logical is a political and constitutional argument based on the Dutch understanding of the separation of powers: matters of policy and regulation should be dealt with by the executive and legislative power. This prohibition is currently heavily criticized and debated in the Netherlands. See Voermans 2017 and de Poorter and Capkurt 2017, pp. 84–95.

regulations and administrative decisions.[7] The broad rulemaking competences allow the ACM to weigh different regulatory options, come to unilateral decisions and intervene in the energy sector. As the ACM has gained broader regulatory powers to intervene in- and regulate the energy market, it is of key importance that the ACM can be controlled and can be hold accountable for the exercise of its regulatory powers, which is necessary to make sure that the ACM's market-interventions and regulations happen in a fair, transparent, and legitimate way.

Some authors have claimed that constitutional positioning of the ACM is in tension with the principle of separation of powers.[8] Those authors mainly hold on to the transmission belt theory to justify the democratic legitimacy of rulemaking. Within the transmission belt theory, the administration can be seen as a "mere implementer" of regulation that has ex ante been decided upon by the legislator within the legislative process.[9] However, the transmission belt theory of administrative law,[10] in which legislation serves as a transmission belt which transfers democratic legitimacy to the NRAs actions, is problematic in the field of energy regulation. The ACM is bound by law to stringent European independence rules, since Article 35 of the Electricity Directive obliges Member States to guarantee the independence of the regulatory authority.[11] These strict independence requirements aim to guarantee impartial and transparent regulation and administrative decision-making by NRAs.[12] The ACM is therefore held at arm's length of parliament and the responsible minister of Economic Affairs. This means that the ACM can exercise its regulatory powers without specific political interference, particularly from parliament and the responsible minister. The responsible minister is only allowed to give general policy guidance to the ACM. In this sense, the ACM cannot simply be qualified as "the executor of the political will", but instead has an independent role within the administration. Besides, even if these tight requirements regarding the ACM's political independency would not exist, it would still be problematic for parliament to effectively control and monitor the ACM's energy

[7] Article 41 Dutch Electricity Act 1998 and Article 81 Gas Act, Articles 27, 31 and 36 Dutch Electricity Act 1998 and Articles 12a, 12b and 12f Gas Act. Dutch Administrative law qualifies these regulations as generally binding regulations (algemeen verbindende voorschriften). Whereas Article 8:3 GALA prohibits the judicial review of generally binding decisions, an exception is made for energy regulations.

[8] Verhey and Verheij 2005, pp. 159, Zwart and Verhey 2003 and Caranta et al. 2004.

[9] Coglianese 2015, Van Gestel 2014 and Stewart 1975.

[10] See Van Gestel 2014.

[11] Article 35 of Directive 2009/72/EC and Article 39 Directive 2009/73/EC.

[12] This is particularly important, considering that the energy market is strongly intertwined with the government, since the Dutch Ministry for Financial Affairs is also a sole shareholder in TenneT, the transmission system operator in the Netherlands that operates the national electricity transmission. This Ministry is also the sole shareholder of the Dutch Gas Transmission Network (Gas Transport Services). See Hancher et al. 2003, pp. 361–362.

regulation. Parliaments often do not have the means, time and expertise to effectively scrutinize every regulation that the ACM issues.[13]

A central theme in the literature concerns the way in which this decrease in parliamentary control on the ACM's regulatory competences can somehow be counterbalanced in order to enhance the legitimacy of the ACM's delegated rule-making competences. Organizing stakeholder participation in the promulgation of regulations,[14] and judicial review of the ACM's regulatory decisions are two mechanisms that can be used to check and counterbalance the ACM's regulatory powers.[15] The focus of this chapter will be on the latter. The Dutch General Administrative Law Act (GALA) designates *het College van Beroep voor het bedrijfsleven* (the Dutch the Appeals Tribunal and Industry, hereafter: CBB) as a special court in appeal procedures regarding regulatory decisions taken on the basis of the Electricity Act and Gas Act.[16] As specialized court, the CBB acts in both first and only instance in reviewing regulatory decisions.[17] Consequently, the CBB holds an important position in reviewing regulations of the ACM taken on the basis of the Electricity Act and Gas Act,[18] In any event, there is no possibility to appeal after an appellant has reached the CBB. For this reason, it is of great importance that the CBB reviews appealed decisions in a correct manner.

The aim of this chapter is to review the role of the CBB in providing regulatory oversight in the energy sector. This chapter will therefore provide an analysis of key judgments of the CBB in energy cases. We will particularly focus on cases in which the CBB scrutinized generally binding regulations in the energy sector between 2002 and 2013, which covers the first regulatory periods in which the CBB had to judge on complicated regulatory matters in the energy sector for the first time. Finally, this chapter will reflect on some recent developments in judicial review of regulatory decisions in the energy sector between 2015 and 2018.

The research question that leads this chapter reads as follows:

> How does the highest administrative court in the Netherlands, scrutinize decisions that the ACM takes based on its discretionary regulatory powers within the energy sector – and how does the standard and intensity of judicial review relate to the principle of separation of powers and the need for subjecting the ACM regulatory decisions to adequate checks and balances?

---

[13]Gilardi and Maggetti 2011, p. 201.

[14]Lavrijssen 2016, pp. 51–57.

[15]Meuwese et al. 2009.

[16]As provided in Appendix 2, Article 4 Awb (General Administrative Law Act).

[17]However, if there is a criminal charge, there should be the possibility of higher appeal. As provided in Article 14 para 5 of the International Convention for Civil and Political Rights, which holds that that 'everyone convicted of a crime shall have the right to his conviction and sentence being reviewed by a higher tribunal according to law'.

[18]*Parliamentary Documents II*, 2003/04, 29702, nr. 3, p. 123. If for instance a fine is issued on the basis of the Electricity Act or Gas Act, the appeal of first instance is the district court of Rotterdam, with the possibility for higher appeal at the CBB. In such cases, the CBB is the judge in second and final instance.

This question has political, theoretical, and societal relevance. First, judicial review can serve as a control mechanism for reviewing the soundness and fairness of the ACM's energy regulation.[19] The importance of having a well-functioning control mechanism that can counterbalance the ACM has greatly increased through the expanding regulatory competences and increased independence of the ACM towards the parliament. This shift of rulemaking competences from the legislator to the administration and the limited political control of the ACM could hence partially be counterbalanced by the possibility of effective judicial review by administrative judges.[20] Second, effective judicial review is also of key societal relevance, as a highly marginal review by judges leaves the actions of regulatory agencies effectively absent of control, which could negatively impact the consumer's right to effective judicial protection. To illustrate: if the judge does not assess all aspects of a regulatory decision or reviews the substantive parts of a decision in a restraint way, there is a great risk that inadequate decisions are left in place, which could then damage the interests of the energy consumers. Third, it is worthwhile from a scientific point of view to assess how the administrative judge deals with the review of regulatory discretionary powers of NRAs, and what effect this has on the judicial protection of, amongst others, consumers.[21]

The structure of this chapter is as follows. Section 8.2 presents the main regulatory principles that underpin energy regulation in the Netherlands. Section 8.3 examines the way in which the CBB has exercised judicial review in some landmark cases. An important question that will be assed concerns how the CBB's standard and intensity of review can be evaluated in light of the principle of separation of powers. Different cases will be analysed and assessed in order to illustrate in what way judicial review by the CBB has been carried out over the years. The selection of cases is focussed on cases in which the interests of the energy consumer were at stake. The reason for this selection of cases and focus on the consumer is that one of the core objectives of EU energy law is precisely to promote the interests of the consumer, by guaranteeing access to affordable, sustainable and secure energy supply. In this chapter the perspective of different types of consumers are researched, including household consumers, large business users and small and medium sized business users.[22] Section 8.4 analyses the current doctrinal positions in legal literature on the judicial review of generally binding regulations and will make suggestions as to how the legal review of regulatory decisions of the ACM could be improved. Finally, a conclusion will be presented that is formed on the basis of the results.

---

[19] Lavrijssen et al. 2016.

[20] Mak 2012.

[21] Lavrijssen and Kohlbacher 2018.

[22] On this, see Lavrijssen 2014. In the third energy directive, the term customer is used which encompasses various groups of customers: wholesale customers, household customers, non-household customers, vulnerable customers. See Pront-van Bommel 2010, p. 44.

## 8.2 Energy Regulation in the Netherlands

The operators of energy networks have a natural monopoly. To prevent abuse of the dominant position of these operators, a system of tariff regulation has been developed on the basis of which the ACM regulates the requirements and tariffs for access to the energy networks (connection and transportation of energy). This regulation encourages operators to work in a cost-efficient manner and to keep the tariffs affordable for energy consumers. European and national energy regulation further aims to secure a sustainable and secure energy supply.[23] Directive 2009/72/EC provides the goals national NRAs need to consider when conducting their work, such as the promotion of a competitive, secure and an environmentally sustainable internal market. However, the Directive leaves the Member States with considerable freedom to give further shape to such tariff regulation.[24] A core principle that applies is that regulation should be both transparent as well as non-discriminatory.[25]

In the Netherlands, the method of benchmark regulation has been implemented.[26] This means that the whole of in- and output of regional operators are assessed, of which the mean is then used as benchmark. For national operators, a comparison is made with other national operators.[27] This benchmark then sets the permissible income levels for the operator. If this income level is exceeded, the ACM will correct the operator in the subsequent regulatory period through an efficiency discount (also known as x-factor).[28] This way, efficiency from the operator's side is encouraged.[29] The efficiency discount is based on a method decision of the ACM, which provides how the costs of the system operators should be compared, which costs should be taken into account and which weight should be granted to certain elements of the costs.[30] Following the x-factor decision, every operator will propose a tariff. Subsequently, the ACM sets a maximum tariff.[31]

---

[23] *Parliamentary documents II 2008/09*, 31901, no. 1–2, p. 44.

[24] Article 36(f) Directive 2009/72/EC. For Directive on gas, see Article 40(f) Directive 2009/73/EC.

[25] Article 35(5) Directive 2009/72/EC and Article 39(5) Directive 2009/73/EC.

[26] Articles 41b and 41c Electricity Act.

[27] It not always turned out to be feasible to establish a benchmark to compare different national network operators. As an example, for a long time the ACM used for the GTS a benchmark that was not based on the performance of other national operators. See: *Parliamentary documents II* 2008/09, 31901, no. 1–2, p. 48.

[28] *Parliamentary documents II 2008/09*, 31901, no. 1–2, p. 11; attached with consultation document 'STROOM'.

[29] Hakvoort et al. 2013, p. 5.

[30] *Parliamentary documents II 2008/09*, 31901, no. 1–2, p. 46.

[31] Lavrijssen et al. 2014, p. 26.

Note, in this context, that this system possible will be subject to changes in the near future with new proposals for modernisation of the *Electriciteitswet* and *Gaswet* (Electricity Act and Gas Act) to enable the facilitation of the energy transition.[32]

## 8.3 Judicial Review by the CBB Between 2002 and 2018

### *8.3.1 Traditional Standard and Intensity of Review of Policy- and Discretionary Powers*

As many textbooks in administrative law have emphasized, the theory of the separation of powers prescribes that the administration should be given discretionary powers to enact administrative decisions and regulations. Each legal system interprets this theory differently, due to different historical developments in constitutional law. The Dutch interpretation of judicial review of administrative discretion is heavily influenced by German Administrative law.[33] The extent of judicial review depends on the standard of review as well as its intensity. The standard of review determines which elements of a decision can be held subject to review. The intensity of review is then a different matter, but one that is effectively connected to the standard used. After all, the elements that are held subject to review can in turn be either held subject to a full or marginal review.[34] Effective review of regulatory decisions by the administrative judge constitutes a key component of effective judicial protection. Both procedural as well as substantive elements of a regulatory decision must be held subject to effective judicial review. In principle, one could say that the more elements of a decision are subject to a judge's assessment—thus the more stringent the review—the more the principle of effective judicial protection is upheld.

It depends on the type of discretionary powers that the legislator has delegated to the ACM what types of standard and intensity of judicial review will be performed by the administrative courts.[35] According to Dutch Administrative law, the term *discretion* has at least three meanings: policy freedom (beleidsvrijheid), margin of appreciation (beoordelingsvrijheid), and objective margin of appreciation (beoordelingsruimte).[36]

[32]Minister van Economische Zaken, Wetgevingsagenda en energietransitie, brief van 11 december 2017, met kenmerk DGETM-EI, 17192414.

[33]Duk 1988 and Schlössels and Zijlstra 2010, p. 164.

[34]Different standards of review can be distinguished. Lavrijssen and De Visser speak of a 'slippery scale', where basically four different standards of review can be discerned, from extremely limited to highly intensive. Lavrijssen and de Visser 2006; Stroink 1995.

[35]Wade and Forsyth 2014, pp. 308–310; and Van den Berge 2017a, b, pp. 204–233.

[36]It is important to note that the judge always has the last word in interpreting the law.

Policy freedom implies that the ACM can choose between possible actions within the circumstances of a specific situation.[37] The ACM has a margin of appreciation when a legal provision contains a vague and undefined term or norm, which needs to be clarified by the ACM in practice.[38] Administrative law then provides that, if the legislator has provided the ACM freedom to interpret and apply legal norms and concepts, the judge will only exercise a marginal review of the ACM's assessments of the facts, but remains to have the competence to fully review the law.[39] The ACM has an objective margin of appreciation if a legislative provision is vague as result of the inability of the legislator to ex ante enhance its clarity. As in this case it is not the legislator's explicit aim to attribute discretionary powers to a regulatory authority, but is forced to do so in the absence of other alternatives, the judge can carry out a full review of the law, the facts and the assessment.[40] In each specific case, the judge is to assess—on the basis of the wordings of the relevant provisions—whether it was the legislator's aim to attribute the ACM discretionary powers. If the ACM establishes in the assessment phase that the requirements for a lawful execution of powers with a margin of appreciation have been met, then it will be necessary in the consecutive policy phase to assess whether and how such discretionary powers can be exercised. In this phase, the ACM has discretion.[41] For this purpose, it needs to balance different interests. The assumption in administrative law is that the judge, in such cases, will carry out a marginal review of this balancing act.[42] In the following section, several judgments on important regulatory decisions by the ACM in the field of energy law (method-, tariff- and code regulatory decisions) will be discussed.

### 8.3.2 *Case Law Analysis*

The analysis of the case law will start by focusing on judgments of the CBB where a decision concerning the regulation of tariffs for access to the national gas transport network has been appealed.[43] In these cases, the CBB left the method decisions for establishing values for calculating the tariffs for access to the transmission network of Gas Transport Services (GTS),—namely the setting of starting costs, the opening RAB (regulatory asset base) and the Weighted Average Cost of Capital (WACC)-

[37] Schlössels and Zijlstra 2010, p. 164.

[38] Michiels 2011, p. 139.

[39] Schlössels and Zijlstra 2010, p. 161.

[40] Michiels 2011, p. 140.

[41] Van Wijk and Konijnenbelt 2005, pp. 141–151.

[42] Schlössels and Zijlstra 2010, p. 170.

[43] CBB 30 November 2006, ECLI:NL:CBB:2006:AZ3365; CBB 29 June 2010, ECLI:NL:CBB:2010:BM9470 and CBB 8 November 2012, ECLI:NL:CBB:2012:BY2307.

intact. The ACM is required to establish the WACC on the basis of Article 82 of the Gas Act.[44] Indicators for the selection of the judgments are:

i. The appeal was initiated by a consumer interest group;[45]
ii. The decision that has been appealed has a significant effect on energy tariffs or the reliability of energy supply for consumers;
iii. The CBB in its judgement deals with the role, independence or competences of the ACM.

#### 8.3.2.1 Starting Costs

In the first case, the appellant—the Organization for Energy, Environment and Water (hereafter VEMW), an association for (corporate) energy consumers—lodged objections against the way in which the starting costs that had been used as basis for the regulation of the energy tariffs had been calculated.[46] VEMW argued that the actual network costs of the previous regulatory period should not have been used as starting costs, as these were not actually the efficient costs. According to the appellant, using the actual network costs as a basis for regulation is in tension with Article 3 of Regulation 1775/2005/EC.[47] VEMW substantiated its arguments by

---

[44] Article 82 Gas Act provided as follows at that time:

1. In contrast to Article 80, the tariffs for exercising the tasks by the network operators of the national gas transport network, referred to in Articles 10 and 10a, first paragraph, section b, c, d and e, as well as the tariffs for services needed for transportation are established in accordance with this article.
2. For each of the tasks of the network operator of the national gas transport network, referred to in the first paragraph, the Board of the competition authority determines the method of regulation, for a period of minimally three and maximum five years, after consultation with the joint network operators and with organizations representing parties in the gas market and taking into account the importance of efficiency of business operation and the promotion of the most efficient quality of the operation of these tasks.
4. The Board of the competition authority determines an efficiency discount after consultation with the joint network operators and representing organizations. This decision applies in the same period as the decision on the basis of the second paragraph. The efficiency discount has as goal to promote efficient business operation.
5. The Board of the competition authority determines on a yearly basis the tariffs that can differ for the tariff carriers as distinguished. (own translation)

[45] Organizations representing parties on the energy market, including consumer organizations, have a privileged position. They are amongst others regarded as having an interest in all decisions made on the basis of the Dutch Electricity Act and the Dutch Gas Act, excluding administrative orders (beschikkingen). See Article 82 Dutch Electricity Act 1998 and Article 61 Dutch Gas Act.

[46] CBB 8 November 2012, ECLI:NL:CBB:2012:BY2307.

[47] Article 3 para 1 of Regulation 1775/2005/EC holds as follows: "Tariffs, or the methodologies used to calculate them, applied by transmission system operators… shall be transparent, take into account the need for system integrity and its improvement and reflect actual costs incurred, insofar as such costs correspond to those of an efficient and structurally comparable network operator and are transparent".

emphasizing that it follows explicitly from both Article 3, para 1, Regulation 1775/2005/EC as well as Article 13, para 1, Regulation 715/2009/EC that the actual, *efficient* costs need to be used as basis for the calculation of tariffs of access to the national gas transmission network operated by Gas Transport Services (GTS). Furthermore, VEMW held that although Article 25, para 4, of Directive 2003/55/EC does not explicitly mention efficient costs, the Notice of the European Commission 'Commission Staff Working Document on tariffs for access to the natural gas transmission networks regulated under 3 Article of Regulation 117/2005' does provide that the Directive should be understood as implying efficient costs. VEMW argued that by using the actual network costs as starting costs, while using efficient costs for GTS only over the course of the regulatory period, the tariffs for GTS where set higher than the efficient costs for a great part of the period. VEMW pointed thus that a transition period had been allowed for, while EU law does not provide any leeway in this regard. The establishment of a method decision for the regulatory period of 2006–2009 was, in consequence, in violation of EU law according to the VEMW.[48] The CBB provided the following judgment:

> (…) The main issue for the VEMW is that the Nederlandse Mededingingsautoriteit (NMA), when establishing the starting costs as of 1 January 2006, has not decided these on the basis of efficiency but has rather assumed the actual costs of GTS at that point in time to represent the efficient costs. VEMW has in this regard not been able to establish what other benchmark NMA could have used to establish the efficient costs at that point in time. NMA has rightly pointed out in this regard that on 1 January 2006 there was no benchmark with costs of other network operators available. NMA was thus not in the position to compare the costs with the performance of other operators. Furthermore, the NMA could assume that on 1 January 2006 the costs where efficient at least to a certain extent, as also prior to that date there was a form of regulation of GTS on the basis of the "Guidelines Gas transmission". VEMW has not substantiated why the NMA should have regarded the costs established at the end of 2005 as not sufficiently efficient to be used as a basis of a new regulation with a newly established level of efficiency at the end of the regulation period.[49] (own translation)

In other words, instead of assessing whether the starting costs could indeed be deemed as efficient, the CBB judged that appellant VEMW had not substantiated why the starting costs as of 1 January 2006 were not efficient and that the VEMW should have elaborated upon what other methods for the assessment of the efficiency of costs NMA could have used. This is striking, as the CBB stated in an earlier decision that the network operator is awarded a certain number of years to bring back the actual costs to the level of efficient costs. The CBB points at the method decisions and explains:

> In the method decisions the NMA has provided it seeks to achieve the goals set by the legislator by decreasing its tariffs over the course of the regulatory periods through application of the x-factor. By doing so, the tariffs gradually develop towards an estimated level of efficient costs in the final year of the regulatory period. The idea behind this is that,

[48] CBB 8 November 2012, ECLI:NL:CBB:2012:BY2307, para 3.3.1.

[49] CBB 8 November 2012, ECLI:NL:CBB:2012:BY2307, para 3.3.3.

> this way, a network operator is awarded with a certain amount of years to bring his costs down to the efficient level. The starting costs of 2006 have been set by the NMA, briefly put, on the basis of the actual costs of 2005 (the year prior the start of the regulatory period).[50] (own translation)

While VEMW thus had a solid argument by putting into question the efficiency of the costs applied, the CBB dismissed the action by stating that VEMW had not been able to prove that the starting costs were not efficient and that it had not provided an alternative way of calculating efficient costs. Critical remarks can be made on three points of the marginal review by the administrative judge.

First, the CBB is unclear about evidence gathering and the apportionment of the burden of proof. The CBB expected a type of evidence gathering from the VEMW that went significantly beyond the *sufficiently plausible* criterion. Dutch Administrative procedural law does not provide a single general evidence standard. Instead, it uses as criterion that if a party submits facts, these should be substantiated in a *sufficiently plausible way*, as long as they can to a reasonable extent create doubt as to the factual basis of a regulatory decision.[51] In this case the judge required the appellants not only to make their own arguments sufficiently plausible, but also to make plausible in what alternative ways the tariffs and the method decisions should have been established. In this context, one should note that in administrative procedural law, the civil law axiom 'who states should prove' does not apply.[52] Within administrative procedural law, the judge has the freedom to apprise the evidence provided,[53] where the basis of a decision, the weight of different interests at stake and the reliability of the evidence at hand are examined.[54] It is noteworthy that the CBB held that VEMW should have explained which benchmark should have been used. The appropriation of the burden of proof here goes beyond the sole duty to make it sufficiently plausible that the costs used were not efficient.

As explained before, in cases concerning discretionary powers of NRAs, the administrative judge is to respect the NRA's assessment of the facts, although the judge should also assess the question whether the establishment of the facts presented by an NRA is legally tenable.[55] This brings us to the second observation. The administrative judge in many cases follows the establishment of facts by the NRA, while this should in fact be reviewed intensively. This is paradoxical, as the judge in administrative law should take an active and thus non-passive approach to compensate the inequality between citizens and regulatory agencies that exists with regard to both expertise and factual power.[56] The CBB, later on in its judgment,

[50] CBB 8 November 2012, ECLI:NL:CBB:2012:BY2307, para 3.3.1.

[51] Schlössels and Zijlstra 2010, p. 1121 and Damen 2013, p. 308.

[52] Schuurmans 2005, p. 213.

[53] Damen 2013, p. 308.

[54] Schuurmans 2005, p. 21.

[55] Damen 2006, p. 21.

[56] Damen 2013, p. 290.

seems to assume that the actual costs as starting costs were, to certain extent, efficient. However, it was in no way clear that these costs were actually efficient. After all, the CBB knew that network operators possess a statutory monopoly and consequently have a dominant position in the sense of Article 102 TFEU and Article 24 Mededingingswet ('Dutch Competition Act'). It was also known to the CBB that prior to the start of the regulatory period, the costs and tariffs for gas transmission had been barely scrutinized. The CBB had, after all, previously established that whilst the costs prior 2006 were regulated by the Gas Transport Guidelines, these directives were not binding upon the ACM and GTS.[57]

Third, the judge's reasoning concerning the interpretation and application of the concept of (efficient) costs in the Gas Act and Gas Directive is noteworthy, as this is factually a legal question, on which the judge has the final say. In this particular case, the judge has neglected to provide an interpretation of this unclear norm in EU law. The CBB held, without providing a substantial evaluation of the norm, that Article 3 Regulation 1775/2005 and the accompanying interpretative Notice of the Commission had not yet entered into force on 1 January 2006. Furthermore, the CBB held that although Directive 2003/55 was in fact in force at that time, this Directive did provide much more than that 'the tariffs should be proportionate and a reflection of the costs'. However, from the preamble of Directive 2003/55 it appears that in the context of the implementation of the Directive, efficient costs did actually play a role.[58] The judge has the duty to interpret national legislation in light of the goals and preambles of relevant EU law. In this case the court seems to have neglected to fulfil this duty, as he did not take into account the efficiency aims flowing from the preamble of the applicable Directive. Besides an incorrect interpretation of the law, the CBB also failed to substantially review the establishment and the qualifications of the provided facts in light of EU law. The only consideration made was that the VEMW had not sufficiently made clear that the actual costs were not, in fact, efficient costs. This whilst it was sufficiently plausible that the choice for actual costs as starting costs for the regulation of the energy tariffs had major consequences for the energy tariffs for the consumer.

#### 8.3.2.2 Opening RAB

The second aspect examined in the cases under consideration is the determination of the opening regulatory asset base by the ACM. The ACM was obliged to determine this value on the basis of Article 13(1), Regulation 715/2009.[59]

---

[57] CBB 10 September 2004, ECLI:NL:CBB:2004:AR2366 and CBB 23 April 2004, ECLI:NL:CBB:2004:AO9530.

[58] Directive 2003/55/EC of the European Parliament and of the Council of 26 June 2003 concerning common rules for the internal market in natural gas and repealing Directive 98/30/EC (OJ 2003, L176/57).

[59] Article 13 para 1 of Regulation 715/2009 reads "*Tariffs, or the methodologies used to calculate them, applied by the transmission system operators and approved by the regulatory authorities*

The CBB started its reasoning by pointing at a previous judgment in which it was held that the ACM has discretion when choosing the method of determining the opening RAB and the supposed length of depreciation period.[60] The opening RAB comprises the costs for the legal duties of GTS. These include the capital costs of the GTS assets. The value of the assets of GTS can be determined in different ways. The applicants held that the applied valuation method resulted in a situation in which consumers had to pay for certain costs twice. This also became apparent from a report of Oxera Consulting Ltd, commissioned for the ACM. Here, the following was stated:

> If this interpretation of the historical context is correct then, by construction, using the DHC methods (both nominal and real) to set the RAB would lead to customers paying again for costs previously factored into energy tariffs.[61]

A similar conclusion was drawn in a report by Brattle:

> On this basis, setting the GTS's RAB above €5.8 billion would appear even less fair. Gas users would pay not only the costs of maintaining the Dutch investment environment, but an additional cost for a network they have largely already paid for.[62]

The CBB again did not agree with the arguments of the applicants, and instead considered as follows:

> 3.4.6 (…) The tribunal concurs the stance of the NMA that the aforementioned Article 13 provides more opportunity for the balancing of different interests when deciding the method for determining the opening RAB than the VEMW pertains. Even when the method does not result in an exact compensation of the actual costs, other elements that can be taken into account, such as the interests of the network operators and its investors following a reasonable and predictable return on investment, if considered, can make the method acceptable. (own translation)

According to the CBB, the determination of the valuation method for the RAB fell within the ACM's margin of discretion. In holding so, the CBB failed to assess whether the valuation method complied with the rules and aims of the EU energy regulation, including the protection of consumer interests. The CBB only briefly

---

*pursuant to Article 41(6) of Directive 2009/73/EC, as well as tariffs published pursuant to Article 32(1) of that Directive, shall be transparent, take into account the need for system integrity and its improvement and reflect the actual costs incurred, insofar as such costs correspond to those of an efficient and structurally comparable network operator and are transparent, whilst including an appropriate return on investments, and, where appropriate, taking account of the benchmarking of tariffs by the regulatory authorities. Tariffs, or the methodologies used to calculate them, shall be applied in a non-discriminatory manner".*

[60] CBB 23 December 2011, ECLI:NL:CBB:2011:BU9127, para 4.1: *"The Tribunal holds first and foremost that the NMA, in deciding how the NMA can most effectively realize the goals provided in the Gas Act, has a margin of discretion, in which context in principle different approaches would be legitimately possible." (own translation)*

[61] Oxera 2011, p. 15.

[62] Brattle 2007, p. 3.

discussed the question whether it is fair for the consumers who paid for certain costs twice. It held in this regard:

> 3.4.6 (…) the Tribunal holds that the NMA, contrary to the view of the GTS, does not exclude that the method decision for determining the opening RAB, including the length of the depreciation period for the pipe lines, can result in a situation where assets have been included for which already payments have been received in a previous period. NMA, however holds, as has been established before the Tribunal, that the aforementioned Article 13(1), has not been breached by the decision (…) VEMW has provided that the taking into account of a reasonable return of investment when determining the RAB results in a double counting of compensation of the WACC in the tariffs. The Tribunal follows the argumentation of the NMA that determination of the RAB and WACC are time-sequential. First the decision is made for the method of determination of the opening RAB. Here, the interests of investors are taken into account on a solid basis. Subsequently, the WACC is calculated while taking the aforementioned RAB into account. Here, the Tribunal concludes there is no case of unacceptable double counting. The question posed in the first paragraph of this section concerning whether the NMA has exceeded its margin of discretion can thus be answered in the negative. Henceforth the appeal by VEMW and Energie Nederland is dismissed. (own translation)

The judicial reasoning and review in this case was found wanting with regard to two main aspects. First, the judicial reasoning regarding the interpretation of EU law and the scope of the margin of discretion that can be exercised by the ACM was overtly brief. The CBB has here reviewed the interpretation of EU law by the ACM in a marginal fashion. To elaborate, it was unclear whether the approach adopted by the ACM was even in line with the wordings and substance of Article 13 of Regulation 715/2009. The administrative judge has the competence to conduct a full review of a regulatory authority's interpretation of a vague legal norm but failed to do so in the present case.[63] One could wonder whether it was not more to be expected from the CBB to instigate a preliminary reference procedure and ask the CJEU for guidance on how to interpret this vague legal norm. What is the meaning of the requirements that the "[t]ariffs, or the methodologies used to calculate them, applied by the transmission system operators… reflect the actual costs incurred, insofar as such costs correspond to those of an efficient and structurally comparable network operator and are transparent, whilst including an appropriate return on investments, and, where appropriate, taking account of the benchmarking of tariffs by the regulatory authorities" for the valuation of the assets and costs of the gas network in light of the aims of EU energy regulations. It seems the judge had not distinguished between the interpretation of laws by the ACM on the one hand, and the qualifying decision by the ACM on the other hand. With regard to the interpretation of laws, the judge always has the final say. If the CBB had subjected the legal arguments, the factual substantiation and the balancing of interests regarding the choice for the valuation method to a further and deeper investigation, providing throughout its judgment a well-motivated distinction between the establishment of facts, the assessment and the legal interpretation, it would have enhanced the right to effective judicial protection for users of energy networks to far greater extent.

---

[63] Schlössels and Zijlstra 2010, p. 161.

Second, the court was unclear in the judgment regarding the assessment of the margin of discretion and how exactly account had been taken of the different interests at stake. The CBB could, at the very least, have motivated in what ways the ACM had balanced the different interests at stake in a reasonable manner when making its decision.[64] Has the ACM justifiably come to the decision that the interests of network operators and investors hold greater weight than those of the consumers and, if so, on what basis? The reasoning of the CBB does not demonstrate in what way the interests of the consumers have been taken into account by its judgement and the decision under appeal.

#### 8.3.2.3 WACC

Third and finally, the applicants challenged the valuation method of the WACC. Here as well, the CBB pointed towards the margin of discretion of the ACM and concluded, after a very marginal review of the decision at stake that the ACM had indeed acted within its margin of discretion. The CBB provided that:

> 3.5.4 First of all, the Tribunal holds that it follows from its established case law that the WACC constitutes a (weighted) average of the costs that a regulated enterprise makes for the attracting of own respectively foreign capital. This is a given and there is no margin of discretion for the relevant regulatory authority. This does omit, however, that for determining the different parameters of the WACC, different methods can be used and that regulatory authorities have broad discretionary powers in deciding on the methods to be used.
>
> Thus the Tribunal does not conclude from the abovementioned statement that the NMA has gone beyond its margin of discretion. (own translation)

#### 8.3.2.4 The LUP Cases

The CBB has further issued different judgments relating to the national uniform producer tariffs (hereafter: LUP cases). In the Netherlands, the costs for feeding energy into the distribution network are allocated to the consumers of energy. The producers thus do not have to pay for these costs; they are exempted from paying transport tariffs.[65] Producers that feed in energy into the national high-voltage power lines traditionally had to pay 25% of the costs for transportation. Producers who fed in energy on regional grids did not have to pay any costs.

In different procedures regarding the LUP, the question arose whether this exemption aligned with the EU principles of non-discrimination and of costs reflectiveness of the network tariffs, which can be found in Electricity Directive

[64] As the CBB has considered in the case discussed below on the right to having a gas connection. See CBB 22 April 2014, ECLI:NL:CBB:2014:134.

[65] See, in this regard, Crespo and Lavrijssen 2013.

2009/72/EC and preceding directives.[66] In the first LUP case, the principle of non-discrimination was discussed.[67] The CBB was asked to interpret and apply (at the time) Articles 27[68] and 36[69] of the Electricity Act 1998 as well as Article 3.5.1. of the Tariff Code (TCE).[70] The applicants, *inter alia* Electrabel Nederland, Essent and E.ON Benelux, initiated their claim by holding that the exclusive levying of a producer transport tariff for Dutch producers infringed Article 36(1)c–d of the Electricity Act 1998. The producers that fed in energy into the national high-voltage power lines argued that the regulation pertained to a breach of the principle of non-discrimination, for establishing an illegitimate distinction between different producers. Second, the applicants held that there was discrimination between users, as decentralized (regional) suppliers did not have to pay the LUP costs, whereas central (national) suppliers were in fact obliged to do so. According to the applicants, Article 3.5.1. Tariff Code infringed upon Article 29 Electricity Act 1998, as the latter did not allow for such a distinction to be made. This, the applicants continued, constituted a breach of Article 7(5) of Directive 96/92/EC which states

[66] An exception to the prohibition of discrimination can only be made if an actual objective distinction can be made between the different situations. See, in this regard, Case C-17/02 *VEMW and others* [2005] ECLI:EU:C:2005:362, para 48. See also para 36 of Directive 2009/72/EC where the principle of cost reflectiveness is referred to. The European directives are grounded in the assumption that network tariffs should reflect the costs (fixed and variable costs along plus a reasonable return on investment).

[67] CBB 2 August 2002, ECLI:NL:CBB:2002:AE6773.

[68] Article 27 Electricity Act 1998.

1. The joined network operators send the director of the service a proposal concerning the tariff structures that lists the method of calculating the tariff for which users will be connected to a network, the tariff for which the transportation of electricity, including the feeding in, the consumption and transit of electricity, for the users will be carried out and of the tariff for which the system services will be conducted and the energy balance will be maintained. (…)
3. The tariffs the network operators of the national high voltage network charge for maintaining the energy balance are objective, transparent, non-discriminatory and reflective of the costs. (own translation)

[69] Article 36 Electricity Act 1998.

> "1. The director of the service establishes the tariff structures and conditions while taking into account:
>
> The proposal of the joined operators as referred to in Articles 27, 31 or 32 and the results of the consultation, referred to in Article 33, first paragraph, the importance of the secure, sustainable, efficient and environmentally sound functioning of energy supply, the importance of the promotion of the development of trade on the electricity market, the importance of promoting efficient operation of users and the importance of good quality of service provision by network operators." (own translation).

[70] Article 3.5.1. Tariff Code provides as follows: for producers with means of production that are connected to a network on EHS_ or HS_ level "a nationwide uniform producers transport tariff applies (LUP)." (own translation).

that grid operators must refrain from any form of discrimination between users or categories of users of the grid.

The CBB concluded however that the ACM, by determining the producer tariffs in this particular way, had not acted beyond the margin of discretion that it has been awarded pursuant Article 36 of the Electricity Act 1998. This is because the principle of cost reflectiveness (the costs must be compensated by the party that causes them) and the principle of efficient business operation were held to be a determinate factor in the decision made by the ACM.[71] Furthermore, the CBB held that the different producers have not been discriminated against, as the producers that feed energy into the national grid simply make use of a different service than producers that do so on the regional grid.

In the second LUP case, different parties appealed the decision by the ACM to set the transport tariff for feeding electricity into the national grid at 0%.[72] The rationale behind this decision was to create a level-playing-field by bringing the producer transport tariff more in line with the transport tariffs for producers abroad. The decision was controversial as the Electricity Act 1998 at the time provided that the tariff for transport of electricity was connected to the feeding of electricity into the network, as well as the consumption of electricity by the network users. The Electricity Act further provided that the tariff would be charged to every user connected to a network managed by a network operator. The tariffs for electricity could differ per user, depending on the voltage levels of the networks into which electricity was fed. The point of law of consideration here was whether the ACM was allowed to set the transport tariff for producers at 0%. In this context, most prominently Articles 27, 29 and 36(1) (old) of the Electricity Act 1998 were relevant.[73]

VEMW alleged that this decision breached the principle of cost reflectiveness. This principle, which according to VEMW followed from the (at the time effective) Article 29(2) Electricity Act 1998,[74] provided that the costs for feeding electricity into the network should be divided amongst the producers and the users of the network. By setting the transport tariff at 0%, producers were not required to compensate for the costs of feeding energy into the network. The CBB held that it

[71] CBB 2 August 2002, ECLI:NL:CBB:2002:AE6773, para 6.1 and Lavrijssen et al. 2014, p. 56.

[72] CBB 11 February 2005, ECLI:NL:CBB:2005:AS7083.

[73] See preceding footnotes.

[74] Article 29 Electricity Act 1998.

1. The tariff at which the transport of electricity will be carried out for the user, relates to the consumption of electricity by a user, regardless of the place of generation of the electricity and the connection where the electricity has been brought into the Dutch net, or the feeding in of electricity by a user, regardless of the place of receiving electricity.
2. The tariff, as referred to in the first paragraph, is charged to every user with a connection to a network that is administered by a network operator. The tariffs for the consumption of electricity can vary for the different users, depending on the voltage level of the network from which the electricity is taken, and the tariffs for the feeding in of electricity can vary for different users, depending on the voltage level of the network the electricity is fed into. (own translation)

was within the margin of discretion of the ACM to decide on the application of the principle of cost reflectiveness. The CBB held:

> 6.4 (…) Applicant further holds that the disputed decision is in breach with the so called principle of cost reflectiveness. The Tribunal first concludes that the Electricity Act 1998 does not explicitly hold that this principle always needs to be applied. It is apparent from the legislative history that the defendant is free to apply the principle. However, as mentioned above, the defendant can exercise discretion when establishing or amending the Tariff Code; when exercising this discretion the defendant is free to decide whether or not to assign transport tariffs to the party that causes the costs of transport. (own translation)

Contrary to the first LUP case, the CBB did not seem to require here that the principle of cost reflectiveness was actually complied with. The CBB held that it was up to the ACM to make its own deliberations and, by doing so, assess whether the strong competitive position of energy producers in the EU should be decisive, even where it is to be expected that the consumer will in the short term incur financial losses due to the decision. Finally the CBB concluded that there was no reason to assume that the ACM had balanced the interests at stake in an inappropriate fashion.[75] This observation is relatively remarkable. First of all, the principle of cost reflectiveness followed from the Electricity Directive in place at that time.[76] The CBB is required to guarantee a consistent interpretation of national laws in light of EU laws and regulations. The CBB should at the very least have referred to the relevant provisions in the Electricity Directive for its interpretation of national law. In doing so it should have motivated why the principle of cost reflectiveness would not apply in the case at hand.[77] As far as uncertainty still existed concerning the interpretation of this principle, it would have been reasonable to expect from the CBB to send a preliminary reference to the CJEU.[78] Second, the administrative judge has not elaborated in what way the balancing of interests has been reviewed in this case. Because the transport tariff was set at 0%, the users, i.e. the consumers, became responsible for the costs of feeding energy into the grid, resulting in a disadvantaged position for the consumer. After several general considerations that point to a very marginal review of the correctness and consistency of the legal and economic reasoning of the decision of the ACM, the appeal was dismissed.[79]

In an interlocutory judgment on tariff regulations, the applicants challenged that the tariff codes charged all costs for feeding in electricity to the end users, while 0% of the costs were attributed to the producers.[80] In this case, the applicants amongst others held that the method decision was in breach of Articles 29 and 41b sub a of the

[75] Lavrijssen et al. 2014, p. 57.

[76] Directive 2003/54/EC of the European Parliament and of the Council of 26 June 2003 concerning common rules for the internal market in electricity and repealing Directive 96/92/EC (OJ 2003, L176/37).

[77] See consideration 18 of Directive 2003/54/EC.

[78] Lavrijssen et al. 2014, p. 59.

[79] CBB 11 February 2005, ECLI:NL:CBB:2005:AS7083, paras 6.4–6.6.

[80] CBB 11 December 2011, ECLI:NL:CBB:2011:BU7936.

Electricity Act 1998, because the method decision regarding the decentralized feeding in of the joined output incorrectly did not distinguish between transport tariffs for consumption and tariffs for feeding in.[81] According to the applicants, Article 29 para 1 and 41b para 1 sub a Electricity Act 1998[82] provide that the consumption of and feeding in of electricity on the net should be separated. Accordingly, the principle of cost reflectiveness should be adhered to, which would mean that the costs of feeding in of electricity should be attributed to the producer, while the user should only have to cover the costs for the consumption of electricity.

The CBB decided in favour of the applicants and held that, indeed, on the basis of Article 29 para 1 Electricity Act 1998, a distinction should be made between the feeding in and consumption of electricity.[83] The costs thereof need to be attributed to the tariff carrier for these services as provided in Article 41b, para 1 under a, of the Electricity Act 1998. The CBB confirmed in a later judgment that the feeding in of electricity and the consumption of energy are two distinct services.[84]

In the final LUP case of 17 October 2013, the central question that was assessed concerned the issue whether the abovementioned also meant that the costs for the feeding in of electricity can constitute part of the user tariff. Article 29[85] and Article 41b, para 1, under a Electricity Act 1998 and Article 3.4.1. Tariff Code Electricity (TCE) are key here. VEMW held that, as the CBB had previously confirmed that the feeding in of electricity and the consumption of electricity are two separate services, the decision of 2009 in which the costs for the feeding in of electricity on the basis of Article 3.4.1. were allocated to the tariff for the supply of electricity breached Article 29 in conjunction with 41b para 1, under a of the Electricity Act 1998.

However, the CBB did not contend with the argumentation of the VEMW.[86] The CBB summarized its conclusion, while referring to the two abovementioned cases, as follows:

> 3.4.4 (…) in the judgement of 2 July 2013 the Tribunal has explained that the judgment of 16 December 2011 cannot be interpreted as providing that the costs for feeding in can in no way be allocated to network users via the transport tariffs. This does not follow from Article 29 of the Act. As VEMW has attested, the present situation is different to such extent that a tariff carrier is available. This is without prejudice to the starting point accepted by the Tribunal that Article 29 of the Act does not exclude the possibility for a different attribution

[81] CBB 11 December 2011, ECLI:NL:CBB:2011:BU7936, para 4.4.1.

[82] Article 41b provides as follows:

1. Every network operator every year sends, prior to 1 October, a proposal to the board of directors of the competition authority with the tariffs that the operator will apply at most for exercising the tasks referred to in Article 16, para 1, taking into account:

   a. The principle that costs are awarded to the tariff carriers for the services that give rise to these costs, (…)" (own translation)

[83] CBB 11 December 2011, ECLI:NL:CBB:2011:BU7936, para 4.4.3.

[84] CBB 2 July 2013, ECLI:NL:CBB:2013:52, paras 3.1 and 3.2.

[85] See Footnote 74.

[86] CBB 17 October 2013, ECLI:NL:CBB:2013:204, paras 3.4.1–3.4.4.

> of costs than what would follow from the application of the principle of cost reflectiveness. The tariff carrier is necessary to determine the extent of the relevant costs and can also be used to establish by what party they have been caused, but the presence of the tariff carrier plays no role in the decision to whom the costs are ultimately allocated. This decision requires a balancing of interests. The Tribunal points in this context to its judgment of 11 February 2005 on the setting of the LUP tariff at 0%. The Tribunal has held herein that it can be reasonable for the ACM to have attached greater weight to the promotion of a healthy European energy market with a level playing field than to the consequences of the allocation of costs to the consumer.[87] (own translation)

The ACM can thus derogate from the principle of cost reflectiveness, as it is free to attach a decisive weight to the attainment of a strong and healthy European energy market, even where this goes at the cost of the tariffs for net usage for end users.[88] The CBB reviewed the interpretation of EU law and the balancing of interests made by the ACM in a highly marginal fashion. The CBB and the ACM attributed, without a substantial explanation, less value to the interests of energy consumers than to those of energy companies. At the very least, the CBB could have motivated in a better and more transparent way why in this case the outcome of the balancing of interests was justified in light of the provisions and goals of the relevant European and national energy laws.[89]

#### 8.3.2.5 The Negative X-Factor

Finally, the CBB has dealt with the negative x-factor in certain cases. The x factor decision, which is taken on the basis of Article 81 Gas Act,[90] has as core goal to promote efficient business operations by network operators. For this reason, the efficiency discount corrects excessive incomes of a previous regulatory period by lowering tariffs in the subsequent period.[91] In 2010 the ACM attributed negative values to the x-factor decisions. In consequence, incomes of network operators did not decrease but increased, with higher tariffs for the energy consumer as a result.

In the first case on the negative x-factor, the applicant (FME, an organisation representing the interests of corporations active in the technology industry) held that the negative x-factor decision of the ACM infringed the law, as the x-factor here was labelled as a discount for consumers.[92] The CBB acknowledged however that

---

[87] CBB 17 October 2013, ECLI:NL:CBB:2013:204.

[88] CBB 17 October 2013, ECLI:NL:CBB:2013:204.

[89] See e.g. consideration 16 of the preamble of Directive 2009/72/EC, which provides that tariffs should not be discriminatory and should be reflective of the costs.

[90] Article 81 Gas Act provides as follows: (…)

The discount to promote efficient business operation has as amongst others as goal to make sure that the network operator can in any case not attain higher returns than what would be usual in the economy and the promotion of equality in the efficiency of network operators.

[91] See also Article 41a para 1a of the Electricity Act 1998: "the discount to promote efficient business operation" (own translation).

[92] CBB 23 April 2013, ECLI:NL:CBB:2013:CA1052.

neither the law nor the parliamentary history anticipate a negative x-factor. However, this does not mean that the option of having a negative x-factor is henceforth excluded. As the CBB provided:

> 3.3 (…) More generally what has been held by the ACM justifies, looking at the text of Article 81, para 1, Gas Act and related legislative history, where a decrease in tariffs was practically continuously assumed, not without question the use of a negative x-factor. The Tribunal deems however that it cannot be assumed that there are no circumstances in which a negative x-factor can be suitably applied in a system of bench mark regulation. (own translation)

It remains unclear in what circumstances a negative x-factor can be justified. The CBB did not further elaborate this consideration in its judgment. In subsequent cases on the negative x-factor, the CBB referred to this specific case.[93] Here, the CBB demonstrated a highly marginal method of review of the interpretation of the Gas Act and the substantive elements of the decision of the ACM. It seemed to accept the negative x-factor without subjecting its legality and reasonability to a thorough substantive review in light of the provisions and goals of European and national energy laws.[94]

## *8.3.3 Is the CBB Heading Towards a More Intensive Judicial Scrutiny of the ACM's Regulatory Decisions Beyond 2013?*

### 8.3.3.1 Right to Be Connected to the Gas Grid (Gas Connection Case)

More recently the CBB seems to have assessed the balancing of interests carried out by the ACM more critically in several cases. For instance, in the case concerning the right to be connected to the gas grid the CBB had a more critical look at the substance of the cases.[95] In this case, Article 12b, para 1, under f[96] and Article 12f,

[93] CBB 13 February 2014, ECLI:NL:CBB:2014:50; CBB 13 February 2014, ECLI:NL:CBB:2014:46. See also Sauter's case note for CBB 13 February 2014, ECLI:NL:CBB:2014:50, AB 2014/227.

[94] Lavrijssen et al. 2014, p. 60. See in this context also Articles 36 and 37 of Directive 2009/72/EC and Articles 40 and 41 Directive 2009/73/EC.

[95] CBB 22 April 2014, ECLI:NL:CBB:2014:134.

[96] Article 12b, first paragraph, section f Gas Act.

1. With due consideration of the rules referred to in Article 12 and the net codes provided in Article 6 of Regulation 715/2009 the joined network operators send a proposal to the Authority Consumers and Market for the conditions applied to users regarding: (…)

   f. The zoning of the network operators for exercising the task, referred to in Article 10, para 6, whereby certain areas can be excepted if the area is located in a district with a heat network, as meant in Article 1, section c, of the Heat Act or will be located in such an area

para 1[97] of the Gas Act played a key role. In principle, the rule was that every person has the right to be connected to the gas grid. This follows from Article 10, para 6 of the Gas Act (old). Excluded are people that are located in an area connected to a heating system, as provided in Article 1, under c of the Act on District Heating.[98] The ACM decided that the borders provided in the Zoning document are to be interpreted as being merely indicatory in the decision being under appeal. By doing so, the ACM gave the network operator the competence to decide on the specific borders in a specific area. Applicant VEMW held that this decision gave rise to uncertainty as it did not provide for exact borders. According to the VEMW, the fact that the ACM neglected to decide on the precise zoning borders infringed upon Article 12f, first paragraph, of the Gas Act and the interest laid therein of advancing the efficient operation of network users.[99] In this case, the CBB reviewed the substance of the decision in a more intensive way. The CBB concluded that the ACM had delegated its task of determining the relevant zoning details to network operators, while it did not have the required competences for doing so. As such, the ACM acted in infringement of Article 12f of the Gas Act. The CBB explains that:

> [T]his single reference to the definitions laid out in the Heat Act provides to the judgment of the Tribunal not sufficient evidence of an (identifiable) balancing of the interests at stake. Following the matters at stake the ACM, prior to taking the disputed decision, has taken no account of the consequences of zoning in this form for (future) users and for the operation of the network operators. Furthermore, it has not assessed the possibilities and difficulties that can come into play in relation to the applicable legislation in this domain. (own translation).

---

or if it is an area where the network operator cannot have a functioning gas transportation network, nor maintain or develop one under economic conditions (own translation).

[97] Article 12f, first paragraph, Gas Act.

1. The Authority for Consumers and Markets establishes the tariff structures and conditions in due regard of:
    a. the proposal of the joined network operators as referred to in Articles 12a, 12b or 12c and the results of consultation, as provided in Article 12d;
    b. the importance of secure, sustainable, efficient and environmentally sound functioning of gas provision;
    c. the importance of the advancement of trade on the gas market;
    d. the importance of the promotion of efficient operation of network users;
    e. the importance of good quality service provision of network operators, and
    f. the importance of the objective, transparent and non-discriminatory balancing of the national gas transportation network, in a manner that reflects the costs;
    g. the rules referred to in Article 12;
    h. Regulation 715/2009;
    i. the Directive (own translation).

[98] Article 12b, first paragraph, under f Gas Act.

[99] CBB 22 April 2014, ECLI:NL:CBB:2014:134, para 3.2.1.

### 8.3.3.2 Method Decision Fourth Regulatory Period

Subsequently, the CBB provided another judgment in which it demonstrated a more intensive type of review of the substance of a decision, whilst it should be noted that several aspects of the decision were still annulled on procedural grounds.[100] This case concerned the method decisions for determining the x-factor, q-factor and the calculation volume for the period 2014–2016 (the fourth regulatory period). These elements are decisive for the determination of network tariffs.[101] The ACM took these decisions on the basis of Article 82, first and second paragraph of the Gas Act[102] and on the basis of Article 13 of the Gas regulation 715/2009 (provision concerning determination of tariff methods).[103] Network operators amongst others appealed the method decision regarding the calculation of own capital, the compensation arrangements in place, the amendment of the opening RAB and regarding the approach for dealing with the decentralized feeding in of energy. The applicants were successful on none of these points. The CBB did decide in favour of the applicants with regard to certain other points, in which it conducted a more intense method of review several times. In the subsequent section, the CBB's reasoning

---

[100] See the comparable cases for national and regional network operators respectively. CBB 5 March 2014, ECLI:NL:CBB:2015:44 and CBB 5 March 2014, ECLI:NL:CBB:2015:45.

[101] See Sauter's case note for the abovementioned cases, *AB Bestuursrechtspraak* 5 June 2015.

[102] Article 82 Gas Act.

1. In contrast to Article 80, the tariffs for exercising the tasks by the network operators of the national gas transportation network, referred to in Articles 10 and 10a, first paragraph, section b, c, d and e, as well as the tariffs for services needed for transportation are established in accordance with this Article.
2. For each of the tasks of the network operators of the national gas transport network, referred to in the first paragraph, the Board of the competition authority determines the method of regulation, for a period of minimally three and maximum five years, after consultation with the joint network operators and with organizations representing parties in the gas market and taking into account the importance of the efficiency of business operation and the promotion of the most efficient quality of the operation of these tasks, as well as the importance of a secure energy supply, sustainability and a reasonable return on investment.

[103] See Article 13, para 1 of Regulation 715/2009: "Tariffs, or the methodologies used to calculate them, applied by the transmission system operators and approved by the regulatory authorities pursuant to Article 41(6) of Directive 2009/73/EC, as well as tariffs published pursuant to Article 32(1) of that Directive, shall be transparent, take into account the need for system integrity and its improvement and reflect the actual costs incurred, insofar as such costs correspond to those of an efficient and structurally comparable network operator and are transparent, whilst including an appropriate return on investments, and, where appropriate, taking account of the benchmarking of tariffs by the regulatory authorities. The tariffs applied by transmission system operators, or the methods used for calculating tariffs that have been agreed upon by the regulatory authorities in accordance with Article 41, para 6, of Directive 2009/73/EC, as well as the tariffs that are published pursuant Article 32, para 1, of that Directive, are transparent, take into due regard the need for system integrity and the promotion thereof and reflect the actual costs. Tariffs, or the methodologies used to calculate them, shall be applied in a non-discriminatory manner" (own translation).

concerning the compensation of foreign capital in the WACC and the dynamic efficiency parameter (the efficiency parameter) will be discussed.

#### 8.3.3.3 Amount of Efficiency Parameter

In this interlocutory judgment of the CBB, the GTS appealed the method decision on gas of 1 January 2014 until 31 December 2016 and the resulting x-factor decision of the ACM. Through its method decision, the ACM decided on its method for determining the discount for efficient business operation (the x-factor) and the method for determining the calculation volume for every tariff carrier of each service for which a tariff is determined (calculation volumnia). The tariffs applied by the GTS are determined on the basis of this decision. The GTS has successfully appealed the application of the dynamic efficiency parameter for the period of 2014–2016 to the period of 2012–2013 in this case. According to GTS, there were no solid reasons for the ACM to use output price variations over the period of 1989–2007 as basis for the efficiency parameters. This differed from the way in which the ACM made such decisions in previous periods. For the method decision 2010–2013, the ACM had used a measuring period of four business cycles (1970–2007). Furthermore, GTS held that the amount of the efficiency parameter of 1.3% was incorrect, as it was not in line with the previous determination of productivity improvement in the period 2010–2013, which constituted 1%. GTS contended that they should be allowed to keep the additional yielded returns. As a result of the decision by the ACM, GTS was yet required to make up for the difference between 1.3 and 1%. Regarding the absence of explanation from the side of the ACM as to why this difference in method applied for determining the efficiency parameter, the CBB concluded that, indeed, the ACM had not fulfilled its duty to state reasons. Also with regard to the amount of the efficiency parameter the CBB followed the position of the GTS. The CBB concluded:

> 3.3.2. With respect to the method by which the ACM has determined the amount of the efficiency parameter, the Tribunal considers that, as follows from the explanatory note of the Gas Act, a key component of the system of tariff regulation is that corporations that perform better than the efficiency goals may keep any additional returns. By discounting the final incomes used for the x-factor decision in such a way that the GTS should also in 2010–2013 have satisfied a frontier shift of 1.3%, the ACM has acted in breach of the system of tariff regulation on the basis of the Gas Act. The Tribunal decides in favour of this aspect of the appeal by GTS.[104] (own translation)

[104]CBB 5 March 2015, ECLI:NL:CBB:2015:44, para 3.3.2. The administrative loop (bestuurlijke lus) enables the administrative judge to request the responsible public body to correct certain irregularities within the administrative decision-making procedure with regard to defects in the motivation of the administrative decision. The responsible public body can issue a new administrative decision or elaborate on its motivation for the already issued administrative decision. Backes et al. 2014.

Ultimately, the CBB annulled the part of the method decision relating to the application of the dynamic efficiency parameter. Doing so, the CBB demonstrated a more intensive review of the margin of discretion of the ACM. The ACM is not allowed to apply a so called 'catch-up' provision, as this would infringe upon an essential component of the system of regulations in place.[105] The CBB has however provided the ACM with the remedy to recover its faults through an administrative loop.[106]

#### 8.3.3.4 Compensation for Foreign Capital in the WACC

With regard to a number of other considerations, the conclusion can be drawn that, although the CBB has reviewed the substance, formally it still annulled the case on the basis of a lack of the provision of adequate reasons. To provide an example, the CBB approved amongst others the complaint of the applicants concerning the way in which the ACM had included a compensation for costs of foreign capital into the WACC. The ACM determined the weighed average cost for foreign capital, in contrast to previous years, on the basis of the costs for new foreign capital. These did not cover the costs associated with current foreign capital, such as the interest on long-term loans. The CBB followed the position of network operators, but nonetheless concluded that the ACM had made its decision in a correct manner, but it had to provide sufficient reasons as to why it had changed its practice of the previous years. As the CBB explained:

> 1.5.4. Now the ACM is adjusting the weighed averaged costs for foreign capital in the WACC on the basis of costs for new foreign capital, we cannot exclude the possibility that the interest compensation for foreign capital as included in the final incomes does not fully cover the costs for foreign capital, as the costs of outstanding loans in the coming regulatory period – given the decrease of interest that we have seen in previous years – are higher than the estimated costs for attracting new foreign capital. In the previous regulatory period, the ACM has explicitly taken into account the (phased refinancing of) current loan portfolios of network operators. The choice to leave this practice has been accompanied with insufficient reasons.[107] (own translation)

In reality, the CBB reviewed the decision in a full manner, after which it agreed in light of the facts at hand that the ACM could not reasonably have come to its decision. The CBB concluded that indeed the costs for current foreign capital possibly are not covered. Nonetheless, in its annulment decision the CBB referred back to procedural grounds, namely a breach of the duty to provide reasons. Also in other parts of the judgment where complaints of the applicants were deemed

[105] W. Sauter, case note on CBB 5 March 2015, ECLI:NL:CBB:2015:45.
[106] CBB 5 March 2015, ECLI:NL:CBB:2015:44, para 6.1.
[107] CBB 5 March 2015, ECLI:NL:CBB:2015:45, para 1.5.4.

ill-founded, the CBB concluded, after a substantial review of the assessment, that the ACM had not provided sufficient reasons for its decision.[108]

An example is the challenge raised by regional network operators regarding the efficiency improvement (dynamic efficiency). Here, the applicants held that the ACM should have involved the cost development of the gas connection service when calculating the expected efficiency changes instead of merely basing this on the cost development of the transportation service. The CBB came to the conclusion here that "*the ACM was not obliged to involve the cost data of the connection service in the determination of efficiency developments and has made sufficiently clear that the cost data for transport services would suffice*"[109] *(own translation).* As the decision was deemed incorrect purely on procedural grounds, the CBB returned the decision to the ACM through means of an administrative loop. The ACM was required to amend the issues within six months or take a new decision.

## 8.4 Judicial Review in the Modern Regulatory Administrative State

### *8.4.1 Analysis Case Law Between 2002 and 2013 and Beyond*

The abovementioned analysis of the CBB's case law shows that between 2002 and 2013, the CBB reviewed regulatory decisions by the ACM in a very marginal way. It illustrates that the CBB often limited its examination of the regulation, by only scrutinizing the *unreasonableness* of the ACM's energy regulations.[110] The criterion that courts use within the marginal unreasonableness test is that courts can only set aside regulations if: the administrative body could not reasonable have reached the contested regulatory decision, or if arbitrary action exists that was manifestly unreasonable or if the administrative body, in weighing the interests involved, could not reasonably have reached the contested action. The method of review of the CBB with respect to the interpretation of EU law and the application of the law, both regarding establishment and evaluation of facts, can in these cases be described as very marginal. The judicial reasoning regarding the (economic) evidence, the balancing of interests, the interpretation of relevant laws and the turning point in which parties have made their arguments sufficiently plausible, all remained very unclear

[108] Another example of this is the interlocutory judgment between the ACM and TenneT, CBB 11 August 2015, ECLI:NL:CBB:2015:272, para 2.5. Here, the ACM was awarded the discretion to either rectify the issues, or take a different decision in line with the guidance provided in the judgment.

[109] See also Lavrijssen et al. 2016.

[110] In landmark case Maxis and Praxis, the administrative court rules that courts should limit themselves to a restrained control of the use of administrative discretionary powers of the executive power. Dutch Council of State 9 May 1996, ECLI:NL:RVS:1996:ZF2153.

in this context. Additionally, our analysis has shown that the court rarely differentiates between the different types of discretionary powers that the ACM has according to Dutch Administrative law.[111]

This marginal standard of judicial review of the ACM's energy regulation is inherently intertwined with the existing Dutch interpretation of the separation of powers, and in particular, the place of administrative courts within the constitutional order and regulatory processes. Courts, in this view, should not operate as "regulatory watchdogs" by substantially reviewing the rationale and quality of regulations. The expert-regulator, it has been said, should focus on the substance of the regulation, whereas the court should instead focus on reviewing the procedure leading to the enactment of the regulation.[112] The refrained way in which the CBB scrutinized the ACM's energy regulations between 2002 and 2013 also seems to be based on these theoretical presumptions, since the CBB has frequently refrained from substantially scrutinizing the matter at hand by pointing at the margin of discretion of the ACM, without further going into the complaints brought forward by the applicants, while the applicants brought legal and factual arguments to the stage that deserved a more intense substantive review in light of the provisions and goals of EU and national law. As a result of this marginal judicial review of the ACM's energy regulations, it has been extremely hard for appellants to realise effective judicial protection in the period between 2002 and 2013.[113] It seems there is a risk that, by applying the standard of marginal review based on a strict application of the theory of separation of powers, the ACM falls between two stools in case both the legislator and minister as well as the judge act with great restraint in checking the ACM in the domain of energy regulation decisions.

### *8.4.2 Marginal Judicial Review Criticised*

The question can be asked whether the traditional assumption in administrative procedural law on the marginal review of regulatory discretionary decisions still holds within the modern administrative state. Recently, many scholars have fiercely criticized the way in which judges marginally review (regulatory) discretionary powers of (independent) regulatory authorities and other parts of the administration.[114] Hirsch Ballin, the former chairman of the Administrative Jurisdiction Division of the Council of State and former Minister of Justice in the Netherlands, has argued that due the marginal judicial review, regulatory decisions that NRAs such as the ACM generate escape scrutiny from both parliament (due to the weakened parliamentary control) and the judiciary (due to the marginal judicial

[111] See § 3.1 for an overview of three types of discretion in Dutch administrative law.

[112] De Waard 2016.

[113] Lavrijssen et al. 2014, p. 62.

[114] See for example, Van den Berge 2017a, pp. 98–99 and Van den Berge 2017b, pp. 203–234.

review). Therefore, he and various other scholars have pleaded that the marginal judicial review in Dutch administrative law needs to be reconsidered and to be substituted by a more demanding judicial scrutiny.[115] A strict application of the theory of the *trias politica*, on which the marginal review by the administrative judge seemed to based, is untenable in light of the independent position of the ACM within the *Rechtsstaat*.[116] It has been argued that the sharp distinction that Dutch administrative law traditionally makes between three types of discretion (beleidsvrijheid, beoordelingsvrijheid and beoordelingsruimte), is very excessive. From a practical point of view, it has been argued that in practice often no differentiation is made between these three types of administrative discretion.[117] The intensity of the judicial control applied by administrative judges in the energy sector should therefore not follow these distinctive types of administrative discretion and the corresponding differentiated standard of judicial review. Instead, it has been argued that the intensity of judicial review should follow functional considerations. The Administrative Division of the Dutch Council of State, responding to this criticism, has stated in its annual report that it will refrain from using the term "marginal review" while reviewing the administration's actions.[118] Interestingly, as has been discussed in para 3.3., in some important recent judgments after 2013, the CBB has imposed a more heightened scope and intensity of judicial review than it did in the past when scrutinizing the ACM's regulatory decisions. It has annulled some important regulatory decisions after a critical review of the substance (the facts and the assessment) of the case, and requiring the ACM to take a new decision with sufficient motivation.[119] Recently the CBB even referred a preliminary question regarding the interpretation of the principle of cost reflectiveness of Article 13 Regulation 715/2009 to the European Court of Justice. The contested interpretation of Article 13 played a crucial role in previous court cases, but was somewhat circumvented by the ECJ by deferring to the discretion of the ACM. By bringing

[115] Hirsch Ballin 2015, pp. 42–43. See also de Poorter and Capkurt 2017, pp. 84–95; Lavrijssen et al. 2016, pp. 142–161; Voermans 2017. Barkhuysen 2015; Verhey 2015; Schuurmans 2015, pp. 19–20. See also the conclusion of Advocate-General R. Widdershoven written for the Administrative Jurisdiction Division of the Dutch Council of State on the scope and intensity of exceptive review of generally binding regulations in the Netherlands, ECLI:NL:RVS:2017:3557, accessed via https://www.raadvanstate.nl/uitspraken/zoeken-in-uitspraken/tekst-uitspraak.html?id=93494.

[116] Hirsch Ballin 2015, pp. 33–34.

[117] Schlössels and Zijlstra 2010, p. 165.

[118] Dutch Council of State 2017, p. 61.

[119] See also the judgement in case 14/291/, NornNed-kabel, 16 June 2016, ECLI:NL:CBB:2016:264 and see also CBB, 8 December 2016, Rendo et al. versus ACM, ECLI:NL:CBB:2016:374. See CBB, 24 July 2018, case numbers 16/886, 16/887, 16/888, 16/890, 16/905, 16/906, 16/907, 16/908, 16/909, 16/910, 16/911, 16/912, Stedin et al. versus ACM, ECLI:NL:CBB:2018:348, CBB, 24 July 2018, case number 16/902, 16/903, 16/904, TenneT versus ACM, ECLI:NL:CBB:2018:347 and CBB, 24 July 2018, case number 17/409 en 17/410, GTS et al. versus ACM, ECLI:NL:CBB:2018:346.

the case to the ECJ, the CBB has demonstrated more willingness so engage with the substance of regulatory decisions, while it tends to refer decisions back to the ACM to restore them on procedural grounds.[120]

### 8.4.3 Risks of Substantive Review

While it is agreed that administrative courts can play a more constructive role in reviewing the ACM's energy regulations, it is argued that the CBB should refrain from scrutinizing the ACM's energy regulations too substantively by replacing the assessment of the ACM with its own assessment. This would amount to an appeal on the merits, which is being conducted by the UK Competition Appeals Tribunal.[121]

Although the CBB is a specialized administrative court, it still suffers from several institutional disadvantages in reviewing the ACM's energy regulations substantively. First, the CBB has less personnel and financial resources and little economic expertise in regulatory matters in comparison to the ACM. So it would be undesirable for practical reasons if the judge would acts as a "regulatory watchdog". The problem with a too substantive judicial review then is that legally trained judges have little knowledge of technical subjects such as energy regulation and are not adequately trained to fully assess complex (economic) evidence.[122] Unlike, for example, members of the Competition Appeal Tribunal in the UK, the CBB does not have cross-disciplinary in house expertise on economics.[123] In fact, the past decade, the CBB has, partly for financial- and partly for pragmatic reasons, never appointed an economic expert itself.[124] When the CBB reviews the ACM's energy regulations, it needs to take into account that the ACM, who has special expertise on this matter, is better equipped to formulate regulations and that legally trained judges have less expertise than the ACM in assessing complex economic matters. Therefore the CBB is not in the best position to reconsider the economic assessments that the ACM has made. Secondly, Dutch administrative procedural law also does not provide the court with the appropriate tools for a full review of the merits of energy regulations. In principle, Article 8:3 GALA prohibits administrative courts to directly examine the legality of generally binding regulations; generally binding regulations issued by the ACM in the energy sector are exempted from this prohibition.[125] Due to this prohibition, Dutch administrative procedure law is

[120] See also CBB, 12 June 2018, Tarief besluit GTS, ECLI:NL:CBB:2018:283.

[121] Graham 2009, p. 250.

[122] Mak 2012; Kerkmeester 2016.

[123] Lowe et al. 2013, para 3.1.3.

[124] Kerkmeester 2016, p. 90.

[125] This prohibition is currently heavily criticized and debated in the Netherlands: de Poorter and Capkurt 2017; Voermans 2017; Schuurmans 2015; van Male 2016, pp. 127–129; Scheltema 2014, p. 242; Schueler 2015, p. 435; Schuurmans and Voermans 2010, p. 811.

mainly developed for administrative proceedings on an individual basis and offers the administrative courts little tools to exercise control on the merits over regulations. The underlying structural logical of this prohibition is a political and constitutional argument based on the Dutch understanding of the separation of powers, namely that matters of policy and regulation should be dealt with by the executive and legislative power. The procedural judicial tools and standard for judicial review as developed in Dutch Administrative Procedure Law are mainly developed in light of scrutinizing individual administrative decisions (beschikkingen). Administrative courts in the Netherlands are therefore not used to examine generally binding regulations. Consequently, it is difficult for courts to develop a substantive standard for the judicial review of energy regulation in the Netherlands. Thirdly, judges do not have the democratic legitimacy to substantially review the merits of energy regulations by the ACM. A (full) substantial review raises the danger that courts will substitute their own judgment for that of the ACM. Laws cannot anticipate on all issues that are relevant for energy regulations. Regulatory discretion is indispensable for the ACM: the ACM needs to have regulatory discretion in order to be flexible and responsive in regulating the energy market. This, however, should not mean that the administrative judge should fully refrain from reviewing regulatory decisions more substantively, by reviewing the correctness and the establishment of the facts.

Administrative courts in the Netherlands now are facing a dilemma when reviewing the ACM's generally binding regulations. On the one hand, they need to defer to the ACM's technical expertise and respect their discretionary powers by not reviewing the ACM's decisions on the merits. On the other hand, administrative courts somehow need to review ACM's regulatory powers in order to make sure that they are taken in a fair matter. Although various scholars have pointed out that the judiciary fails to provide effective regulatory oversight in controlling the administration marginally, they omit to provide a clear alternative for a suited review method of decisions made by these agencies.[126] In the following section, several suggestions are made as to which type of judicial review could be applied by the CBB in order to review the ACM's energy regulations. It will be explored how the administrative judge could provide regulatory oversight in these matters by balancing between the need for effective review on the one hand and the need for regulatory discretion for the ACM on the other hand.

### *8.4.4 The Scope and Intensity of Judicial Review: Procedural-Proportionality Review?*

Based on a critical review of the abovementioned case law, it is suggested that the CBB continues its more recent thorough review of regulatory decisions and in

[126] Hirsch Ballin 2015, p. 43.

doing so applies a two-stage procedural proportionality test. This test allows the CBB to review the reasonableness of the ACM's energy regulations in a meaningful and transparent way.[127] Under this procedural proportionality test, courts should ideally apply the principle of proportionality in a procedural fashion. This allows courts to scrutinize both procedural as well as substantial aspects of administrative regulations, without intervening the ACM's discretionary powers. A limited procedural proportionality test allows courts to examine both the procedure (full procedural) and substance (limited substantive review) of the ACM's energy regulations, which allows the judge to make sure that regulations are made in an accountable and transparent way, without intruding the regulatory discretion of the ACM.[128] This test consists of two parts, namely procedural review and proportionality review.

**Part 1: Procedural-Proportionality Test**

The proportionality principle regulates the (causal) relationship between the purpose of an administrative action and the means used to achieve that purpose. The principle of proportionality has an important role and function in administrative law, as it is employed by (administrative) courts across the world as a tool to control the actions of the administration. In essence, the principle of proportionality asks the administration to justify its administrative actions on substantive grounds.[129] The proportionality test traditionally consists of a three-staged test.[130] The first test, the suitability test, refers to the causal relationship between the means and the end. It asks the question whether the chosen measure is suitable in order to achieve the given aim. The second test, the necessity test, implies that the courts reviews whether the chosen measure is necessary to achieve the aimed goal. The question asked is whether the chosen measure is least restrictive given the aim of the regulation. Finally, the third test, proportionality *stricto sensu*, the question is asked whether a necessary and suitable measure is disproportionate because it imposes an excessive burden on the individual.[131]

However, in order to determine whether a certain energy regulation is proportionate or not, the CBB needs to know the rationale that underpins energy regulations. Courts will not be able to review the necessity and the suitability of the measure if they are not informed of the policy choices that the regulator made

[127] In doing so, the CBB's standard of judicial review of regulations would also be in alignment with the standard of review that the Judicial Division of the Dutch Council of State applies while reviewing the (un)lawfulness of administrative regulations via exemptive review. See de Poorter and Capkurt 2017. See also the conclusion of Advocate-General R. Widdershoven written for the Administrative Jurisdiction Division of the Dutch Council of State on the scope and intensity of exceptive review of generally binding regulations in the Netherlands. Accessible via https://www.raadvanstate.nl/uitspraken/zoeken-in-uitspraken/tekst-uitspraak.html?id=93494.

[128] See, for a more detailed analysis, Eijkens 2015, p. 48.

[129] Cohen-Eliya and Porat 2011.

[130] Harbo 2010, p. 165.

[131] Harbo 2010, p. 165.

during the promulgation of the regulation. Article 2.3 of the Dutch 'Guidance document for drafting regulations' (Aanwijzingen voor de regelgeving) provides a framework which steps an administrative body must take before the promulgation of an administrative regulation:

(a) knowledge of the relevant facts and circumstances shall be acquired;
(b) the objectives being aimed at shall be defined in the most specific, accurate terms possible;
(c) it shall be investigated whether the objectives selected can be achieved using the capacity for self-regulation in the sector or sectors concerned or whether government intervention is required;
(d) if government intervention is necessary, it shall be investigated whether the objectives in view could be achieved by amending or making better use of existing instruments, or, if this proves impossible, what other options are available;
(e) the various options shall be compared and considered with care.[132]

This provision (informally) creates a right to justification of regulations. The rationale underpinning this justification is that, without this information, other actors involved in the regulatory process (such as parliament) are not able to form an (informed) opinion on the regulation. The problem in the Dutch context, is that courts cannot legally enforce these guidelines. These guidelines are, unlike, for example, the American Administrative Procedure Act, not formalized by law. Therefore, these guidelines do not have legally binding and judicially enforceable effect. Besides these guidelines, Dutch Administrative procedure law does not provide a procedural framework for the promulgation of regulations. Consequently, a general legally enforceable procedure for the promulgations of regulations does not exist in the Netherlands. Nevertheless, this procedural lacuna can be filled in another way. The CBB can review the procedure that has led to the promulgation of the regulation, in an indirect procedural fashion, by reviewing whether the ACM's energy regulations are in conformity with procedural requirements and general principles of good administration (algemene beginselen van behoorlijk bestuur), such as the principle of careful and impartial examination, the principle of transparency, the principle of due care, and the duty to provide reasons.[133] The duty to provide reasons and the principle of careful[134] and impartial examination[135] form the core of the principle of good administration and are particularly important in this sense. Both principles aim to ensure that administrative regulations are taken on the basis of a complete overview and assessment of the relevant facts of the case.

The duty to provide reasons is a key aspect of procedural review which can aid courts to scrutinize the ACM's energy regulations. In order to comply with the duty

---

[132] Translation provided by Van Gestel and de Poorter 2016.

[133] Articles 3:2, 3:46 and 3:47 GALA.

[134] Articles 3:46 and 3:47 GALA.

[135] Article 3:2 GALA.

to provide reasons, the ACM must reflect on the rationality of the reasoning of its regulations and, since the ACM must justify how it has exercised its regulatory discretionary powers, it must provide a reasonable explanation for its energy regulations. As part of the duty to provide reasons, the ACM should in particular motivate the factual, legal, and scientific considerations that underpin energy regulations in a transparent way.[136] Second, on the basis of the principle of careful and impartial examination, the competent public body is, first, required to examine all relevant elements of a case carefully and impartially. Additionally, the competent body should motivate whether different regulatory options have been examined and assessed by the regulator. This principle of sound administration is particularly interesting, since it has been developed by the CJEU as a procedural guarantee to counterbalance the wide discretionary powers that the European Commission has in the assessment of complex economic and risk regulations.[137]

**Part 2: Limited substantive review**

The duty to provide reasons and the principle of careful and impartial examination can be seen as an instrument that can institutionalize the principle of proportionality as a tool for administrative courts to review the relationship between the purpose and aim of an administrative regulation and the means to achieve that aim. This is beneficial for three reasons. First, applying a procedural means-end proportionality review can aid the democratic deficit of energy regulations. Applying the proportionality test has the potential to improve the quality of the regulatory process. It places a strong burden of proof on the ACM if it regulates the energy sector. Applying the principle of proportionality in a procedural fashion thereby structurally institutionalizes a right to justification, since it clearly incentivizes the ACM to motivate its regulations. It should motivate whether the means used in regulation are necessary and appropriate, what objective the regulation aims to achieve, which regulatory measure is chosen to achieve this objective, whether other regulatory measures have been considered. Applying a proportionality test can thereby strengthen the rationality of the ACM's energy regulations.

Secondly, applying this test can also strengthen the role that the CBB can play in monitoring the ACM's regulatory actions, while not intervening with its regulatory discretionary actions. The duty to provide reasons (which is a procedural requirement) also enables the CBB to scrutinize whether the substantive information underpinning the ACM's energy regulation is reasonable in light of the underlying national legislation/directive/regulation. This limited substantive review with the aid of the proportionality test can only be performed by the CBB if the CBB has sufficient background information on the relevant regulatory issue. Without this

[136] This is also in alignment with the standard of judicial review that the CJEU applies in competition law cases. See ECJ, Case C-12/03 *Commission v. Tetra Laval* [2005] ECLI:EU:C:2005:87, para 39.

[137] See Case C-269/90, TU München [1991] ECR I-5469, ECLI:EU:C:1991:438, at paras 13 and 14; Case C-525/04 P, Spain v Commission [2007] ECR I-9947, ECLI:EU:C:2007:698, at paras 58 and 59 and Hofmann et al. 2011, pp. 190–204.

information, the CBB cannot review the ACM's reasoning or evidentiary basis for energy regulations. In order words: if the ACM provides clear and understandable reasons for the promulgation of its energy regulations, the CBB will be in a better position to carry out the proportionality test and review the reasonableness of the ACM's energy regulations. Through the enforcement of the duty to provide reasons and the principle of careful and impartial examination, courts will be able to apply the first and second step of the three-staged proportionality test (suitability and necessity test) and review the suitability and the necessity of energy regulations, without intervening with the ACM's technical choices and regulatory discretionary powers. Thirdly and finally, the application of a procedural-proportionality test structures the information-flow between courts and regulators and decreases the information asymmetry between courts, regulators and citizens affected by the regulation.[138] In doing so, the principle of proportionality can pursue a dialogue function between the court and the regulator. Finally, this means-ends rationality also serves a broader goal, namely that of transparency and accountability. If the ACM regulates the energy market, citizens (and the scientific community) then will be better able to understand the reasons that underpin the ACM's energy regulations. This will not only strengthen the transparency of the ACM's regulatory decisions, but also strengthens the accountability of the ACM towards the public.

## 8.5 Conclusion

The question how a relatively novel constitutional player such as the ACM can be checked by the judge in an effective manner is very relevant for ensuring the ACM is subject to adequate checks and balances. This chapter has shown that in the large majority of CBB cases on energy regulatory decisions in the period between 2002 and 2013, the judge applied a doctrinal restraint when reviewing discretionary decisions by the ACM, which has had its effect on its judicial reasoning. The method of review of the CBB with respect to the interpretation of EU law and its application of the law, both regarding establishment and evaluation of facts, can in these cases be described as limited to such extent that the question arose whether one can actually still speak of effective review in light of the right to effective legal protection that EU citizens derive from EU law. The judicial reasoning regarding the applied/desired provision of evidence, the balancing of interests, the interpretation of relevant laws and the turning point in which parties have made their arguments sufficiently plausible, all remained very unclear in this context. Often the CBB set aside claims by pointing at the margin of discretion of the ACM, without further going into the complaints brought forward by the applicants, while the applicants brought legal and factual arguments to the stage that deserved a more intense substantive review in light of the provisions and goals of EU and national

[138] Mantzari 2015.

law. As a result of judges reviewing energy decisions in this way, it has been extremely hard for consumers to realise effective judicial protection.[139] It seems there is a risk that the control on the ACM falls between two stools in case both the legislator and minister as well as the judge act with great restraint in checking the ACM in the domain of energy regulation decisions. A strict application of the theory of the *trias politica*, on which the marginal review by the administrative judge is based, is untenable in light of the independent position of the ACM within the *Rechtsstaat*.[140]

The main question then remains how a relatively novel constitutional player such as the ACM can be checked by the judge in an effective manner without intruding the ACM's discretionary powers. This contribution provides several suggestions for the improvement of the effectiveness and the transparency of the standard and intensity of judicial review of energy regulatory decisions applied by the CBB. It is proposed that the procedural-proportionality judicial review provides a very practical and comprehensive interpretation of the requirement of effective review under the current legality test.[141] By applying a procedural-proportionality review, courts will be given more instruments, to ensure that energy regulations are made in a fair, well-informed and transparent way, which, could enhance both the democratic legitimacy of energy regulations and the democratic accountability of the ACM. Due to this kind of judicial review, the ACM can no longer hide behind its regulatory discretionary powers. Instead, it means that the ACM, on the basis of the duty to provide reasons, should justify its regulatory actions in a transparent and substantive way; It requires the ACM to make transparent the goals of the regulations, its reasons, the way these reasons relate to the will of the legislator and the proportionality of measures.

In its recent case law, in several recent judgements between 2015 and 2018, the CBB showed more willingness to review the substance of the regulatory decisions of the ACM, which led to the annulment of several key energy regulation on procedural grounds. These developments show that the tide may be turning at the CBB, though a more intensive research of recent case law will be needed to substantiate whether the CBB will really have a less restraint approach towards the substance of regulatory decisions of the ACM.

## References

Backes C, Hardy E, Jansen A, Polleunis S (2014) Vier jaar bestuurlijke lus – success-story of teleurstelling? [Four years administrative loop – success-story or disappointment?]. Jurisprudentie Bestuursrecht Plus [Jurisprudence Administrative Law Plus] 16(4):207–225

---

[139] Lavrijssen et al. 2014, p. 62.

[140] Hirsch Ballin 2015, pp. 33–34.

[141] Lavrijssen 2014, p. 225.

Barkhuysen T (2015) Een revolutie in bestuursrecht [A revolution in administrative law]. NJB (Dutch Jurists Journal] 24:1583–1583
Caranta R, Andenas M, Fairgrieve D (2004) Independent Administrative Authorities. British Institute of International and Comparative Law, London
Coen D, Thatcher M (2005) The new governance of markets and non-majoritarian regulators. Governance and International Journal of Policy and Administration 18(3):329–346
Coglianese C (2015) Administrative law: the US and Beyond. In: Wright D (ed) International Encyclopedia of Social & Behavioral Sciences. Elsevier, Amsterdam, pp 109–114
Cohen-Eliya M, Porat I (2011) Proportionality and the Culture of Justification. The American Journal of Comparative Law 59(2):463–490
Crespo A, Lavrijssen S (2013) A legal assessment of the exemption of electricity producers from transport tariffs under EU law. European Engergy and Environmental Law Review 22(6):245–262
Damen L (2006) De bestuursrechter. Van materiële waarheidsvinder naar marginaal toetsende achteroverleuner? [The administrative judge. From material truth finder to marginally reviewing judge]. In: Asser W, Damen L Knigge G (authors) Partijautonomie of materiële waarheid? [Party autonomy or material truth?]. Boom Juridische Uitgevers, The Hague, pp 21–32
Damen L et al (2013) Bestuursrecht 2: Rechtsbescherming tegen de overheid, bestuursprocesrecht [Administrative Law 2: Legal protection agains the government, administrative procedural law]. Boom Juridische Uitgevers, The Hague
De Poorter J, Capkurt F (2017) Rechterlijke toetsing van algemeen verbindende voorschriften. Over de indringendheid van de rechterlijke toetsing in een toekomstig direct beroep tegen algemeen verbindende voorschriften [Judicial review of generally binding rules. About the penetration of the judicial review in a prospective direct appeal against general connection regulations]. NTB [Dutch Journal of Administrative Law] 3:84–95
De Waard B (2016) Proportionality: Dutch Sobriety. In: de Waard B, Ranchordás S (eds) The Judge and the Proportionate Use of Discretion. Routledge, London, pp 109–124
Duk W (1988) Beoordelingsvrijheid en beleidsvrijheid [Margin of appreciation and policy freedom]. RM Themis 4:157–158
Dutch Council of State (2017) Annual report Dutch Council of State. Accessible via http://jaarverslag.raadvanstate.nl/2017/visueel/uploads/2018/03/Webversie-jaarverslag-2017-Raad-van-State.pdf
Eijkens J (2015) Effective review of energy regulation in the Netherlands (master thesis). Tilburg University Press, Tilburg
Graham C (2009) Judicial Review of the Decision of the Competition Authorities and the Economic Regulators in the UK. In: Essens O, Gerbrandy A, Lavrijssen S (eds) National Courts and the Standard of Review in Competition Law and Economic Regulation. Europa Law Publishing, Groningen, pp 241–264
Gilardi F, Maggetti M (2011) The Independence of Regulatory Authorities. In: Levi-Faur D (ed) Handbook on Regulation. Edward Elgar, Cheltenham, pp 201–214
Hakvoort R, Knops H, Koutstaal P, van der Welle A, Gerdes J (2013) De tariefsystematiek van het elektriciteitsnet [The tarrif systematics of the power grid]. D-cision, ECN and TU Delft, Zwolle
Hancher L, Larouche P, Lavrijssen S (2003) Principles of good market governance. Journal of Network Industries 4(4):339–374
Harbo T-I (2010) The Function of the Proportionality Principle in EU Law. European Law Journal 16(2):158–185
Hirsch Ballin E (2015) Dynamiek in de bestuursrechtspraak: Over de betekenis van veranderingen in economie, politiek en samenleving voor de bestuursrechtelijk rechtsontwikkeling [Dynamics in administrative law: About the meaning of changes in economics, politics and society for the administrative law development]. In: Hirsch Ballin E, Ortlep R, Tollenaar A (authors) Rechtsontwikkeling door de bestuursrechter [Development in Administrative law by the administrative judge]. Boom Juridische Uitgevers, Den Haag, pp 1–58

Hofmann H, Rowe G, Türk A (2011) Administrative Law and Policy of the European Union. Oxford University Press, Oxford

Kerkmeester H (2016) Economic evidence in competition law: the experience from a national administrative court. In: Kovac M, Vandenberghe A (eds) European Studies in Law and Economics: Economic Evidence in EU Competition Law. Intersentia, Antwerp, pp 85–102

Lavrijssen S (2014) The Different Faces of the Energy Consumers: Towards a Behavioural Economics Approach. Journal of Competition Law and Economics 10(2):257–329

Lavrijssen S (2016) Waarborgen voor de energieconsument in de energietransitie [Guaranteeing for the energy consumer in the energy transition]. Tilburg University Press, Tilburg

Lavrijssen S, de Visser M (2006) Independent administrative authorities and the standard of judicial review. Utrecht Law Review 2(1):111–135

Lavrijssen S, Eijkens J, Rijkers M (2014) The role of the highest administrative court and the protection of the interest of the energy consumers in the Netherlands. TILEC, Tilburg

Lavrijssen S, Eijkens J, Capkurt F (2016) Rechterlijke toetsing van energieregulering door het CBb en het recht op effectieve rechtsbescherming [Judicial Review for energy regulation by the CBb (Board of Appeal for business) and the right to effective legal protection]. Tijdschrift voor Europees en economisch recht [Journal for European and economic law] 4:142–16

Lavrijssen S, Kohlbacher T (2018) EU electricity network codes: good governance in a network of networks. TILEC, Tilburg

Lowe P, Marquis M, Monti G (2013) European Competition Law Annual 2013: Effective and Legitimate Enforcement of Competition Law. Bloomsbury Publishing, Oxford

Mak E (2012) Judicial Review of Regulatory Instruments: The Least Imperfect Alternative? The Theory and Practice of Legislation 6:301–319

Mantzari D (2015) Economic Evidence in Regulatory Disputes: Revisiting the Court-Regulatory Agency Relationships in the US and the UK. Oxford Journal of Legal Studies 36(3):565–594

McLean J, Tushnet M (2015) Administrative Bureaucracy. In: Tushnet M, Fleiner T, Saunders C (eds) Routledge Handbook of Constitution Law. Routledge, London/New York, pp 121–130

Meuwese A, Schuurmans Y, Voermans W (2009) Towards a European Administrative Procedure Act. Review of European Administrative Law 2(2):3–35

Michiels F (2011) Hoofdzaken van het bestuursrecht [Essentials of administrative law]. Kluwer, Deventer

Oxera (2011) The opening regulatory asset base of the Dutch gas transmission system. https://www.acm.nl/sites/default/files/old_publication/bijlagen/4229_Regulatory%20Asset%20Base.pdf. Accessed 27 September 2018

Pront-van Bommel S (2010) De energieconsument centraal? [The Energy Consumer Central?]. In: Pront van-Bommel S (ed) De Consument en de andere kant van de elektriciteitsmarkt [The Consumer and the other side of the Electricity Market]. University of Amsterdam, Centrum voor Energievraagstukken [Centre for Energy Issues], Amsterdam, pp 44–50

Rose-Ackerman S, Jordao E (2014) Judicial Review of Executive Policymaking in Advanced Democracies: Beyond Rights Review. Administrative Law Review 66:1–73

Scheltema M (2014) Internationale regelgeving buiten de staten om: de behoefte aan bestuursrechtelijke beginselen over regelgeving [International legislation outside the states: the need for administrative principles on legislation]. NTB [Dutch Journal of Administrative Law] 28:236–241

Schlössels R, Zijlstra S (2010) Bestuursrecht in de sociale rechtsstaat [Administrative Law in the social constitutional state]. Kluwer, Deventer

Schueler B (2015) De verschuivende functies van de Awb [The shifting functions of the General Administrative Law Act]. RegelMaat 30(6):422–436

Schuurmans Y (2005) Bewijslastverdeling in het bestuursrecht: Zorgvuldigheid en bewijsvoering bij beschikkingen [Burden of proof in administrative law: Carefulness and reasoning with decisions] (thesis Amsterdam VU). Kluwer, Deventer

Schuurmans Y (2015) Van bestuursrechtelijke detailhandel naar maakindustrie [From administrative retail sector to manufacturing industry]. Inaugural address Leiden University, Leiden

Schuurmans Y, Voermans W (2010) Artikel 8:2 AWB: weg ermee! [Article 8:2 General Administrative Law Act: get rid of it!]. In: Barkhuysen T, den Ouden W, Polak J (eds) Bestuursrecht harmoniseren: 15 jaar Awb [Harmonising administrative law: 15 years of the General Administrative Law Act]. Boom Juridische Uitgevers, The Hague, pp 809–832

Stewart R (1975) The Reformation of American Administrative Law. Harvard Law Review 88 (8):1667–1813

Stroink F (1995) Judicial control of the administration's discretionary powers. In: Bakker R, Herringa A, Stroink F (eds) Judicial control, comparative essays on judicial review. Metro Publishing, Antwerp-Apeldoorn, pp 81–99

The Brattle Group (2007) GTS's RAB and implications for tariffs and investments. https://www.acm.nl/sites/default/files/old_publication/bijlagen/3824_BP.pdf. Accessed 28 September 2018

Van den Berge L (2017a) The relational turn in Dutch Administrative Law. Utrecht Law Review 13(1):99–111

Van den Berge L (2017b) Montesquieu and Judicial Review of Proportionality in Administrative Law: Rethinking the Separation of Powers in the Neoliberal Era. European Journal of Legal Studies 10(1):204–233

Van Gestel R (2014) Primacy of the European Legislature? Delegated Rule-Making and the Decline of the Transmission Belt Theory. The Theory and Practice of Legislation 2(1):34–59.

Van Gestel R, de Poorter J (2016) Putting Evidence-based lawmaking to the Test: The Judicial Review of Legislative Rationality. The Theory and Practice of Legislation 4(2):155–185

Van Male R (2016) Bestuursrechter is meest gerede rechter voor toetsing van bestuurswetgeving [Administrative judge is most obvious judge for review of administrative legislation]. NTB [Dutch Journal of Administrative Law] 15:127–129

Van Wijk H, Konijnenbelt W (2005) Hoofdstukken van bestuursrecht [Chapters of administrative law]. Elsevier, The Hague

Verhey L (2015) De markttoezichthouder als wetgever [The market monitor as legislator]. RegelMaat [Regularity] 30(3):165–169

Verhey L, Verheij N (2005) De macht van de marktmeesters [The power of the market masters]. Toezicht (Handelingen Nederlandse Juristen-Vereniging) [Control (Proceedings Dutch Jurists Association)]. Kluwer, Deventer, pp 153–330

Voermans W (2017) Besturen met regels, volgens regels [Control with rules, according to rules]. In: Voermans W, Schutgens R, Meuwese A (eds) Algemene regels in het bestuursrecht [General rules in adminstrative law]. Boom Juridische Uitgevers, The Hague, pp 10–84

Wade W, Forsyth C (2014) Administrative law. Oxford University Press, Oxford, pp 308–310

Zwart T, Verhey L (2003) Agencies in European and Comparative Law. Intersentia, Antwerp

# Part III
# Final Observations

# Chapter 9
# Judicial Review in Administrative Governance: A Theoretical Framework for Comparative Analysis

**Peter Lindseth**

## Contents



**Abstract** This chapter explores elements of a theoretical framework to better understand judicial review in administrative governance from a comparative perspective. It proceeds from the premise that administrative governance cannot sustain itself without maintaining a legitimating connection to the *trias politica*—legislative, executive, and judicial—in some historically or legally recognizable sense. Judicial review, together with political oversight by legislative and executive

Olimpiad S. Ioffe Professor of International and Comparative Law, Director of International Programs, University of Connecticut School of Law, USA; e-mail: peter.lindseth@uconn.edu.

P. Lindseth (✉)
University of Connecticut School of Law, Hartford, USA
e-mail: peter.lindseth@uconn.edu



J. de Poorter et al. (eds.), *Judicial Review of Administrative Discretion in the Administrative State*, https://doi.org/10.1007/978-94-6265-307-8_9

actors, serve as complementary mechanisms of mediated legitimacy in this sense. In addition, from a principal-agent perspective, judicial review can also be understood as reducing asymmetric information risks and the so-called agency-cost problem. To understand these functions more robustly, however, a historical, constructivist and genealogical approach is also needed. Such an approach allows us to understand the role played by judicial review in reconciling tensions between three ideal types of rule in administrative governance: democracy, technocracy, and juristocracy. Building on this theoretical foundation, we can better analyse, in comparative terms, how different polities have responded to several basic questions regarding judicial review in administrative governance: 'which' (judge/forum), 'whether' (preclusion), 'when' (admissibility/timing), 'who' (standing), 'what' (scope/depth/intensity or review), and ultimately 'why', i.e., the overarching purpose of judicial review in relation to sound regulatory decision making, democratic politics and the protection of fundamental rights.

**Keywords** Administrative governance · agency-cost problem · asymmetric information risk · constructivism · democracy · *dualité de juridiction*, expertise · historical and genealogical method · judicial review · juristocracy · mediated legitimacy · principal-agent theory · process review · regulation · rule of law · technocracy · *trias politica*

## 9.1 Introduction

This chapter explores elements of a possible theoretical framework to better understand judicial review in administrative governance from a comparative perspective. By judicial review, I am referring to forms of independent legal control exercised by judges sitting on either ordinary judicial courts or venerable court-like administrative jurisdictions (for example, the French *Conseil d'Etat* or the Dutch *Raad van State*).[1] This sort of independent legal control has been essential to the legitimation of administrative governance, i.e., the various forms of regulatory power (rulemaking, enforcement, or adjudication) that have diffused and fragmented away from the classic *trias politica*—legislatures, executives, and courts—over the last century, if not more. The key drivers in the growth of administrative governance have been intensifying regulatory demands posed by such phenomena as urbanization and industrialization; the movement of people, goods, and capital across borders; the increase in environmental threats, including of a trans-boundary character; and more recently digitalization and associated risks, just to name a few. A complex and variegated administrative sphere has developed in response to these phenomena, comprised of ministerial departments, agencies, bureaus, commissions, tribunals, public corporations, and the like. This sphere today operates at all levels

[1] Cf. Lindseth 2005a.

—subnational, national, supranational, and international—and indeed it often transcends what is traditionally understood as the public-private divide.[2]

And yet, while the growth and importance of administrative governance cannot be denied, its legitimacy remains suspect, despite its evident functional benefits. The problem is that administrative governance is perceived as operating in tension with our historic commitments to democratic and constitutional self-government represented in the classic *trias politica*. The administrative sphere often enjoys a significant degree of autonomy, whether de jure or de facto; nonetheless, it lacks the capacity to fully legitimize its output in autonomous terms. Legal empowerment and expertise in the face of functional demands all provide some measure of legitimacy for administration governance, albeit only incompletely. Experience shows, rather, that diffuse and fragmented administrative governance cannot sustain itself without 'maintaining the connection' to the more robustly legitimate *trias politica* in some historically or legally recognizable sense.[3] We can call this the 'mediated legitimacy' of administrative governance.[4]

As will be further explained in this chapter, judicial review is one of the core mechanisms of such mediated legitimacy, along with legislative and executive oversight. Institutional density and the complexity of the administrative sphere, along with its effective autonomy and broad discretion, all suggest the need for intensive judicial review. Nonetheless, we should never lose site of the equally important need from mediated legitimacy provided by political oversight, both legislative and executive. It is only by working together that these three complementary mechanisms provide the mediated legitimacy that administrative governance needs to sustain itself durably. Together the three mechanisms help modern societies reconcile the complex realities of administrative governance with our deeply held commitments to democratic and constitutional self-government inherited from the past.

## 9.2 Judicial Review as a 'Fire Alarm': The Perspective of Principal-Agent Theory

Our point of entry into this discussion is admittedly at a high level of abstraction. We begin with so-called principal-agent (PA) theory and, more specifically, the problem of reducing agency costs. This latter concept, derived from economics, refers to the challenge of reducing the risk to principals that their agents will pursue their own preferences rather than those of the principal. Modern states are, of course, rife with PA relationships and therefore agency-cost problems. These include, for example, the relationship between the electorate itself (the enfranchised

[2] See, e.g., Auby 2010; Verkuil 2007; Freeman 2006; Lindseth 2006.

[3] Cf. Strauss 1987, p. 493, and the discussion in Sect. 9.4 below.

[4] Lindseth 2004, 2010.

portion of the demos) and elected officials (government); between the legislature and the executive writ large; or, finally, between the political summit of the executive—e.g., a president or prime minister (depending on the system) as well as cabinet ministers—and the dense and complex administrative apparatus operating either under them or beyond the confines of the state. Legal control by judicial or administrative courts can play a crucial role in policing these various PA relationships, with the aim of reducing, if not eliminating entirely (an admittedly impossible task), the agency-cost problem.

At the heart of that problem are so-called asymmetric information risks, which flow from the fact that agents necessarily enjoy a good deal of autonomy and discretion, much of which is intended, via broad delegations to pursue functionally beneficial tasks that the principal is unable to pursue on its own. These tasks may include the regulation of a whole range of economic, social, environmental, or financial risks. As a consequence of this functionally-demanded autonomy, agents will necessarily possess more information about their regulatory activities than do their principals, which generally remain centralized. For that reason, principals must develop strategies to disgorge information from agents in order to make it possible to exercise oversight (at a minimum) or even outright control (if needed in the extreme), thus working to reduce agency costs.

One can understand judicial review of administrative action, at least in part, as one of several means by which principals manage asymmetric information risk and thus the agency-cost problem. In particular, judicial review can be understood as a vehicle by which a principal (normally a legislature) empowers third-parties (litigants) to pull what we can metaphorically call a *fire alarm*,[5] thus enlisting the aid of a judge to adjudicate whether the executive or administrative agent has acted unlawfully or unreasonably. Together with so-called *police patrols*—that is, hierarchical oversight and control by political actors (legislative and executive)—these mechanisms seek to overcome information asymmetry and thus reduce agency costs.[6] (They also, as noted above and developed further below, provide mediated legitimacy to the administrative sphere.)

PA theory is typically understood as a rational-choice approach to institutional analysis,[7] focusing on the incentives that purport to arise in any instance where one party (a principal) delegates power to another party (an agent) to pursue actions on the principal's behalf.[8] Like all abstract rationalist models, however, PA theory serves only as a starting point for analysis, focusing our attention—'as a matter of parsimony if nothing else'[9]—on certain basic incentives that operate in any system

[5] For an application of this concept in a comparative analysis of judicial review of administrative action, see, e.g., Ginsburg 2008, p. 63.

[6] The initial development of these concepts trace to McCubbins and Schwartz 1984.

[7] For an overview of the development of the theory, see Miller 2005. See also Karagiannis and Guidi 2017, pp. 16–18.

[8] For a succinct summary, see Pollack 2007.

[9] Langevoort 2018, p. 276.

of diffuse power. Nonetheless, to get a more complete picture of the governance system, we should not assume PA relationships operate according to some timeless and decontextualized logic or set of incentives. Rather, what we need to understand is how these relationships have actually evolved in the historical construction of particular systems of governance over time. In other words, we need to combine PA theory with a more constructivist and historical approach.[10] This tact is justified because, once we move from theoretical abstraction to an analysis of historical granularity (essential to comparative analysis), several complications and complexities necessarily intrude on our understanding of how PA relationships actually work, whether over time or in particular locations.

## 9.3 Complications and Complexities: Constructivism, History, and Genealogy

The most basic complication flows from the varied ways in which potential 'principals' and 'agents' in a governance system (e.g., the 'people', the 'legislature', the 'executive', the 'administration', etc.) have been historically constructed or reconstructed across time and place. Indeed, the very concepts of *delegation* between *principal* and *agent* have a normative and political history of their own, one that any comparative or theoretical perspective must take into account.[11] We must dispense, for example, with an idealized understanding of a 'Westphalian' constitutional principal with unbridled control over regulatory outcomes within a particular territory, an ahistorical reading of sovereignty if there ever was one.[12] As a consequence of institutional complexity, the power of control over administrative agents, whether de facto and de jure, is often greatly diminished, if sometimes nearly relinquished entirely, except in all but the most extreme circumstances.[13] Over the course of the twentieth century in particular, constitutional principals have often needed to settle for something less than actual control—perhaps merely

[10]This effort is in line with those who seek to draw 'on insights from both rationalist and constructivist scholarship' as a basis for better theorizing (Graham 2014, p. 367).

[11]See Lindseth 2010, pp. 54–55.

[12]See Sheehan 2006.

[13]In his contribution to this volume, John Bell discusses the PA model as merely one several possible models by which to understand accountability in administrative governance. The PA model is characterized, in his view, by hierarchical control, which he distinguishes from the 'representative-elector' model and the 'trustee' or 'fiduciary' model, which are characterized by less hierarchy and capacity for control. The present chapter takes the position that these are all merely different types of PA relationships, distinguished by the degree of effective autonomy in the agent or limits (legal or otherwise) on the capacity of the principal to exercise control. They are different in degree, but not in kind.

supervision or coordination—what an American might call oversight,[14] or a German *Steuerung*, or steering.[15]

Moreover, sometimes the complexity of modern governance seems to defy, at least empirically, the claim that a delegation of power in any meaningful sense has even occurred.[16] Particularly in the modern world of diffuse and fragmented regulatory power, whether within or beyond the state, it might seem that we are living in a world of 'agents without principals'.[17] What needs to be recognized, however, is that the psychology of actors in such a system is still often tied to PA notions—what I have called elsewhere the 'normative yearning for legitimate political control'.[18] Even without explicit articulation, this psychology often shapes the behaviour of individual actors and, through them, that of the system itself in a PA direction.[19] This is particularly the case where certain actors in the system—say, legislatures, chief executives—command significantly greater 'legitimacy resources' as compared with merely administrative actors, no matter how otherwise autonomous.[20]

What the presence of this psychology suggests is that our ability to interpret institutional relationships from a PA perspective is itself historically and culturally contingent, dependent on a particular normative-political evolution, which will in turn have a bearing on, but also be reciprocally shaped by, the co-evolution of various structural and procedural norms operating in the system. These may include, most importantly, the distinction between the constitutional and sub-constitutional—indeed administrative—realms, the former being the supposed domain of principals and the latter being that of agents. The reality is usually much messier. As Quentin Skinner has usefully reminded us, concepts that are 'so deeply enmeshed in so many ideological disputes over such a long period of time'—and constitutional and administrative certainly qualify—cannot be said to have an 'essence or natural boundaries'.[21] Rather, in a somewhat Nietzschean way, we are compelled to explore them *genealogically* (just as Ernst Hirsch Ballin seeks to do in his contribution to this volume).

The genealogical approach must therefore confront the varying understandings of notions like separation of powers—say, Westminster-style parliamentarism versus US presidentialism, as well as many variants in between and beyond[22]—

[14] See, e.g., Lindseth et al. 2008.

[15] Voßkuhle and Wischmeyer 2017.

[16] See, e.g., Grant and Keohane 2005 (noting the non-delegated nature of the power of most important global actors).

[17] Lindseth 2006.

[18] Lindseth 1999, p. 693.

[19] See, e.g., Lindseth 2006, 2002.

[20] Lindseth 2010, p. 11; see also Lindseth 2018.

[21] Skinner 2009, p. 326.

[22] On the fate of the classic *trias politica* in modern administrative governance, see, e.g., Ackerman 2010.

along with the demands of due process, to use the American terminology (other systems may of course use other terms). But it must also confront norms of a seemingly sub-constitutional character, which may derive from the aggregation of organic statutes, enabling acts, and general administrative procedure acts (although the accumulation of these various pieces of legislation could well be experienced as quasi-constitutional for a particular community).[23]

## 9.4 Reconciling Democracy, Technocracy, and Juristocracy

Another level of complexity arises from the challenge of reconciling tensions between three ideal types of rule—democracy, technocracy, and juristocracy—that typically operate to some degree in all systems of administrative governance. Judicial review plays a crucial role in this process of reconciliation while also being the protagonist in the final ideal type (about which more below).

### *9.4.1 Democracy*

We begin with *democracy* (rule by the demos, or 'people'), which arguably remains the overarching normative commitment in most modern polities. It also, however, is an 'essentially contested concept',[24] one whose substantive content and institutional realization is subject to significant debate and variation across time and place. The classic understanding of democracy, at least in the North Atlantic world, is generally associated with a particular institutional technology—the elected assembly as it emerged in the nineteenth century.[25] This technology operates against the background of certain liberal guarantees of publicity as well as freedom of expression, association, and of the press. But again, given the extent to which modern governance necessarily entails the diffusion and fragmentation of normative power into a complex administrative sphere, the challenge of vindicating this democratic vision—that is, of 'maintaining the connection'[26] between administrative governance and the elected assembly as the privileged expression of self-government—has been a significant one, particular over the last century.

In the face of this complex challenge, some actors in the system—and indeed many scholars—have been tempted to claim that democracy itself is taking on (or at

[23]The US Administrative Procedure Act (APA) is a classic example.
[24]Gallie 1956.
[25]Cf. Eley 1995, pp. 106–115.
[26]Strauss 1987, p. 493.

least should take on) a new, specifically 'administrative' form.[27] This new form of administrative democracy seeks to respond, in effect, to one of the core 'broken promises' of traditional electoral democracy identified by Norberto Bobbio in the 1980s,[28] notably the incapacities of centralized democratic sovereignty in the face of plural power centres and the triumph of neo-corporatist interest representation over political representation. Among those who hope to reconstruct democracy in a more administrative direction, alternative technologies beyond the elected assembly —typically transparency, participation, and reasoned decision-making within the administrative sphere itself—are seen as playing a crucial role. Procedural rights of this type in effect seek to replace what Bobbio called the 'centripetal' ideal of democracy—in which 'the many' become 'one'—with a resigned acceptance of the 'centrifugal' nature of society as a *polyarchy* with multiple power centres.[29] Through such rights, the complex plurality of interests in society can ideally assert themselves directly within administrative governance, through what some scholars call a 'directly-deliberative polyarchy'.[30]

The precise relationship between classical (electoral) and novel (administrative) forms of democracy, however, remains unclear in many systems. There can be no doubt that modern systems of administrative governance increasingly rely on forms of transparency, participation, and reasoned decision-making, often enforced through judicial review. Nonetheless, these mechanisms have not displaced traditional forms of hierarchical oversight and control by political actors, whether legislative or executive. What this lack of displacement suggests is that, as normative and regulatory power has diffused into a complex system of administrative governance, the *trias politica* has continued to serve, through various means of oversight and steering, as conduits through which the legitimacy of the new forms of administrative governance could be mediated in a historically recognizable, if still evolving, sense.[31] This is precisely the mediated legitimacy that I emphasized at the outset of this chapter.

### *9.4.2 Technocracy*

The effort at reconstructing the very meaning of democracy and separation of powers in modern administrative governance is very often seen as necessitated by the rise of *technocracy* (rule by experts), or at least by the pervasiveness of technocratic values as competing source of legitimation. The felt need for heightened transparency, participation, and reasoned decision-making is a testament to the

[27] See, e.g., Lamasurier 1980; Frug 1990; Im 2001; Daugeron 2011; Psygkas 2017.

[28] See generally Bobbio 1987.

[29] Bobbio 1987, p. 28.

[30] Cohen and Sabel 1997.

[31] See Lindseth 2004, pp. 1414–15; see also Lindseth 2010.

ever-increasing power of (purported) expertise both within and beyond the state, as well as the difficulty of 'maintaining the connection' in a classic sense.[32]

In this regard, doctrines of administrative law become an important site of contestation and renegotiation in this process of historical reconstruction (about which more in the next section). Perhaps the most prominent example is the well-known struggle to define a workable distinction between *politics* and *policy*, a distinction that can be said to underpin both legislative delegations as well as the constitutionalized demarcations that exist in certain systems between the realms of legislation and regulation.[33] In a similar vein one can look to the distinction between *policy* and *law*, which can be said to underpin doctrines of judicial deference to administrative determinations. The emergence of these sorts of distinctions can be understood, at least in part, as a vindication of technocratic values in the face of countervailing demands for political or judicial control of the administrative process.

### 9.4.3 *Juristocracy*

These distinctions can also be seen, however, as a way of warding off *juristocracy* (rule by judges). Indeed, one of the very interesting phenomena in modern administrative governance is the extent to which all actors in the system, judges perhaps above all, have internalized at least some measure of respect for the prerogatives of both scientific expertise and democratic politics as essential to defining the proper contours of the legal control of administrative action.

This internalization has, of course, not been absolute, particularly as concerns over proportionality and human rights have intensified over the last quarter century. Judges retain, *in extremis*, a sense of law's ultimate supremacy—the 'rule of law' in the most generic sense, even as that phrase may have a more specific meaning in some systems but not in others. This ultimate supremacy of the law can manifest itself in any number of ways, but allow me to stress two. First, judges sometimes find that the normative commitments to legal supremacy may require the enforcement of legislative mandates against technocracy, thus allying juristocracy with the elected assembly. Second, judges sometimes conclude that even the product of a momentary democratic majority—legislation—needs to give way to commands of a constitutional nature, in which case juristocracy is the ally, at least in theory, of the constituent power. But the linkage between judicially pronounced constitutional norms and the constitutional text can sometimes be tenuous (as in the

---

[32] Strauss 1987, p. 493.

[33] Articles 34 and 37 of the French Constitution of 1958 is the classic example of such a textual demarcation. However, this demarcation has a judicial counterpart, in judge-made doctrines that seek to specify certain 'reserved domains' (*Vorbehalt des Gesetzes*, *riserva di legge*) in which the legislature must define the controlling norms itself, as a protection against a return to dictatorship through legislative abdication. See generally Lindseth 2004.

case, say, of judicially articulated 'general principles of law'). As the linkage to the constitutional text becomes ever more distant in some instances, we may well be in the realm of juristocracy *tout court*.[34]

In carrying out these ultimately juristocratic tasks (even if only episodically, given the nature of administrative litigation), judges are often motivated by the classic ideal of rendering justice in the particular case. Nonetheless, concerns over the systemic consequences of particularized decisions are generally never far from the surface; that is, invoking a higher-law norm to protect a litigant from unlawfully or unreasonably exercised public power can almost always be justified as a means of promoting systemic legitimacy. In these instances, the litigant has successfully enlisted the aid of a judge to vindicate that party's particular interest over that of the public (or 'general') interest putatively represented by the administrative actor exercising authority delegated from the legislature. How aggressively the judge undertakes this role, responding to the 'fire alarm' on behalf of litigants, will necessarily have a bearing on, but also be informed by, the dominant understandings of the proper balance of power between general and particular interests (including human rights), as well as between democracy (politics), technocracy (expertise), and juristocracy (law) in the system.

## 9.5 Elements of a Framework for Comparative Analysis

### *9.5.1 Five Basic Questions (and the Historical Genealogy That Might Help Answer Them)*

Armed with this theoretical background, we can now ask: How have these types of complications and complexities manifested themselves in various systems of judicial review? To answer this overarching question, we could usefully consider five even more basic sub-questions that every system must answer: (1) *which* judge should be charged with the task of legal control of administrative governance; (2) *whether* there are any matters categorically beyond the legal cognizance of the judge (what Americans call 'preclusion' of judicial review that arises in some instances); (3) *when* is it appropriate for the judge to intervene in the administrative process in response to a litigant's complaint (admissibility/timing); (4) *who* may properly invoke the power of the judge to exercise legal control (standing); and (5) *what* types of questions (fact/law/policy) may the judge properly address and in what depth when exercising the power of legal control?[35] These questions might

[34]For a critical take on the phenomenon from the perspective of political economy, discursive politics, and redistributive outcomes, see Hirschl 2007.

[35]I make no claim of originality in posing these questions, which in some form are often used as a basis for teaching judicial review in introductory administrative law courses in the United States. See, e.g., Lawson 2007. Note also that I reserve a final, ultimate question of 'why' (the overarching

appear of a technical nature (for example, admissibility/timing and standing, as in questions 3 and 4). But we should also recognize how, upon closer examination, they are sites of contestation and negotiation over the more fundamental complications and complexities outlined in the prior section, as well as several others outlined below.

To analyse how systems have answered these questions, comparative analysis must again adopt a genealogical approach, seeking to uncover historical and cultural underpinnings that might help explain variations across time and place. Limiting myself here to stereotypical 'common law' versus 'continental' distinctions (which I intentionally caricature for purposes of provoking further reflection), these underpinnings might include: divergent understandings of the relationship between state and society (a *state* which shapes society through 'representing the general interest' vs. a *society* which constrains the state through what might be called a 'constitution of liberty'); a different understanding of the relationship between administration and sovereignty (administration as somehow possessing an elemental state power over society vs. administration as enjoying only delegated power within a limited/constrained state); a different understanding of the relationship between administration and justice (administration as an instrument of 'the general interest' vs. justice as the defence of 'particular interests' and thus somewhat suspect); a different set of legal-cultural images of the administrative actor (variously a Hegelian *pouvoir neutre* existing above social divisions, or a Weberian/rational technocrat bearing the authority of the general-interest state, vs. a mere bureaucrat who is the product of interest-group politics, susceptible to capture, and thus in need of constraint); a different conception of the locus of administration within the state (administrative centralization and hierarchy vs. administrative diffusion/fragmentation and polyarchy); and finally a different conception of the relationship of administration to legality (administration as unable to act without clear legal authority—the 'legal state', *Rechtsstaat*, *état de droit*, etc.—vs. a system which accepts/tolerates administrative discretion to a much greater degree, within the broad limits of the 'rule of law').

These varying historical distinctions obviously pull in different directions. Moreover, in the European case, they may well have been overwhelmed by the functional and normative demands of European integration over the last seven decades, as reflected in the respective legal edifices constructed by the European Court of Justice and the European Court of Human Rights (as several contributions to this volume suggest). The extent to which such historical distinctions continue to impact our five questions—perhaps as trace elements, given significant convergence over the last half century; perhaps with continuing salience despite the apparent convergence, albeit below the surface—is too great an analytical task for this brief chapter to undertake. Rather, the focus of the remainder of this section will instead be on the first and last of our five questions and how they manifest

purpose of judicial review in relation to sound regulatory decision making, democratic politics and the protection of fundamental rights) for the conclusion to this chapter.

themselves in various systems in Europe—notably in the UK, at the EU level, and, most importantly, in the Netherlands—as suggested by the other contributions to this volume.

### 9.5.2 Which Forum? Which Judge?

We begin with the UK, which serves as a useful reminder that legality is merely one dimension of administrative accountability more generally. John Bell's contribution notes how in the UK, as in many other systems, legal review by courts is necessarily supplemented by review by ombuds on questions of maladministration as well as specialized tribunals (often comprised of subject matter experts) on the actual merits of the administrative decision under challenge. Bell argues that accountability in the fullest sense requires 'braiding' among the various types of review mechanisms; external control of legality alone is insufficient. Deni Mantzari, in her chapter on the UK, makes a similar point. She notes that the fragmentation of the various channels of accountability reflects what Richard Rawlings has called 'multi-streamed jurisdiction' in the UK.[36] Focusing specifically on how this fragmentation manifests itself in the competition law space, Mantzari discerns a tripartite relationship among, first, expert regulators at the agency level; second, an expert tribunal—the Competition Appeal Tribunal (CAT)—charged with merits review; and third and finally, the generalist Court of Appeal charged with review on questions of law. What emerges out of this tripartism is a system of review of varying intensity along a continuum, in which the interaction between specialists and generalists plays a crucial role determining the scope and depth of review at each point.

We might pause here to consider an interesting historical irony in this fragmentation of the various channels of administrative accountability in the UK. What it suggests is that, in the face of the functional demands of regulation, the UK has seen fit over the last half century to move well beyond even the classic *dualité de juridiction* in the French sense—something infamously denounced by Dicey as anathema to British sensibilities—to a multiplicity of jurisdictions in order to meet the challenge of accountability in modern administrative governance. Indeed, the classic justification of separate judicial and administrative courts—*juger l'administration, c'est encore administrer* (to judge the administration is still to administer) —arguably applies to this multiplicity with even greater force, particularly as between merits tribunals and courts. This fragmentation suggests the need for a judge not merely imbued with *le sens de l'Etat*—the classic French justification for separate administrative courts—but *le sens de l'expert*, or deep subject-matter knowledge and understanding. This perhaps explains, as mentioned by Mantzari, the multiplicity of fragmented merits tribunals along sectoral lines in the UK, e.g.,

[36] Rawlings 2008, p. 96.

for water (OFWAT), communications (OFCOM), and energy (OFGEM). And yet, even with the creation of specialized agencies and tribunals to bring expertise to bear in these various regulatory domains, the system still preserves an appeal on the law to more robustly legitimated judges on the Court of Appeal, thus preserving mediated legitimacy and in some sense reconciling new regulatory demands with older commitments to the rule of law as represented by the judicial courts.[37]

The process of European integration over the last seven decades can be understood as facilitating a kind of jurisdictional fragmentation as well, only now between the national and supranational levels. The EU's system of judicial remedies, especially the ECJ's seemingly exclusive interpretive jurisdiction under the preliminary reference procedure, arguably manifests an analogous principle—*juger l'intégration, c'est encore intégrer*—to judge integration is still to integrate. The theory goes something like this: Judicial review of EU law can have a direct impact on the success or failure of market integration on a supranational scale; consequently, the drafters of the treaties placed exclusive jurisdiction over treaty interpretation in an adjudicative body that was autonomously supranational, imbued with *le sens de l'Union* (so to speak) and therefore reliably committed to the 'EU interest'.[38] Of course, the EU courts can act directly as a judge of administrative legality vis-à-vis the regulatory decision making of Union bodies. The paradigmatic case is in the competition law context, where firms can appeal from Commission-imposed fines and penalties, first to the General Court, and then to the ECJ. But as Rob Widdershoven stresses in his contribution here, the vast majority of instances in which EU law is enforced against private parties takes place at the national level, by national authorities. Disputes over these national-level administrative applications of EU law come before a supranational judge by way of preliminary reference.

### 9.5.3 *What Scope of Review? What Depth of Review?*

The EU case is also helpful as we turn from the question of which forum/judge to what scope/depth of review. ('Scope' refers to the range of questions the judge might examine—law, fact, policy discretion—whereas 'depth' refers to the extent to which the judge will undertake a de novo examination of these questions or defer in some measure to the determinations of the administrative actor.) As Widdershoven emphasizes, in the EU case the level of review is often a function of the regulatory context: less intensive review demanded in technically complex domains, where regulators enjoy a margin of discretion or appreciation; more intensive review, particularly with regard to proportionality, demanded in cases imbued with concerns over fundamental rights. However, in the great sweep of

[37] For additional historical perspective on how this process of mediated legitimacy and reconciliation has worked, cf. Lindseth 2005a, b.

[38] For a scholarly defense of this position, see Baquero Cruz 2008, pp. 414–15.

cases, in which the national regulator enjoys a margin of discretion in technically complex domains (the core of modern risk regulation and administrative governance), Widdershoven discerns a clear trend in EU law toward 'process review', paralleling what the ECJ applies to the review of the EU's own regulatory acts.[39]

Process review is particularly illuminating of several of the tensions explored in Sect. 9.4, notably as between the proper realms of 'policy' and 'law'. It is also something well familiar to US administrative lawyers, because a similar form of review is dominant in our administrative law. In theory, such review is not on the policy merits (out of fear of violating the great taboo in administrative justice today—in which a generalist judge substitutes his or her judgment for that of the more expert regulator). Rather, the focus is on the quality of the regulator's decision-making *process*, understood not strictly in terms of procedure (although procedural legality of course matters) but rather in terms of the adequacy of the evidentiary record and the rational relationship between the evidence found and the regulatory choice made.

In its way, this balance can be understood as the translation of the admonition of *juger l'administration, c'est encore administrer* into the question of the intensity of review. Process review is meant to be deferential on matters of policy, as long as it remains within the bounds of the law (who decides that legal question is also potentially subject to deference—a strong point of contrast between some systems).[40] Within those bounds, regulators should be able to choose any outcome reasonably supported by the evidentiary record, as long as that record is not vitiated by manifest errors in the establishment of the facts (a highly deferential standard). Nonetheless, process review still requires judges to examine the regulators' claim of a rational relationship between the facts found and the policy choice made. That claim must be supported by an adequate statement of reasons, transparent to regulated interests, regulatory beneficiaries, as well as the reviewing court. In effect, the judge must examine whether the regulator can defend the policy choice *in technocratic terms* by reference to evidence and well-articulated explanations. Only then will judicial deference be appropriate. In this way, the court both acknowledges the need for deference while nonetheless asserting that the deference cannot be absolute, consistent with the demands of the judicial role in providing mediated legitimacy and oversight.

One might fairly ask whether this is really judicial deference at all or merely an elaborate jurisprudential pretext for courts to interfere in administrative decision making. Perhaps it is both. But in some sense there is no real answer to the objection, because, genealogically speaking, the question implicates one of the deepest debates in the history of administrative governance: how to distinguish between the proper realms of justice and administration?[41] Just as the adage *juger*

---

[39] Cf. Lenaerts 2012.

[40] See, e.g., Craig 2017.

[41] In fact, this debate goes back several hundred years. See, e.g., Boulet-Sautel 1980; see also Mannori and Sordi 2009, 2013.

*l'administration, c'est encore administrer* reflects one perspective in that debate, so too does the famous counter-point advanced by a leading member of the *Conseil d'Etat* in the mid-nineteenth century: *juger, c'est juger.*[42] In short, to judge is to render justice, which requires a forum independent of the 'active' administration, bringing to bear the historical concerns of law—procedural fairness, lack of bias, fact gathering by way of probative and relevant evidence, respect for legal rules and principles, and the logical coherence of decision making.[43]

### 9.5.4 The Dutch Context

Today, the effort to distinguish justice from administration is less jurisdictional and more substantive, manifesting itself primarily (but hardly exclusively)[44] in the debate over of the proper scope of judicial review. And indeed, if the contributions in this volume are any guide, this debate appears to be particularly alive in the Dutch context. That is not to say that the Dutch debate is without an important jurisdictional dimension: As Tom Barkhuysen and Michiel van Emmerik outline in their contribution, the Dutch system is characterized not only by a *dualité de juridiction* in the French sense (as between the ordinary judicial courts and the Council of State as the general administrative court) but also by fragmentation among other sectoral jurisdictions in the direction of what we also see in the UK. A leading example is the *College van Beroep voor het bedrijfsleven* (the Appeals Tribunal for Trade and Industry, or CBB), the focus of the contribution of Saskia Lavrijssen and Fatma Çapkurt on judicial review in the energy sector. Further complicating the jurisdictional picture in the Netherlands is, as elsewhere in Europe, the existence of supranational courts, both in the EU (the ECJ in Luxembourg) and in the Council of Europe (the ECtHR in Strasbourg). Decisions by both jurisdictions have played catalytic roles in Dutch administrative justice, both in terms of the availability[45] and the intensity of external legal control.[46]

---

[42] Vivien 1852, p. 130.

[43] A version of this debate appears in other systems as well. The contribution of Tom Barkhuysen and Michiel van Emmerik in this volume contains a nice summary of the debate among Dutch scholars (notably Struycken and Loeff) on this very question.

[44] Obviously, questions of preclusion and timing of judicial review, as well as of standing—our second, third, and fourth basic questions—implicate these concerns as well. Regarding the latter, for example, John Bell notes that UK administrative law has moved away from a rights-based model of standing to a public interest model. Such a doctrinal shift opens the way for a significantly broader category of potential litigants to pull the 'fire alarm' in a PA-theoretical sense, thereby inviting greater judicial scrutiny of administrative action. Contrast this with the restrictive *Plaumann* formula (derived from case 25/62, *Plaumann & Co. v. Commission*, 1963 E.C.R. 95) that has long dominated the standing jurisprudence of the ECJ in the review of EU level acts. See Meuwese 2013.

[45] ECtHR, October 23, 1985, No. 8848/80, *AB*, 1986, 1 (*Benthem*).

[46] ECJ, Case C-12/03 *Commission v. Tetra Laval* [2005] ECLI:EU:C:2005:87.

While the availability question is now reasonably well-settled in the Netherlands, the intensity question appears to be in a continuing state of flux. That flux derives, apparently, from the challenge of reconciling two conflicting legal-cultural currents: on the one hand, the vestigial commitment of some judges to constrained forms of legal review in favour of political oversight; and, on the other, pressures coming from domestic commentators—as well as arguably from the EU level—to intensify judicial review at least in certain regulatory domains (for example, deepening the proportionality analysis where fundamental rights are at stake).

Ernst Hirsch Ballin has been at the forefront of this debate, arguing for intensified judicial review both in his 2015 report *Dynamiek in de bestuursrechtspraak* ('Dynamics in Administrative Adjudication'),[47] as well as in this book. His call for a rethinking of the proper balance between political oversight and judicial review—born of concerns over the diffuse and fragmented realities of modern administrative governance, as well as what appears to be an unusually deferential approach of Dutch judges—seems to be having its intended effect. Hirsch Ballin's call has garnered the support of all his fellow Dutch contributors to this volume, including the current chair of the Administrative Jurisdiction Division (AJD) of the Dutch Council of State, Bart Jan van Ettekoven, one of Hirsch Ballin's successors in that role. Van Ettekoven contributes an illuminating overview of the AJD's recent efforts to expand the scope and depth of its review in various domains, including the review of secondary legislation—generally binding regulations—a topic examined in detail in a chapter by Jurgen de Poorter as well.

Given the higher visibility of such regulations, this type of administrative action would be likely to attract greater (and more robustly legitimate) political scrutiny, thus perhaps justifying more judicial deference. Consequently, any intensification of judicial review in this domain leads us to an ultimate question with which we shall close: what is or should be the purpose of judicial review relative political oversight of administrative action?

## 9.6 Conclusion: Why Judicial Review?

There are many possible answers to this ultimate question. Judicial review must of course never lose sight of the obligation to render justice in the individual case, most importantly by protecting any applicable fundamental rights. But beyond that broadly shared goal, what should be purpose of judicial review of administrative action, particularly in relation to promoting sound policy-making as well as reinforcing democratic oversight and control?

From one perspective, courts should resign themselves to the current realities of technocracy, enforcing transparency and participation rights, as well as reason-giving obligations by administrative actors, in order to realize a sort of

[47] Hirsch Ballin 2015.

non-hierarchical, bottom-up form of ‘administrative democracy’. From another perspective, judges might adopt a more juristocratic strategy, recognizing that, because hierarchical political control by legislative and executive actors can no longer serve a robust legitimating function (given the realities of bureaucratic density and complexity, along with broad discretion within the administrative sphere), intensified judicial review is needed to counter-act those trends.

In their concerns about the possibilities of traditional electoral democracy or effective political oversight, these two perspectives bring to mind a famous observation of Léon Aucoc, a French *conseillier d'Etat* under the Second Empire. Aucoc argued that, in the absence of robust political legitimation in other forms, administrative justice should serve as a kind of ‘safety-valve which should always remain open’.[48] There is much truth in this statement. It is quite similar to the idea, set out in Sect. 9.2 above, that judicial review can serve as a kind of ‘fire alarm’ (apologies for the mixed metaphors), in which litigants enlist the aid of a judge to adjudicate whether the executive or administrative agent has acted unlawfully or unreasonably. But we should always remember that such judicial ‘fire alarms’ are supposed to work in conjunction with ‘police patrols’ by robustly legitimated political institutions. Both the technocratic and juristocratic strategies would seem to greatly discount the value or potential of the latter in favour of the former, creating an ultimately juristocratic safety-valve in the face of the technocratic realities of modern administrative governance.

This chapter concludes on a slightly different note. It retains a perhaps quixotic attachment to democratic self-government as expressed in the *trias politica*, even as functional demands have diffused and fragmented regulatory power into a dense and complex administrative sphere to a considerable extent (and often for sound regulatory reasons). From this perspective, among the core purposes of judicial review of administrative action (including in the enforcement of transparency, participation, and reason-giving obligations) should be to help facilitate democratically legitimate oversight by institutions of representative government, both legislative and executive. Stated in terms of PA theory, the aim should be to reduce asymmetric information risks and agency costs so that democratic and constitutional principals can exercise oversight and perhaps even control over their far-flung agents when needed.

From this perspective, beyond doing justice in the individual case, judges should also seek to mediate the legitimacy of administrative governance in conjunction with the political branches. They should work to achieve a reconciliation between, on the one hand, the inevitability of technocracy and juristocracy in administrative governance and, on the other, our deeply held commitments to democratic self-government inherited from the past. This reconciliation may often favour a balance between deference and scrutiny of the type that process-oriented review

[48] Lampué 1954, p. 380.

seeks to effectuate. Out of such a reconciliation, one hopes, courts can strive to make their own contribution to a durable constitutional settlement for administrative governance over the long term.

## References


Ackerman B A (2010) Good-bye Montesquieu. In: Rose-Ackerman S, Lindseth P L (eds) Comparative administrative law. Edward Elgar Publishing, Cheltenham, pp 128–133

Auby J B (2010) Contracting out and 'public values': A theoretical and comparative approach. In: Rose-Ackerman S, Lindseth P L (eds) Comparative administrative law. Edward Elgar Publishing, Cheltenham, pp 511–523

Baquero Cruz J (2008) The legacy of the Maastricht-Urteil and the pluralist movement. European Law Journal 14:389–422

Bobbio N (1987) The future of democracy: A defence of the rules of the game. University of Minnesota Press, Minnesota

Boulet-Sautel M (1980) Police et administration en France à la fin de l'ancien régime [Police and administration in France at the end of the old regime]. In: Paravicini W, Werner K F (eds) Histoire Comparée de l'administration (IVe-XVIIIe Siècles) [Comparative history of administration (IVth-XVIIIth centuries)]. Artemis, Munich, pp 47–51

Cohen J, Sabel C F (1997) Directly-deliberative polyarchy. European Law Journal 3:313–342

Craig P (2017) Judicial review of questions of law: A comparative perspective. In: Rose-Ackerman S, Lindseth P L (eds) Comparative administrative law. Edward Elgar Publishing, Cheltenham, pp 449–465

Daugeron B (2011) La démocratie administrative dans la théorie du droit public: retour sur la naissance d'un concept [The administrative democracy in public law theory: a look back at the birth of a concept]. Revue Française d'Administration Publique [French Journal on public administration] 137–138:21–37

Eley G (1995) The social construction in Germany, 1871–1933. In: Andrews G R, Chaphman H (eds) The social construction of democracy, 1870–1990. New York University Press, New York, pp 90–117.

Freeman J (2006) Extending public accountability through privatization: From public law to publicization. In: Dowdle M W (ed) Public Accountability: designs, dilemmas and Experiences. Cambridge University Press, Cambridge, pp 83–114

Frug J (1990) Administrative Democracy. University of Toronto Law Journal 40:559–586

Gallie J (1956) Essentially contested concepts. Proceedings of the Aristotelian Society 56:167–198

Ginsburg T (2008) Administrative law and judicial control of agents in authoritarian regimes. In: Ginsburg T, Moustafa T (eds) Rule by law: the politics of courts in authoritarian regimes. Cambridge University Press, Cambridge, pp 58–72

Graham E R (2014) International organizations as collective agents: fragmentation and the limits of Principal control at the World Health Organization. European Journal of International Relations 20:366–390

Grant R W, Keohane R O (2005) Accountability and abuses of power in world politics. American Political Science Review 99:29–43

Hirsch Ballin E M H (2015) Dynamiek in de bestuursrechtspraak: over de betekenis van veranderingen in economie, politiek en samenleving voor de bestuursrechterlijke rechtsontwikkeling [Dynamics in administrative law: about the meaning of changes in economy, politics and society for the development of administrative law]. In: Hirsch Ballin E M H, Ortlep R, Tollenaar A (eds) Rechtsontwikkeling door de bestuursrechter, VAR Vereniging voor Bestuursrecht [Legal development by the administrative judge, VAR Association for Administrative Law]. Boom Juridische Uitgevers, The Hague, pp 7–58

Hirschl R (2007) Towards juristocracy: the origins and consequences of the new constitutionalism. Harvard University Press, Cambridge
Im S (2001) Bureaucratic power, democracy and administrative democracy. Ashgate, Aldershot
Karagiannis Y, Guidi M (2017) Principal-agent models and EU policy-making. In: Zahariadis N, Buonanno L (eds) The Routledge Handbook of European Public Policy. Routledge, New York
Lamasurier J (1980) Vers une démocratie administrative: du refus d'informer au droit d'être informé [Towards an administrative democracy: from the refusal to inform to the right to be informed]. Revue du Droit Public 5:1239–1269
Lampué P (1954) Le développement historique du recours pour excès de pouvoir depuis ses origins jusqu'au début du XXe siècle [The historical development of the recourse for abuse of power from its origins to the beginning of the XXth century]. Revue Internationale des Sciences Administratives 2:359–392
Langevoort D C (2018) Behavioral ethics, behavioral compliance. In: Arlen J (ed) Research Handbook on Corporate Crime and Financial Misleading. Edward Elgar Publishing, Cheltenham, pp 263–281
Lawson G (2007) Federal administrative law, 4th edn. Thomson/West, St. Paul, MN
Lenaerts K (2012) The European Court of Justice process-oriented review. College of Europe, Research Papers in Law 1/2012
Lindseth P L (1999) Democratic legitimacy and the administrative character of Supranationalism: The example of the European Community. Columbia Law Review 99:628–738
Lindseth P L (2002) Delegation is dead, long live delegation: managing the democratic disconnect in the European market-polity. In: Joerges C, Dehousse R (eds) Good governance in Europe's integrated market. Oxford University Press, Oxford, pp 139–166
Lindseth P L (2004) The paradox of parliamentary supremacy: delegation, democracy, and dictatorship in Germany and France, 1920s–1950s. Yale Law Journal 113:1341–1415
Lindseth P L (2005a) "Always embedded" administration: the historical evolution of administrative justice as an aspect of modern governance. In: Joerges C, Stråth B, Wagner P (eds) The economy as a polity: The political constitution of contemporary capitalism. UCL Press, London, pp 117–136
Lindseth P L (2005b) Reconciling with the past: John Willis and the question of judicial review in inter-war and post-war England. University of Toronto Law Journal 55:657–689
Lindseth P L (2006) Agents without Principals?: Delegation in an age of diffuse and fragmented governance. In: Cafaggi F (ed) Reframing self-regulation in European private law. Kluwer Law International, Alphen aan den Rijn, pp 107–130
Lindseth P L (2010) Power and legitimacy: Reconciling Europe and the nation-state. Oxford University Press, Oxford
Lindseth P L (2018) The metabolic constitution and the limits of EU legal pluralism. In: Davies G, Avbelj M (eds) Research handbook in legal pluralism in EU Law. Edward Elgar Publishing, Cheltenham, pp 223–242
Lindseth P L, Aman A C, Raul A C (2008) Administrative law of the European Union: Oversight. ABA Publishing, Chicago
Mannori L, Sordi B (2009) Science of administration and administrative law. In: Hofmann H, Grossi P, Canale D (eds) A treatise of legal philosophy and general jurisprudence, Vol. 9, A history of the philosophy of law in the civil law world, 1600–1900. Springer, New York, pp 225–261
Mannori L, Sordi B (2013) Storia del diritto amministrativo [History of administrative law]. Laterza, Rome
McCubbins M D, Schwartz T (1984) Congressional oversight overlooked: Police patrols versus fire alarms. American Journal of Political Science 28:165–179
Meuwese A (2013) Standing rights and regulatory dynamics in the EU. In: Popelier P, Mazmanyan A, Vandenbruwaene W (eds) The role of constitutional courts in multilevel governance. Intersentia, Cambridge, pp 291–310
Miller G J (2005) The political evolution of principal-agent models. Annual Review of Political Science 8:203–225

Pollack M A (2007) Principal-agent analysis and international delegation: Red herrings, theoretical Clarifications, and empirical disputes [WWW Document]. Bruges Political Research Papers Cah. Rech. Political Bruges No 2 Febr. 2007. http://papers.ssrn.com/sol3/papers.cfm?abstract_id=1011324. Accessed 28 September 2009

Psygkas A (2017) From the "democratic deficit" to a "democratic surplus": Constructing administrative democracy in Europe. Oxford University Press, Oxford

Rawlings R (2008) Modeling judicial review. Current Legal Problems 61:95–123

Sheehan J J (2006) Presidential address: The problem of sovereignty in European history. American Historical Review 111:1–15

Skinner Q (2009) A genealogy of the modern state. Proceedings of the British Academy 162:325–370

Strauss P L (1987) Formal and functional approaches to separation-of-powers questions–A foolish inconsistency? Cornell Law Review 72:488–526

Verkuil P R (2007) Outsourcing sovereignty: Why privatization of government functions threatens democracy and what we can do about it. Cambridge University Press, Cambridge

Vivien A (1852) Etudes administratives. Guillaumin, Paris

Voßkuhle A, Wischmeyer T (2017) The 'Neue Verwaltungsrechtswissenschaft' against the backdrop of traditional administrative law scholarship in Germany. In: Rose-Ackerman S, Lindseth P L, Emerson B (eds) Comparative administrative law, 2nd edn. Edward Elgar Publishing, Cheltenham, pp 85–101

# Chapter 10
# Observations and Outlook

**Ernst Hirsch Ballin**

Judicial review of administrative acts is one of the core characteristics of a democracy under the rule of law. Several contributions to this volume have demonstrated that the judiciary indeed holds the clue to what Susan Rose-Ackerman refers to as 'the administrative law and policy puzzle'.[1] Moreover, the contributions to this volume have charted, both from an internal and external perspective, how the workings of a judicial review reflect changes in the administrative organization, constitutional processes and society in countries, such as the Netherlands, with a high-level mode of governance and administrative organization.

A question that repeatedly comes to the forefront concerns the legitimacy of judicial powers compared to that of political powers. This question refers to the complexities of constitutional systems. A constitutional system consists of institutions that mutually define each other's position, and the processes of their

[1] Rose-Ackerman 2012, p. 682.

Ernst Hirsch Ballin is distinguished university professor (Tilburg University), professor in human rights law (University of Amsterdam), and president of the Asser Institute for International and European Law. He is also a member of the Scientific Council for Government policy (WRR). Ernst Hirsch Ballin was since 2000 a member and since 2003 the president of the Administrative Jurisdiction Division of the Council of State, until he was reappointed as the Minister of Justice of the Netherlands (2006–2010). He recently published on the future of the European Union, citizens' rights and fundamental rights protection, and trust in the rule of law; e-mail: ballin@uvt.nl.

E. Hirsch Ballin (✉)
Tilburg University, Tilburg, The Netherlands
e-mail: ballin@uvt.nl

E. Hirsch Ballin
University of Amsterdam, Amsterdam, The Netherlands



J. de Poorter et al. (eds.), *Judicial Review of Administrative Discretion in the Administrative State*, https://doi.org/10.1007/978-94-6265-307-8_10

interaction. Building on the rich variety of insights and experience in the preceding chapters, we conclude this volume with a brief exploration of the constitutional status of judicial review in a democracy under the rule of law (*democratische rechtsstaat*) such as the Netherlands.

While the notion of the separation of powers—legislative, judicial and executive in Montesquieu's *trias politica* theorem—obviously comes to mind here, the functions of the administrative state extend beyond the confines of the traditional trio. On the one hand, administrative acts under judicial review exceed what could be seen as merely the execution of laws, while, on the other hand, many of these acts are based on powers attributed to agencies and bureaucracies that are not or not fully subject to political oversight. This is one of the reasons why contributions to this volume have questioned the traditional justification of judicial self-restraint.

Apart from the fact that functions and powers not fitting into the *trias politica* theorem have been identified,[2] the constitutional significance of judicial review has as much to do with relations between the state powers as with their separation. A mature democratic constitution gives voice to citizens in lawmaking and policymaking, recognizes and implements their fundamental rights, and provides them and the society as a whole with norms and services based on the expertise of those performing public service. Chapter 7 of this volume acknowledges the constitutional theory presented by Daniel Halberstam as a suitable basis for analysing present-day constitutional complexities because of its orientation on three foundational constitutional values: voice, rights and expertise.[3]

Notwithstanding the rise—often for good reasons—of autonomous agencies, a large part of the public administration continues to function under political guidance or supervision. In both cases, the political legitimation resources with respect to individual decisions are limited. As Peter Lindseth explains in his contribution, they require complementing by other sources of 'mediated legitimacy' in the 'triangle of democracy, technocracy, and juristocracy'. In other words, judicial review does not replace or supplant political legitimation. It is needed not only as a protection against politically motivated intrusion in the individual's interests, but also contributes positively to the (mediated) legitimacy of administrative action in a democratic state. In Peter Lindseth's words (in the final section of the chapter), 'among the core purposes of judicial review of administrative action (including in the enforcement of transparency, participation, and reason-giving obligations) should be to help facilitate democratically legitimate oversight by institutions of representative government, both legislative and executive.'

Future research may further elaborate on the outlook for a synergetic interaction between judicial review and democratic legitimation. This essentially depends on our understanding of democracy, and specifically whether we view democracy as the electoral empowerment of authorities, or as a 'debate and discussion aimed at

[2] Such as the governing function, which consists in giving political direction to a polity (see Bin and Pitruzzella 2011, p. 77).

[3] Halberstam 2010, p. 193.

producing reasonable, well-informed opinions in which participants are willing to revise preferences in light of discussion, new information, and claims made by fellow participants.'[4] The decades-old debate on the extent to which judicial review is compatible with the democratic legitimation of executive power is based on the former view of democracy and supposes a zero-sum relationship between judicial review and political oversight. But while this view prevailed for much of the 20th century, it is certainly not something belonging only to the past, given the traction it is currently gaining in 'illiberal democracies', where authoritarian rulers rely on the outcome of (more or less) free elections.[5]

Deliberative democratic theory permeates not only the decisions to be taken on legislation and policy by elected officials, but also governmental and administrative processes at large.

As good practices have shown, the quality of administrative decision-making in the administrative state can be greatly enhanced by practices such as those described by Geneviève Cartier from a Canadian perspective. Administrative discretion can be understood as dialogue, which means that the exercise of authority should be 'sensitive to the particularities of the individuals and to the values expressed in the statute and the legal system generally.'[6] Similar approaches in the Netherlands have been referred to as *interactief bestuur*, or interactive public administration. In this sense, administrative law must also allow scope for reciprocity: indeed, this was one of the ideas behind the Dutch General Administrative Law Act, introduced in 1994.[7] While several contributions to this volume recommend a less restrictive approach to judicial review of administrative acts, this does not mean there will be no scope for deference vis-à-vis legitimate policy considerations. Rather, such reviews will have to comply with legal principles, including the principle of proportionality. A deliberative approach in judicial reviews[8] should mean that the procedural and substantive assessments of the proportionality of a decision have to include views from various perspectives, whereby the rapprochement between contentious procedures and mediating approaches would appear to create a suitable procedural context.

The ability of the judiciary, including its highest courts, to meet such expectations depends partly also on its organization. Overburdened judiciaries are overly inclined to 'stick by the rules'. Only when sufficient time is available can courts proceed from a formalistic procedural check to an assessment of due process, including the proportionality check. The degree of specialization also influences the ability and readiness to apply an effective judicial review.

What, lastly, should be emphasized is the intrinsic relationship between judicial review—not only of administrative acts, but also of legislation itself—and the

---

[4] Cartier 2018, p. 59.

[5] AIV 2017, p. 36.

[6] Cartier 2018, pp. 60–61.

[7] Hirsch Ballin 1989, pp. 1–4; see also Hirsch Ballin 1991, pp. 261–265.

[8] Cf. Cartier 2018, p. 64, p. 69.

effective protection and realization of human rights. While courts have a duty to enforce the protection of human rights, unfavorable political conditions may result in the judiciary operating differently. Indeed, courts operating in such conditions can become an antagonist of a free and just society through, for example, an undue constitutionalization of political entrenchments, such as the freedom to carry arms, or inappropriate deference to a ruling party.

The above confirms our belief that democracy and the rule of law should not be sold as separate items, but instead be seen as contributing jointly to the complex, life projects-enabling purpose of the constitution.

## References

AIV (2017) The will of the people? The erosion of democracy under the rule of law in Europe. Adviesraad voor Internationale Vraagstukken [Advisory Council on International Issues], The Hague

Bin R, Pitruzzella G (2011) Diritto costituzionale [Constitutional law]. G. Giappichelli, Turin

Cartier G (2018) Deliberative ideals and constitutionalism in the administrative state. In: Levy R et al (eds) The Cambridge Handbook of deliberative constitutionalism. Cambridge University Press, Cambridge, pp 57–71

Halberstam D (2010) The promise of comparative administrative law: A constitutional perspective on independent agencies. In: Lindseth P L, Rose-Ackerman S (eds) Comparative administrative law. Edward Elgar Publishing, Cheltenham, pp 185–204

Hirsch Ballin E M H (1989) Wederkerig bestuursrecht [Reciprocal administrative law]. Rechtsgeleerd Magazijn Themis afl. 1: pp 1–4

Hirsch Ballin E M H (1991) Rechtsstaat en beleid (Een keuze uit het werk van -) [Rule of law and policy (A choice from the work of -). W.E.J. Tjeenk Willink, Zwolle

Rose-Ackerman S (2012) The regulatory state. In: Rosenfeld M, Sajó A (eds) The Oxford Handbook of comparative constitutional law. Oxford University Press, Oxford, pp 671–685

MIX
Papier aus verantwortungsvollen Quellen
Paper from responsible sources
FSC® C105338

If you have any concerns about our products,
you can contact us on
**ProductSafety@springernature.com**

In case Publisher is established outside the EU,
the EU authorized representative is:
**Springer Nature Customer Service Center GmbH**
**Europaplatz 3, 69115 Heidelberg, Germany**

Printed by Libri Plureos GmbH
in Hamburg, Germany